Napoleon's War in Spain

Napoleon's War in Spain

The French Peninsular Campaigns, 1807–1814

J. Tranie and J.-C. Carmigniani
from the notes and manuscripts of Commandant Henry Lachouque
with original illustrations by Louis de Beaufort

Translated by Janet S. Mallender and John R. Clements
Foreword by David G. Chandler

ARMS AND
ARMOUR

Published in 1982 by Arms and Armour Press,
Villiers House, 41-47 Strand, London WC2N 5JE
Reprinted 1993

Distributed in the USA by Sterling Publishing Co. Inc. 387 Park
Avenue South, New York, NY 10016-8810.

Distributed in Australia by Capricorn Link (Australia) Pty. Ltd.
P.O. Box 665, Lane Cove, New South Wales 2066.

First French-language edition *Napoleon et la Campagne d'Espagne*,
published in 1978 © Editions Copernic, Paris, 1978.
First English-language edition © Lionel Leventhal Limited, 1982.
Foreword © David G. Chandler, 1982.

British Library Cataloguing in Publication Data
Lachouque, Henry
Napoleon's war in Spain, 1807-1814.
1. Peninsular War, 1807-1814
I. Title II. Tranie, Jean III. Carmigniani, Juan-Carlos IV. Napoleon et
la campagne d'Espagne.
English
940.2'7   DC231
ISBN 1-85409-219-7

Printed and bound in Great Britain by Bath Press, Avon

Acknowledgments
We would like to express our gratitude to all those who have helped us
in our research. Our warmest thanks go particularly to:
Raoul and Jean Brunon — whose expertise in the subject is
appreciated by all — who kindly placed at our disposal their study on
the chronology of the events of this war, as well as a selection of
documents from their library.
Commissaire de la Marine, Louis Merllie, Vice-President of *La
Sabretache*, who kindly lent us the plates of the late H. Boisselier, thus
making easier our research into the reconstruction of certain little-
known uniforms.
Vicomte Henri de Beaufort, who once again made available to us his
incomparable library of 'militaria'.
Dr. F. G. Hourtoule for authorizing the reproduction of plates by the
late J. Girbal, from the series *Soldats et Uniformes du Premier Empire*.
Colonel Wemaere, curator of the Musée de l'Armée, whose kindness has
so helped our research.
Mlle. Lenoir and the library of the Ministère des Armées.
Cyril Charbault for his photographs, which permitted us to create the
first mock-up of the work.
Martine Thiebeaux, who kindly helped us with the text.

Contents

1807 15

Relations between Spain and France — The Continental Blockade — Invasion of Portugal by Junot — Capture of Lisbon — Situation in Spain in 1807 — First entry of the French into Spain.

1808 23

Anxiety of the Spanish faced with the arrival of the French — Revolt against Godoy — Abdication of Charles IV in favour of his son Ferdinand — Murat's entry into Madrid — Charles IV resumes his rights to the throne — Insurrection in Madrid (the 'Dos de Mayo') — Bayonne interview — Napoleon gives the crown to Joseph — Scenes of horror in Spain — The French victors at Logroño and Tudela — Sieges of Saragossa and Valencia — Bessières beats Cuesta at Medina del Rio Seco — Disaster of Baylen — Joseph evacuates Madrid — Signing in Portugal of the Convention of Cintra after the Battle of Vimeiro — Junot and his troops repatriated by the British — The Emperor decides to intervene — The Erfurt interview with the Tsar — Composition of the armies engaged — Entry of Napoleon into Spain — Lefebvre victor at Zornoza — Soult at Gamonal — The march on Madrid — Somosierra — Fall of Madrid — Proclamation to the Spanish — Pursuit of Sir John Moore's British army — Second siege of Saragossa.

1809 69

Napoleon enters Astorga and decides to return to France — Soult continues the pursuit towards Corunna — Embarkation of the British, death of Sir John Moore — Capture of Saragossa — Jourdan appointed Chief of Staff — Soult enters Portugal — Capture of Braga and Oporto — Soult halts — Arrival of Sir Arthur Wellesley, future Duke of Wellington — The French are attacked at Oporto and beat a retreat — Portugal is evacuated — Disagreement between Ney and Soult — Victor triumphant at Medellin and Sebastiani at Ciudad Real — Wellesley threatens Madrid — Battle of Talavera — Return of the British to Portugal — Siege of Gerona — The French victorious at Ocaña — Defeat of Marchand at Tamanès — Capture of Salamanca.

1810 95

Andalusian campaign — Capture of Malaga and Seville — Defeat outside Cadiz — Victor blockades the town — French prisoners escape from the hulks — Joseph tries to charm the Spanish — The Kingdom of Spain is dismembered by the Emperor — Useless protestations from Joseph — Soult, proconsul in Andalusia — Wellington organizes the defence lines of Torres Vedras — Masséna appointed to command the Army of Portugal — Capture of Ciudad Rodrigo — Battle of Bussaco — Masséna's entry into Coimbra — The French halt outside Torres Vedras — Withdrawal to Santarem — Drouet d'Erlon arrives from Spain — Suchet Governor in Aragon — Capture of Tortosa.

1811 117

Soult's capture of Badajoz — Masséna's retreat — Incident with Ney who is relieved of his command — Battle of Fuentes de Oñoro — Masséna's disgrace — Soult's problems in Andalusia — Battle of the Chiclana — Beresford besieges Badajoz — Battle of Albuera — Marmont's manoeuvre and meeting with Soult — Relief of Badajoz — Return of Soult to Andalusia — Defeat of Godinot at Tarifa — Suchet — Siege of Tarragona — Attack on Montserrat — Suchet appointed marshal — Siege and capture of Sagunto — Siege of Valencia.

1812 137

Capture of Valencia by Suchet — Capture of Ciudad Rodrigo and Badajoz by Wellington — Soult's manoeuvring — Wellington's capture of Salamanca — Battle of Los Arapiles (Salamanca) — Marmont wounded — Clausel's retreat — The Army of Portugal retires to the Ebro — Suchet in Aragon — Raising of the Siege of Cadiz — Evacuation of Andalusia — Wellington enters Madrid — The Fuente de Higuera interview — Wellington checked outside Burgos — Recapture of Madrid — Wellington's disengagement.

List of Colour Plates

List of Maps

Foreword

By David G. Chandler, MA (Oxon), FRHistS, FRGS,
Head of Department of War Studies and International
Affairs, RMA Sandhurst

It is a particularly welcome event for historians to find an important French work devoted to the history of the Peninsular War, 1807–1814. Apart from the notable multi-volume treatment commenced by General Maximilien Sebastien Foy in the late 1820s (which only extended as far as 1810), there has been a noteworthy lack of monographs devoted to the subject, although many biographies and specialist works have inevitably included significant chapters. The fact is that the 'Spanish Ulcer' formed – and forms – for the French what the Eastern Front 1941–45 represents for the Germans, or Vietnam for the Americans. Hence the interest of this handsomely illustrated volume, now made available to a wide English-speaking readership by the initiative of Arms and Armour Press.

Produced by Jean Tranié and J.-C. Carmigniani from the notes and papers left by the late Commandant Henry Lachouque, the doyen of French Napoleonic scholars writing for a broadly-based market, it should be appreciated that this treatment represents a strongly-Gallic viewpoint. Its given title is not without significance; Napoleon was only present in Spain from early November 1808 until mid January 1809 – or less than one-fourteenth of the 43-month Peninsular struggle – although it is true that he was wholly responsible for the attacks or 'interventions' upon Portugal and Spain, and remained intimately involved in the strategic and policy aspects of the struggle, whether dating his steady flood of orders, exhortations and rebukes from Paris, Vienna, Dresden, Moscow or Leipzig. Nevertheless, the absence of the master from the scene, which he occasionally likened with scorn to a police operation rather than a formal war, was one major factor in producing the end result. Similarly, the French proclivity to name the struggle 'the War in Spain' rather than 'the Peninsular War' indicates a partially-subconscious desire to write-down the equally-important events in Portugal, where the French suffered some of their most humiliating reverses and Wellington and his Anglo-Portuguese Army achieved a number of notable successes. As in so many cases, this is essentially a difference of national outlook, a variation in perception.

Considering this weighting of the approach to the subject, it will not surprise the reader to find that rather more attention is paid to French successes than to Allied operations. Some notable British successes – the spirited cavalry battle of Sahagun on 21 December 1808, for example – receive no mention. Some Allied setbacks, the loss of Almeida by Brigadier-General Cox on 28 August 1810, for instance, are incompletely described; the loss of this important fortress in the Northern Corridor to Marshal Ney after only a 12-day siege being wholly due to a massive explosion of the main magazine, which devastated both town and defences. Even more surprisingly, perhaps, there is no mention of the French 'sortie from Bayonne' on 14 April 1814, the very last action of the Peninsular War, fought four days after the Battle of Toulouse, which indicates the degree of loyalty to the Emperor among his defeated but defiant troops.

Lachouque and his collaborators describe with verve and a fine sense of narration the main developments in this desperate struggle. Rightly, they stress three major contributory factors underlying the French failure in the Peninsula. The inability of the marshalate and the senior generals to work under King Joseph and Marshal Jourdan in effective, complementary teams was indeed a major weakness that Wellington was not slow to exploit to the full. The mutual jealousies and suspicions of the senior commanders – and, a not unimportant point, of their wives (the presence of Massena's comely mistress unconvincingly disguised as an hussar officer was a source of truly major friction and dissension at the official receptions and dinner-parties during the French campaign of 1810 in Portugal) – bedevilled the conduct of the struggle from February 1809 until the redoubtable Marshal Soult took over supreme command after the cataclysm of Vitoria in 1813 – a 'last-ditch' development which led to a remarkable improvement in French martial fortunes, although the broad issue of the war in the Peninsula was already irreversibly settled. Had such a sensible step been taken in 1810, the outcome might have been substantially different.

Secondly, the authors stress the degree of popular hostility to French rule as a major factor in their failure. Again they are absolutely correct, but perhaps they do not bring out the full significance of the point. The scale of the guerrilla war is hard to judge as the monks, ex-soldiers and other leaders of the bands kept few records, either because they were illiterate or because they wished, for understandable reasons, to leave no trace of their looting activities. Far more important than their operations against French couriers, small detachments and convoys or the unfortunate occasional straggler (cumulatively great though these were, particularly in psychological terms), was their all-out vendetta waged against fellow-Spaniards who had welcomed or at least connived at the change of ruling dynasty in 1808. This was the real 'war to the knife' that lay behind the conventional operations of the various armies in the field, and the result of the ceaseless assassinations and blood-purges of real or suspected collaborators was the virtual elimination of much of the enlightened nobility and embryonic educated middle-classes of Spain. A number of Goya's paintings bring out well the horror of this social revolution proceeding within the main war.

Thirdly, the authors pay tribute to Wellington's great tactical skills on the battlefield, and the implacable nature of British hostility and determination as important factors in their defeat. And so they were, but in fact the story does not end there. Wellington was indubitably a master-tactician, but he was also notable as a strategist and logistician. Before leaving for the Peninsula in 1808 to face French troops for the first time since 1794, he confided to a friend that '... a dozen years of victory under Bonaparte must have made them better [soldiers] still. They have, besides, it seems a new system of strategy* which has outman-oeuvred and overwhelmed all the armies of Europe. 'Tis enough to make one thoughtful, but no matter. My die is cast. They may overwhelm me but I don't think they will outmanoeuvre me. First, because I am not afraid of them, as everybody else seems to be; and secondly because if what I hear of their system of manoeuvre is true, I think it is a false one as against steady troops. I suspect all the continental armies were more than half-beaten before the battle was begun – I, at least, will not be frightened beforehand.'

In this passage, Wellington (or Wellesley as he then was) revealed his awareness of the French systems of manoeuvre and, above all, of Napoleon's reliance on psychological shock to win his battles and wars, and as the saying goes,'fore-warned is fore-armed'. It is also clear that he was, from the first or at least from the time of Talavera in 1809, aware that his army's role would be to sustain the remnants of the Portuguese and Spanish armies and, above all, the partisan and guerrilla war. He sensed that a small, well-trained regular Anglo-Portuguese force, allied to a large and diffuse resistance movement (albeit one dogged by indiscipline and unreliability) would be able to tie down a far larger force of French troops and present their commanders with an impossible problem. To contain the guerrillas, the French needed to disperse their forces in garrisons and punitive columns; to face Wellington, they were forced to concentrate their forces, and thus take the pressure off the guerrillas and leave them a virtually free hand. And so it proved between 1809 and 1812: some 230,000 French soldiers were tied down in the Peninsula by barely 45,000 British and 30,000 Portuguese regulars, backed by possibly 70,000 active guerrillas and partisans. The French lost an estimated 200,000 casualties in the Peninsula – an average, over the eight-year duration of the war, of some 300 men a day. Of the total loss, perhaps 60,000 are attributable to direct action with Wellington's forces, and as many more to disease encouraged by underfeeding and exposure to a climate of often harsh extremes; the remainder – over half – were caused by the guerrilla struggle. Need more be said to demonstrate the point?

Thus Wellington's strategic role from 1809 to 1812 was to supply, support and sustain the efforts of the local forces, drawing invaluable intelligence of enemy movements from them, and earning them important respites by his periodic sorties from his Lisbon base and sanctuary deep into enemy-occupied territory to create major distractions – which the bemused French marshals fell for every time, greatly to the cost of both their armies and their individual reputations. After the capture of Ciudad Rodrigo and Badajoz in early 1812 (and Napoleon's coincidental weakening of his armies in Spain as he prepared to invade Russia), Wellington was able to switch over from the defensive to the offensive, and begin the systematic liberation of Spanish soil which, with the occasional setback represented by the Burgos episode, he proceeded to do in the Salamanca and Vitoria campaigns before penetrating the Pyrenean barrier after a herculean struggle against the redoubtable Soult to carry the seat of war into southern France by early 1814. Here, then, was a strategist of the first order.

* A reference to the Napoleonic systems of manoeuvre – using envelopment or the central position.

Wellington was equally aware that Spain was a country 'where small armies are swallowed up and large armies starve.' He had learnt in India the importance of a sound supply system as the *sine qua non* for underwriting a sustained war in a generally inhospitable countryside. These lessons he applied to his conduct of the Peninsular War with telling skill; from first to last his logistical abilities were far superior to those of his opponents, who half-starved their men or over-loaded their limited mule trains. Wellington, aided by his commissariat officers, built up a triple-system of supply to ensure that his Anglo-Portuguese army rarely went hungry or short of ammunition and other essentials of life and war. Using the power of the Royal Navy to convoy supplies from England to Lisbon (and, from mid-1813, to Santander) he built up stock-piles. But this would have been of little use without the means for forward-distribution, and here Wellington's triple system came into its own. First, whenever possible stores were moved by barge and river-boat to intermediate depots perhaps 50 miles in rear of the army. From there, they were carried in ox-cart convoys to forward supply depots and intermediate posts to about ten miles behind the front. At this stage the regimental mule-trains took over the duties of collection, movement and actual distribution. This system, when fully developed by 1811, worked very well, and its success underlay and made possible the achievements of the fighting divisions. There were periodic crises – especially when sufficient gold was not forthcoming from the Treasury in London – but no contemporary force had a better supply system than Wellington's Peninsular army, and of it he was the architect and supervisor. As he once remarked, 'one must follow the history of a biscuit from its leaving Lisbon until it reaches a soldier's mouth on the frontier.' By attention to detail, laborious and time-consuming though this duty was, Wellington brought victory to his arms and liberation to the peoples of Spain and Portugal.

It is hoped that these few paragraphs will serve to supplement the brilliant evocation of the Peninsular War, as seen by French soldiers and scholars, which the pages of this beautiful book represent. Understandably, the authors have played down certain aspects of the struggle and given stronger emphasis to others, but purely objective history makes for very dull reading, and that is a charge that will certainly never be launched at this well-translated volume. Wellington's methods and roles require rather more attention than was found space for in the main body of the book, but it is hoped that something has been done in this Introduction to redress the balance to a slight degree. There is no doubt – as the authors make quite clear – that Napoleon blundered badly in undertaking Portuguese and Spanish adventures in the first place, then in underestimating the scale of the problem. It has been noted that he never chose to return to Spain after January 1809, although for much of 1810 and 1811 he was comparatively free to do so. His insistence on continuing the prosecution of a hopeless war when prudence (although not personal and national pride) would have suggested a cutting of losses and a withdrawal at least to the line of the River Ebro if not to the Pyrenees, as King Joseph occasionally timidly advocated, was a recipe for disaster. Instead, the Emperor insisted on reinforcing failure, with well-known results. Above all, by providing his inveterate British opponents with an opportunity to exploit their command of the sea and to find a location for a large-scale campaign and war-effort on the Continent of Europe, Napoleon doomed his Empire to failure. The 'Spanish Ulcer' cost Napoleon, and France, dear.

Preface

The Spain of Charles IV, in character both Atlantic and Mediterranean, European yet linked with France throughout so much of her history, could but vainly hope to avoid becoming embroiled in the brutal upheaval caused by the French Revolution and Empire.

Victim of her thousands of kilometres of coastline, so tempting for blockade-runners; poor, fanatical, badly governed – she seemed to Napoleon a land easy to subdue, educate and integrate with his vast empire. His failure to appreciate the realities of Spain led to seven years of atrocious and merciless fighting, where quite often no holds were barred.

Ignored and despised, since it was seen as the Emperor's mistake, this war was also disliked because it gave the vanquishers of Europe a bad conscience. This time, it was not a question of fighting a despot or an aristocratic caste, but a whole nation drawn up against the 'Antichrist' and imbued with the spirit of patriotic pride.

The Peninsular War, which began in Portugal in 1807 and was brought to a close at Toulouse in the spring of 1814, prefigures modern wars of liberation. It saw the destruction of regiments that had once caused princes, kings and emperors to tremble. It also saw an army in rags rise from the native soil to help the redcoats drive from Spain the detested French army of occupation.

Whatever cause they served, whatever their language and the colour of their uniforms, it is these men and the officers who led them that this book has attempted to bring to life. Courageous fighting men, they deserve a place in the memory of their nations.

Napoleon in 1808. He was to forget his brother's warning in the Convention – 'Never strike Spain', thinking that the eviction of its wretched dynasty and the promise of 'the blessings of progress' would be welcomed with enthusiasm. The response of the Spanish people was a revolt of the entire nation. (David, Musée de Bayonne)

PROTAGONISTS IN THE STRUGGLE...

Above: Charles IV, King of Spain (1748–1819). Sixty years old, corpulent, a huge eater, his apparent benevolence hid his brutality. His favourite distraction was hunting, to which pursuit he gave most of his time. Each of his minutely ordered days allowed only very little time for affairs of state, consequently he was held in little esteem by his people. Of weak character, he was dominated by his wife and, through her, by Manuel Godoy. (Goya, Prado)

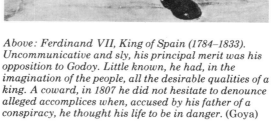

Above: Ferdinand VII, King of Spain (1784–1833). Uncommunicative and sly, his principal merit was his opposition to Godoy. Little known, he had, in the imagination of the people, all the desirable qualities of a king. A coward, in 1807 he did not hesitate to denounce alleged accomplices when, accused by his father of a conspiracy, he thought his life to be in danger. (Goya)

Above: George Canning (1770–1827). Disciple of Pitt, whose policies he adopted after the eviction of the Whigs, Secretary of State for Foreign Affairs from 1807 to 1809, he was responsible for British intervention in Spain, which was followed by a treaty of alliance signed on 14 January 1809. (Painting by Turner after Lawrence)

Left: Richard Wellesley, Second Earl of Mornington, then First Marquis (1760–1842). Formerly Governor-General of India, he became Foreign Secretary in 1809. He provided powerful support for his brother – the future Duke of Wellington.

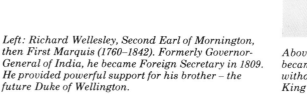

Above: The Prince of Wales (1762–1830). He became Prince Regent to George III, who withdrew from public affairs in 1811. He became King George IV in 1820. (After De Koster)

Above: The Bourbons of Spain. In the foreground King Charles IV – on his right the Queen, Maria-Luisa of Parma, his cousin (lascivious, toothless and incontestably ugly). On the left of the picture and in the foreground, the heir apparent, Ferdinand, Prince of the Asturias, and his wife Maria-Antonia of Naples. Behind the king, Don Luis of Parma, King of Etruria and his wife Pepita. Represented also are the younger brothers of Ferdinand, the Princes Charles and Francis of Paule. In the background, the Infanta Maria-Josepha, sister to Charles IV, and Donna Carlotta, another daughter of Charles IV, married to the Regent of Portugal. 'They led Spain to a state of complete decadence. No more money, no more navy, no more army, no more politics, no authority over the colonies who were ready to rebel, no more respect on behalf of an indignant nation' – Thiers, 'Le Consulat et l'Empire' (Goya, Prado)

Above: Joseph Bonaparte, King of Spain and the Indies (1768–1844). Napoleon's respected elder brother. King of Naples since 1806, he accepted the crown of Spain without enthusiasm. Full of goodwill, extremely benevolent, intelligent and cultured, he tried to make his subjects happier. The first constitutional monarch in the history of Spain, he tried to please and to make himself accepted, but in vain. To the people he remained the 'intruder king', and they gave him all sorts of unmerited nicknames. Disappointed by the affairs of Spain, it was not long before the Emperor took away from him all authority over the French military commanders. (Kinson, Cassel Museum)

Above: Manuel Godoy, y Alvarez de Faria, Prince of the Peace (1767–1851). The son of a noble but poor family, he enlisted in the Company of Life Guards, where he was noticed by the Queen, Maria-Luisa. This liaison raised him to the highest honours. Exploiting the laziness of his sovereign and the vice of the Queen, he was detested by the Spanish people. He controlled the politics of the country until 1806 and, while maintaining the best of relations with France, dealt tactfully with her enemies. Instigator of the First Treaty of Fontainebleau, signed in 1807, which provided for the sharing out of Portugal between France and Spain, he opened Spanish territory to the French Army. In 1807 he was appointed Grand Admiral (a title which the illustrious Don John of Austria had held) and Colonel-General of the military establishment of the King. He intrigued for the changing of the line of succession to the detriment of the Prince of the Asturias, and because of this the country's aversion for him came to a head. (Goya, Academy San Fernando, Madrid)

Above: Viscount Castlereagh, Second Marquis of Londonderry (1769–1822). Secretary for War in 1807, he intervened in favour of Portugal, then Spain where, after the death of General Moore, he had Wellesley appointed head of the expeditionary force. Foreign Secretary in 1812, he carried on the fight against Napoleon on the diplomatic front.

1807

Relations between Spain and France — The Continental Blockade — Invasion of Portugal by Junot — Capture of Lisbon — Situation in Spain in 1807 — First entry of the French into Spain.

Twelve years had passed since the Kingdom of Spain had made peace with Revolutionary France. As allies of the French, the Spanish fared indifferently – especially at sea, where their fleet had been defeated by the British at Cape St. Vincent in 1797 and had foundered under the orders of Villeneuve at Trafalgar. Such reverses caused resentment, and the ties between Spain, with its ancient Inquisition, and France, with its revolutionary fervour, became ever more strained. To make matters worse, in 1806, Napoleon discovered some extremely compromising documents in the papers abandoned by King Frederick William of Prussia during his flight from the battlefield of Jena. Godoy, favourite of the Spanish King, lover of the Spanish Queen, acclaimed 'Prince of the Peace' for having reconciled Spain and France in 1795, had been intriguing with the Allies. Alarmed at being thus discovered, Godoy consented to despatch a contingent of 15,000 Spanish troops, under the Marquis de la Romana, to serve with the French on the Elbe. But this was only a beginning, for the Iberian peninsula was soon to become a burning issue.

By the summer of 1807, a series of legendary victories – Austerlitz, Jena and Friedland – had forced Continental Europe to make peace. At the Treaty of Tilsit, the Yalta of the era, the French and Russian emperors had agreed to divide the world between them. Russia rejoiced. Illuminations were everywhere. And yet one shadow remained: the British would not lay down their arms. Alone for the moment, but certain that the star of the Corsican would fade, they stood fast. To force them to submit, Napoleon had determined to starve them out: to close Europe to their ships, to destroy their commerce, and thereby to force them to make peace. His weapon was the Continental Blockade, decreed in Berlin in late 1806 – but countered on 7 June 1807 by British Orders in Council that sought to block up all French and colonial ports. Meanwhile, British ships made for the areas most vulnerable in Napoleon's system, where trade could still be carried on. One of these was Portugal, which, following the Methuen Treaty of 1703, had been virtually a British colony for a century.

The Emperor threatened. On 15 October 1807, he informed the Portuguese Ambassador, the Count of Lima: 'If Portugal does not do what I want, the House of Braganza will no longer reign in two months.' The Allies tried a ruse. The British Ambassador in Lisbon left for London, and Portugal declared war on Britain on 17 October; but Napoleon was not to be deceived by play-acting. An army of 25,000 stood waiting at Bayonne. At their master's order, they set off to cross Spain and invade Portugal, General Junot, the future Duke of Abrantes, at their head. Spain posed no problem. On 27 October, Godoy signed a treaty to partition Portugal. The north of the country, to be known as 'Lusitania Septentrional', with Oporto as its capital, would pass to the Spanish King's daughter, the ex-Queen of Etruria, in exchange for Tuscany. The Tagus valley and Lisbon would be Napoleon's, for disposal at a general peace. But the south, to be called 'The Principality of the Algarve', would be given to the 'Prince of the Peace' who was beside himself with joy at the prospect. 'I shall march at the head of my hussars', he wrote, 'and that will be sufficient.'

Even before this treaty could be concluded, Junot had crossed the Bidassoa and turned towards Lisbon. His army of virtually raw conscripts was badly trained and its equipment left much to be desired. Nevertheless, anxious to arrive as quickly as possible at Lisbon in order to capture the princes of Braganza, Junot force-marched onwards. Soon a long line of stragglers congested the roads, and

indiscipline reigned. The sight of this throng had a deplorable effect on the Spanish people. If Portugal had wanted to resist, there is no doubt that the operation would have ended in disaster. As it was, Junot's army, reduced to 4–5,000 men, arrived on the outskirts of Lisbon on 27 November. While the royal family escaped with the Treasury and the fleet, the French conquerors installed themselves in the capital on 30 November, and more than 20,000 stragglers slowly caught up.

This brutal dismemberment of Portugal was in no way impeded by the Spanish government, weak and divided as it was. Indeed, at the dawn of the nineteenth century, Spain, with her eleven million inhabitants, was but a shadow of her brilliant past. Still powerful in the New World, where her conquistadors had created kingdoms with the aid of the arquebus and the cannon, she was weak in Europe because of her inefficient rulers and the sway held over her by the clergy and the monks. King Charles IV, a man of perfect honour, like his cousin Louis XVI, was

General Junot (1771–1813). Commanding I Observation Corps of the Gironde, about 26,000 men, he took Lisbon without a fight on 30 November 1807.

Above right: Lisbon at the beginning of the nineteenth century. (From a contemporary engraving)

Right: Victim of denunciation, Ferdinand had to surrender his sword, and was imprisoned in his apartments in the Escurial at the instigation of Godoy, on 27 October 1807. (After F. Motta)

The Spanish Army, La Romana Division, 1807–08

1. Regiment of Zamora (commanded by Colonel Salcedo), drum major.
2. Regiment of Zamora, fusilier, 1807.
3. Regiment of Catalonian light infantry (commanded by Major Borillas), chasseur.
4. Regiment of Catalonian light infantry, officer.
5. Infantry of the line, Regiment of Guadalajara (commanded by Colonel Martorell), grenadier.
6. Infantry Regiment Princessa, (commanded by Colonel San Roman), sapper. The regiment had two uniforms, that of the Ordinance of 1802 and that of 1805.

7. Infantry of the line, Regiment of the Asturias (commanded by Colonel Dellevieilleuze), sapper, 1807-08.
8 & 9. Infantry of the line, Regiment Princessa, grenadier. Figure 9 wears the later uniform.
10. Sapper Corps (engineers, sappers and miners).
11. The King's Regiment of cavalry, officer in service dress. In 1808 the Spanish cavalry totalled twelve regiments.
12. Regiment of dragoons of Almanza commanded by Colonel Caballero. This regiment still wore the uniform of the light cavalry.

The Spanish Army, 1808

1. Captain-general in dress uniform. There was a simpler uniform with braiding on the collar and lapels only, waistcoat and breeches white or buff and a crimson sash with three gold stripes.
2. Brigadier in undress uniform.
3. Officer of the staff.
4. Royal Guard of Halbardiers. 1,000 men formed part of the guard at the royal palace.
5. Officer of the Royal Spanish Guard.
6. Royal Walloon Guard. The two units of royal guards totalled more than 6,000 men. Together with the bodyguard and carabiniers, they composed the royal household troops.

7. Manuel Godoy, Generalissimo of the Army, Admiral of the Fleet and Prince of the Peace.
8. Royal Carabinier.
9. Brigade of Chasseurs, Royal Carabinier. This squadron served as personal guard to Godoy with the title of 'Cazadores espanoles de la guardia de honor del generalissimo'.
10. Royal Guards. There were four companies differentiated by the colour of the carbine sling: Spanish (red), American (crimson), Italian (green) and Flemish (yellow).
11. Brigadier-General Don Mariano Alvarez de Castro, defender of Gerona.

without education, culture or any great intellectual ability. The Queen, vindictive and immoral, ruled her weak husband, while Godoy, lover and favourite, ruled them both. The monks, insolent, libertine and ignorant, lived off the populace which remained poverty-stricken. The villages, many of which were mere collections of huts, were far apart, and the absence of proper roads accentuated their isolation. Woods were sparse and land often lay fallow; the towns themselves were dirty and the streets badly paved. When, at the beginning of 1808, the Emperor summoned General de Beurnonville and demanded from him a report on Spain, the latter made enquiries and wrote: 'There are no roads, no transport, no houses, no shops, no provisions in a country where the people warm themselves in the sun and live on nothing. The Spaniard is brave, daring and proud; he is a perfect assassin. This race resembles no other – it values only itself and loves only God whom it serves very badly.' To that assessment should be added an appreciation of the difficult terrain, often poor or uninhabited, broken up by mountains where communications were by means of passes and narrow plains – an ideal place for the war of ambush and 'coup de main' that was to become famous as 'guerrilla warfare'.

The drama was to be played out with four principal actors: King Charles IV; the Queen, voluptuous, ugly and obstinate; the favourite and ex-lifeguard Godoy, who had achieved the tour de force of becoming a grandee of Spain, of marrying an Infanta and of amassing a fortune thanks to a shameless misappropriation of funds; and, finally, Crown Prince Ferdinand, 27 years old, sly and cowardly, who hated Godoy and was impatient to reign. Influenced by his former tutor, Canon Escoiquiz, who thought himself the stuff of a Ximenes or a Richelieu, Ferdinand sought the support of Napoleon. He wrote to ask for the hand of an imperial princess. The Emperor, who had no princess available, did not reply, but at the same time, he received a letter from Ferdinand's father setting out his grievances against his 'unnatural' son, whom Godoy had just arrested for conspiracy against the state. Appealed to by father and son, Napoleon became the arbitrator of this family quarrel.

On 13 November, on a pretext of reinforcing the Army of Portugal, II Observation Corps of the Gironde, commanded by Dupont, crossed the Bidassoa and made its way towards Valladolid, while the Coastal Observation Corps entered Biscay (9 January 1808). At the other end of the Pyrenees, the Eastern Pyrenean Division, commanded by Duhesme, entered Catalonia.

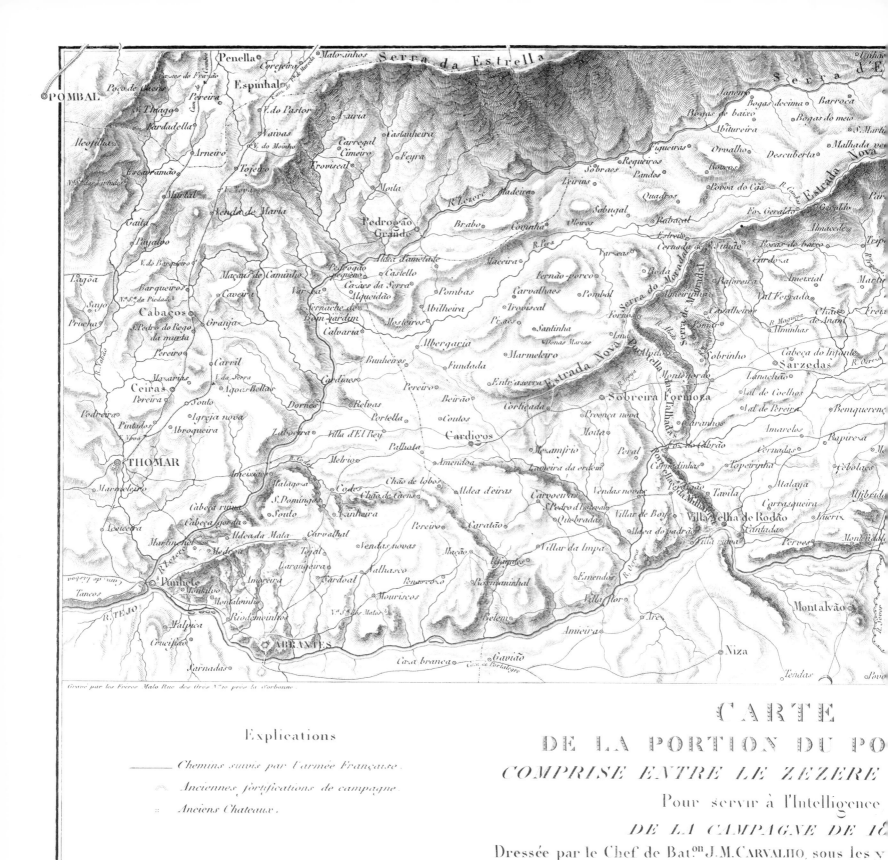

POMBAL

Penella
Serra da Estrella
Serra d E

Espinhal

THOMAR

ABRANTES

Gravé par les Freres Malo Rue des Gres N.º 10 pres la Sorbonne.

Explications

———— Chemins suivis par l'armée Française.

Anciennes fortifications de campagne.

Anciens Chateaux.

CARTE
DE LA PORTION DU PO
COMPRISE ENTRE LE ZEZERE
Pour servir à l'Intelligence
DE LA CAMPAGNE DE 18
Dressée par le Chef de Bat.ᵒⁿ J.M.CARVALHO, sous les y
POUR SON HISTOIRE DE LA GUERRE DE L

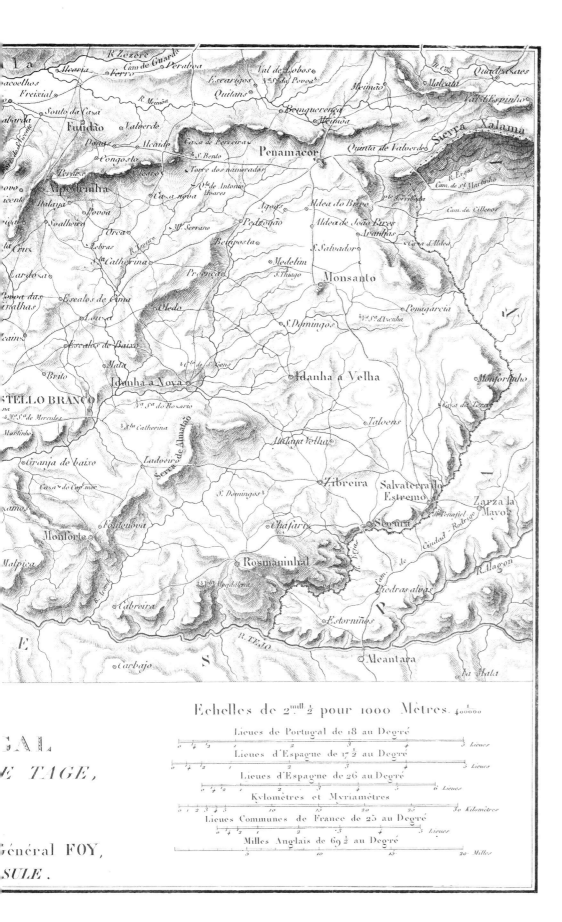

Talleyrand-Périgord, Charles Maurice de, Prince de Benavente, Grand Chamberlain, Vice-Grand Elector, Minister of Foreign Affairs (1754–1838). He was the great instigator of French intervention in Spain, pressing Napoleon, who occupied the place of Louis XIV in Europe, to install a Bonaparte in Madrid, as the great king had established a Bourbon. In his memoirs, Pasquier states several times that he heard from Talleyrand's own mouth the following phrase, 'Since Louis XIV, the crown of Spain has belonged to France's reigning family. It is one of the best parts of the great king's heritage and the Emperor should inherit it in whole; he must, he cannot abandon any part of it'.

Left: One of the maps from General Foy's 'Histoire de la Guerre de la Peninsule sous Napoleon' (1827). It depicts the area of Portugal between the Rivers Zezere and Tagus.

General Lasalle, Count (1775–1809). At the end of 1807 he commanded the reserve division of cavalry destined to intervene in the Peninsula.

Above: The march of General Junot's troops in the Sierra de Goze gorges, November 1807. (Drawing by Philippoteaux)

Left: Ferdinand, Prince of the Asturias.

Below left: Canon Don Juan d'Escoiquiz (1762–1820). Archdeacon of Toledo, tutor then adviser to the Prince of the Asturias, whom he urged to seek Napoleon's protection in order to escape the marriage which Godoy was arranging with his own sister-in-law. Implicated in the plot denounced to Charles IV, the aim of which was to dethrone Charles in favour of Ferdinand, d'Escoiquiz was arrested. Under pressure of public opinion and despite the confession written by the Prince of the Asturias denouncing 'his accomplices' among whom d'Escoiquiz was named, a moderate sentence was delivered at his trial. After losing his ecclesiastical benefices, he was confined in the monastery at Tardon. Made a Counsellor of State at the time of Ferdinand VII's accession, he accompanied him to Bayonne, then to Valençay and was interned at Bourges. He became Secretary of State in 1814.

Above: John, Prince Regent and later King of Portugal (1767–1826). Fleeing from the French invasion, he took refuge in Brazil. In 1816, on the death of his mother, he took the title John VI, but did not return to Portugal until 1821.

1808

Anxiety of the Spanish faced with the arrival of the French — Revolt against Godoy — Abdication of Charles IV in favour of his son Ferdinand — Murat's entry into Madrid — Charles IV resumes his rights to the throne — Insurrection in Madrid (the 'Dos de Mayo') — Bayonne interview — Napoleon gives the crown to Joseph — Scenes of horror in Spain — The French victors at Logroño and Tudela — Sieges of Saragossa and Valencia — Bessières beats Cuesta at Medina del Rio Seco — Disaster of Baylen — Joseph evacuates Madrid — Signing in Portugal of the Convention of Cintra after the Battle of Vimeiro — Junot and his troops repatriated by the British — The Emperor decides to intervene — The Erfurt interview with the Tsar — Composition of the armies engaged — Entry of Napoleon into Spain — Lefebvre victor at Zornoza — Soult at Gamonal — The march on Madrid — Somosierra — Fall of Madrid — Proclamation to the Spanish — Pursuit of Sir John Moore's British army — Second siege of Saragossa.

Above: Marshal Joachim Murat (1767–1815). Grand Duke of Berg, named Supreme Commander of the French army in Spain as Lieutenant of the Emperor on 20 February 1808, and Lieutenant-General of the kingdom on 2 May 1808. (Portrait by François Gérard, Musée de Versailles)

Above right: Murat's army corps crossing the Pancorvo pass, February 1808. (Drawing by Philippoteaux)

The Spanish very soon became disturbed at the arrival of more than 24,000 men. How could they explain a veritable invasion, the only pretext for which was that it was to watch over the coastline of the Peninsula. However, for the moment they did not react, for they thought that the Emperor would bring Godoy, the abhorred favourite, to his senses and install Ferdinand (who had the favour of the people) on the throne.

The various corps, arriving one after the other, formed three distinct armies. On 20 February Murat was given supreme command, with the title of Lieutenant-General of the Emperor, and was left with rather vague instructions: 'I order you to march in a warlike fashion, to keep your divisions in good order and away from action, to provide abundantly for their needs so that they commit no disorderliness, to avoid any incidents, to take no part in the divisions of the Spanish court. ... The rest does not concern you and if I tell you nothing it is because you do not need to know anything.' A legendary cavalier, covered with gold and trimmings, the handsome Murat, son of an

Above: Murat at the Escurial recovers the sword of Francis I, which had been lost at Pavia. 'This courageous man's weapon, in the capital of a nation of courageous men, will in the centuries to come call to mind the century of the great Napoleon and that of Charles V.' The ceremonial and pomp displayed on this occasion was a severe affront to Spanish pride. (Job)

innkeeper, was the Emperor's brother-in-law. His appointment proves how important Napoleon now felt the question of Spain to be. But Murat, who was in fact to show much ability, thought that there was a throne for the taking and that there was certainly an opportunity here for him.

During the month of March, the King and Queen and, naturally, the favourite, who were at the palace of Aranjuez, began to feel uneasy. They planned to withdraw to the vicinity of Cadiz in Andalusia, in order to escape to the Americas if necessary. But the Spanish people would not have this; during the night of 17/18 March, a riot broke out. Godoy, who had hidden in a cupboard, was captured

when, urged by thirst, he tried to leave. Beaten black and blue, he was imprisoned only to be saved from death by Ferdinand. Meanwhile, in order to quell the riot, Charles IV removed his favourite from office. A few hours later, however, fearful on his own account, he abdicated in favour of his son, whose accession was greeted with delirious enthusiasm. It was now 20 March.

At this moment, Murat arrived outside Madrid. He received a letter from the Queen, seeking protection for her husband and Godoy. Two days later, the ex-King himself protested that 'he had abdicated only in order to avoid even greater misfortunes and to prevent bloodshed,

Right: The occupation of the citadel of Barcelona and the palace of Monjuich by the French on 29 February 1808. Under the pretext of reinforcing Junot's army operating in Portugal, the French troops flocked to Spain, growing from 70,000 in January 1808 to more than 100,000 in March. Taking advantage of their position as allies, the French took by surprise and without firing a shot the fortresses of Pamplona, San Sebastian, Figueras and Barcelona. (From the library of R. and J. Brunon)

Right: Entry of Murat into Madrid, 23 March 1808. (Anonymous, nineteenth century)

Far right: Entry of Ferdinand VII into Madrid, 24 March 1808. '. . . they kiss his hands, his knees, his stirrups, and in the midst of all, the cloaks thrown over the highway to make him a carpet, hats, fans and handkerchiefs flying through the air, a rain of flowers in a clamour of delirium, in the clash of bells, the exploding of fireworks, the people's idol makes his way' – J. Lucas-Dubreton 'Murat'. (From a watercolour by L. Rossi)

Right: The arrest of the Prince of the Peace on 19 March 1808. Deprived of all his ranks and posts by the king, dogged by the hatred of the people, Godoy remained hidden during the sack of his palace, but was arrested the next day. Protected with difficulty by his escort of Life Guards, he was thrown, wounded, into the Guards' stables. (Maurice Orange)

Far right: During the night of 17 March, the palace of the Prince of the Peace at Aranjuez was invaded and sacked by a crowd of 'Madrilènes'. (Philippoteaux)

Above: Imperial Guard. From left to right: Mamelukes, chasseurs à cheval and marines. (Philippoteaux)

Below: 9 April at Vitoria. The crowd wants to prevent the departure of Ferdinand for Bayonne. (Drawing by Philippoteaux)

Right: In the early hours of the morning of 2 May, carriages having been brought before the royal palace to take away the last two members of the royal family, the Queen of Etruria and the Prince Don Francis, the crowd ran to arms and started killing isolated Frenchmen. The centre of the insurrection was in the Puerta del Sol; Murat, whose troops were quartered outside the town, gave the order to clear the streets, which operation was executed with energy. Cavalry of the Guard, dragoons and infantry dispersed the multitude. The numbers of victims has never been determined with precision; it having been enlarged or diminished according to needs. The insurgents lost 400 according to Thiers, 1,500 or more according to other historians. French sources seem to agree that the figure was approximately 100. ('El Dos de Mayo', Goya, Prado)

Below: Scene from the Madrid uprising. Townsmen and peasants, among whom can be seen a priest, equipped with makeshift weapons attack a detachment of dragoons of the Guard. In front, an officer is stabbed by a peasant. (Lithograph by Raffet)

Far left: General Grouchy (1766–1847). From February to October 1808 he commanded the cavalry of the Army of Spain, at the head of which he participated in the repression of the insurrection of 2 May. He was Governor of Madrid in May 1808. (Anonymous drawing)

Left: General Daumesnil (1777–1832). He commanded the cavalry of the Guard at Madrid (First Squadron of chasseurs and a company of Mamelukes). (Portrait by Riesener)

which rendered the said act null and void'. This situation was not displeasing to the ambitious Murat, who did not acknowledge Ferdinand VII. The throne remained vacant. The vacancy also gave ideas to Napoleon, who, urged on by Talleyrand, thought the time had come for the Bourbons to be replaced by Bonapartes ... a logical step, as in France. He prepared to leave for Bayonne, to which he 'summoned' the family – the old King, the Queen, Ferdinand and, of course, the favourite (30 April).

In Madrid, the rumble of rebellion could be heard. Murat had received the order to remove the last of the royal household, against the wishes of the people. On 1 May, crowds gathered in the Puerta del Sol. Silently, at nightfall, peasants armed with blunderbusses and knives, came in from the surrounding countryside, and mingled with them. Next morning, 2 May (the famous 'Dos de Mayo'), when the crowd before the royal palace saw Prince Francisco in tears refusing to leave, it erupted. Every isolated soldier encountered in the streets had his throat slit and was disembowelled and mutilated.

Murat reacted immediately. Clearing the square with a battalion of infantry supported by two guns, he sent for troops quartered in the barracks on the outskirts of the city – objective, the Puerta del Sol. Commanded by Daumesnil, a squadron of chasseurs, preceded by Mamelukes, climbed the Alcala road under violent fire, and entered the square, sowing terror and skilfully hacking off heads as they went. The columns of infantry that arrived by order of General Lefranc completed the dispersal of the panic-stricken mob. Thirty or so armed individuals were captured and shot. The riot was quelled. It had been quite a skirmish, finishing well for the French, who remained the victors. But it was also to become a symbol for the Spanish and mark the beginning of an atrocious but

Left: The 'Dos de Mayo'. The charge of the cavalry of the Guard. Led by Daumesnil, chasseurs and Mamelukes charge up the Alcala road towards the Puerta del Sol. (M. Orange)

Right: An episode of the Madrid uprising. Death of Captain Daoiz. (Lithograph from painting by Castellano)

Below: The executions of the night of 2–3 May on the Principe Pio hill. The number of victims of the military courts set up by Murat is passed over in silence by Thiers. According to more recent sources, it would have been in the order of about a thousand. ('El Tres de Mayo', Goya, Prado)

popular war, which indirectly but surely was to contribute to the downfall of the colossus. Within seven years, the Spanish were to enter Toulouse... but for the moment, the time had not yet come for fear or regret on the French side. The Emperor at Bayonne, feigning great anger, left Ferdinand to have his ears boxed by his mother: alarmed, Ferdinand abdicated in favour of his father, who handed over his own rights to Napoleon in exchange for the châteaux of Compiègne and Chambord and an annual allowance of thirty million reales. Ferdinand was sent to the château of Valençay under guard of Talleyrand, who was told to amuse him. There he was to remain until 1814, deliberately ignoring the partisans who, on his behalf, waged a war without mercy.

The Emperor, who distributed crowns generously amongst his family, offered, or rather gave, the throne of Spain to the unwilling Joseph. (Murat departed, annoyed and green with envy.) On 10 May, Napoleon wrote to his brother: 'Through the organ of the Supreme Council of Castile, the nation demands a king. It is to you that I give this crown. Spain is not like Naples. It is eleven million inhabitants, more than 150 millions in revenue, without counting the immense revenues and possessions in America. It is, moreover, a crown that places you in Madrid, only three days from France and entirely covering one of her frontiers. In Madrid you are in France; Naples is at the end of the world. After you have read this letter, I wish you to leave the Regency to whomsoever you wish.... You will receive this letter on the 19th; you will leave on the 20th and you will be here on 1 June....'

There was no possible reply that Joseph could make, so he packed his bags with resignation. Of little use his being

Right: View of Bayonne. (From a painting by Vernet, Musée de la Marine)

Right: Bayonne, April 1808. Stormy interview between Ferdinand VII, Charles IV and Queen Maria-Luisa, in the presence of Napoleon. (F. Blanch)

Above: Abdication at Bayonne, May 1808. The scene represented is fictitious, for the act of abdication itself was not witnessed by all the main protagonists, as depicted here. (Lithograph by C. Motte)

Left: Bayonne, 30 April. Ferdinand VII, wishing to follow Charles IV into his apartments, is halted by the old king. 'Wretched boy, have you not dishonoured my white hairs enough?' (Myrbach)

Above: General Savary, Duke of Rovigo (1774–1833). He was entrusted by Napoleon with escorting Ferdinand VII to Bayonne. He was temporarily in command of the Army of Spain after the departure of Murat (June–July 1808).

Left: Scene during the uprising in the Asturias. A priest endeavours to prevent the massacre of five people in May 1808. This province was the first to organize resistance against the Napoleonic colossus. On 24 May at Oviedo the entire populace, responding to the call of Canon Leano Ponte, seized the arsenal, and on 25 May the Marquis of Santa-Cruz, in the name of the Junta, declared war on Napoleon. (Philippoteaux)

the eldest in the family – you do not argue with such a brother, younger or not.

Next, Napoleon addressed an eloquent proclamation to the Spanish: 'Spaniards, your nation was decaying. ... Your princes have surrendered to me all their rights to the crown of the Spanish territories. I do not wish to reign over your provinces, but I do wish to acquire for all time your eternal friendship and the gratitude of your posterity.

Your monarchy is old; my mission is to rejuvenate it. I shall improve all your institutions and I will see, if you assist me, that you enjoy the benefits of reform, without clashes, without disorder and without upheaval. Spaniards, remember what your fathers have been; see what you have become. The fault is not yours but that of the evil administration that has governed you. Be full of hope and confidence in the present situation, for I want your last

Right: Scene of the uprising in Valencia on 24 May 1808. On the announcement of the events in Bayonne, the population of Valencia rose and formed a junta which decreed a mass uprising. Under the leadership of Canon Calvo, a fanatic who was afterwards to be executed by his fellow-citizens, a troop of ruffians recruited from the dregs of the population massacred more than 300 French who had been locked up in the citadel. (Engraving by Motta)

Right: The oath of the Junta of Cadiz, 24 July 1808. From 22 to 30 May 1808, after the announcement of the abdications of Charles IV and Ferdinand VII, there was a general uprising in all the parts of Spain not occupied by French troops. Insurrectionary juntas (called provincial juntas) were formed, which declared war on France and decreed mass revolt. On 25 September at Aranjuez there was created the 'supreme, central governmental junta of the kingdom' formed by the representatives of the 32 provincial juntas. It was then transferred to Seville where it exercised its supremacy over the others. (Painting by Casado del Alisal)

descendants to keep my memory and say: "he was the regenerator of our homeland".'

This clever eloquence was certainly in the Emperor's style, but unfortunately it did not convince the majority of the Spanish, who, made fanatical by their priests, saw the French as instruments of Satan.

The scenes of horror multiplied. The crowd raised the gallows in Valladolid, which was in flames. At Torquemada, effigies of Napoleon were burned and, to punish the town, anyone found armed was massacred. At Pamplona, an old servant of the Marquis de Clermont-Tonnere stabbed an invisible enemy crying, 'Napoleon, I shall kill you!'. At Salamanca, implements used by the French were burned, the houses they had lived in were purified with holy water, and General René, on his way to rejoin Dupont, was thrown into boiling water by the peasants of the Sierra Morena. The insurrection was essentially of the people, and many notables who refused to associate themselves with it were murdered.

During this time, the French forces were plunging into the blazing countryside. These were not the handsome regiments left on the Vistula. Out of a total of 110,000 men, the front-line troops numbered 30,000 infantry and 3,000 cavalry, which were part of the regular army but came from the depots and had not yet experienced a campaign. Many of them were ill-instructed conscripts who had received little training in marching and manoeuvring. The remaining two-thirds were composed of foreigners (Germans, Swiss, Italians) whose training had been rudimentary. The provisioning of an army of 100,000 men by a population of eleven million was thought to be a simple matter, and no special measures were taken. In short, here were young, impressionable troops, hastily mustered, barely educated or trained, feebly officered, badly equipped and charged with the invasion of a poor, tormented, difficult country, whose inhabitants were fanatical, rebellious and savage.

Napoleon, however, was calm. Junot was guarding Portugal; Dupont's troops were drawn up on the road to Cadiz; Moncey was disposing his men from Madrid to Aranda; Bessières from Burgos to Vitoria; while Duhesme was in Barcelona.

Above: Marshal Moncey, Duke of Conegliano (1754–1842). Doyen of the marshals, in June 1808 he received command of the 'observation corps of the coast' and marched on Valencia at the head of 9,000 infantry and 1,500 cavalry.

Above: General Duhesme (1766–1815). Commander of the 12,000-strong East Pyrenees Division (6,000 French, 6,000 Italians), he contained the Barcelona insurrection, but failed at Gerona, the siege of which he abandoned on learning of the surrender of General Dupont at Baylen.

Above: Marshal Bessières, Duke of Istria (1768–1813). Commanding II Corps he gained the brilliant victory of Medina del Rio Seco on 14 July 1808, over General de la Cuesta. He was General commanding the Northern Army in 1809 and 1811. (Job)

Left: View of Barcelona in 1808. (Bacler d'Albe, Musée de l'Armée)

Above left: Victorious resistance of the inhabitants of Bruch against General Schwarz's column, 5 June 1808. (Engraving by F. Blanch)

Above right: General Count Lefebvre-Desnouëttes (1773–1822). Bessières's chief of staff, commanding the light cavalry of the Guard.

Left: View of Burgos, from a contemporary painting.

Below left: Detachment of chasseurs à cheval in the mountains of Old Castile in June 1808. (L. Sergent)

Above: General José Palafox y Melzi (1776–1847). Nephew of the Duke of Melzi, Vice-Chancellor of the kingdom of Italy. Having served in the Life Guards, his fidelity to Ferdinand VII whom he visited at Bayonne resulted in his proclamation as Captain-General of Aragon by the people (May 1808).

The Spanish Army, 1808–12

1. Irish regiment of Ultonia, fusilier. There were three Irish regiments in the Spanish army. This regiment took part in the defence of Gerona in 1809.
2. Battalion of volunteers of Barcelona. During the period 1805–1811 there were thirteen battalions of light infantry. The coat was dark blue with distinctive colours of yellow, red or maroon.
3. Cadet of the military college of Seville. Numerous military colleges were extant during the Spanish war, including the 'Colegio Militar de Sevilla', the 'Preferencia de Granada', and Tarragona (1810), Murcia (1810), Jaen (1812) and Santiago (1811).
4. Marine, uniform for land service. On board ship this regiment wore a different uniform.
5. 3rd Swiss Regiment (Reding), officer. There were six Swiss regiments in the Spanish Army, known better as 'azules' from the colour of their uniforms. The regiments took the name of their colonel. They totalled about 8,500 men, each regiment having two battalions, one of grenadiers and one of fusiliers.
6. 6th Swiss Regiment (Preux), officer of grenadiers.

7. 3rd Swiss Regiment (N. de Reding), fusilier. At the Battle of Baylen the regiments of J. de Reding and de Preux, attached to General Dupont's corps, found themselves face to face with N. de Reding's Swiss-Spanish regiment. Following custom in the Swiss Army, the colours were paraded in front of the troops who presented arms. Nearly all the men deserted to rejoin the Spanish ranks, so that of a total of 1,300 men, only 170 remained on the French side.
8. Staff officer of the artillery. The staff of the artillery and the engineers had a green uniform with purple-red markings.
9. Royal Corps of Artillery, officer. This corps comprised the foot artillery, horse artillery, field artillery, regimental artillery, a flying company of the Guard and the train.
10. Royal Corps of Artillery, gunner.
11. Fortress artillery. At Gerona, two guns from this unit participated in the defence of the town.
12. Royal Corps of Artillery, drum major.

The British Army, 1807–12

1. 92nd Foot (Gordon Highlanders). Senior officer on horseback in campaign dress.
2. 18th Hussars, officer. From 1809, four hussar regiments served in Spain. The 18th distinguished itself during the retreat to Corunna, and in 1813 was part of Grant's brigade.
3. King's German Legion, 3rd Hussars, 1809. This unit served in Lord Paget's brigade from 1809.
4. 20th Light Dragoons, officer on campaign, 1808. The 20th was the first cavalry regiment to take part in the Spanish war.
5. 6th Foot (1st Warwickshire). Sergeant of centre company.
6. 14th Light Dragoons, officer. They landed at Lisbon in 1808 and won fame at Fuentes de Oñoro, under Captain Brotherton, and then at Vitoria where they seized the carriage and baggage of King Joseph.
7. 52nd Foot (Oxfordshire Light Infantry), 1810. This regiment was present at Vimeiro, Talavera, Bussaco, Badajoz, Salamanca and Vitoria.
8. 10th Dragoons (Prince of Wales Hussars), corporal, 1808. This regiment took part in the retreat to Corunna, particularly distinguishing itself at Benavente against the Chasseurs à Cheval of the Guard.

9. 92nd Foot (Gordon Highlanders), officer in campaign dress, 1810–15. On campaign the grey trousers replaced the kilt.
10. 92nd Foot, light company, campaign dress, 1808–09.
11. 42nd Foot (Royal Highland Regiment or Black Watch), officer in dress uniform 1809. It was the only regiment in which all the companies wore a completely red plume. Arriving in Portugal in 1808, the Black Watch was present at Corunna, Bussaco and Salamanca.
12. 91st Foot (Argyleshire), Corporal in light company, 1808. The company wore the shako; only the pipers wore the plumed bonnet.
13. 71st Highland Regiment of Foot, centre company. In 1809 this regiment became the Highland Light Infantry. The ostrich feathers on their bonnets were sold to fashionable Portuguese ladies.
14. 6th Foot (1st Warwickshire), grenadier, dress uniform.
15. 60th Foot (Royal American), 5th Battalion officer on campaign, 1812. The regiment was part of the 6th Brigade from 1808 to Vitoria. In 1813 it belonged successively to the brigades of Brisbane, Cadogan and Anson.
16. 36th Foot (Hereford), light company officer. In 1809

this unit served at Corunna with Catlin Crawfurd's brigade.
17. 43rd (Monmouthshire) Light Infantry, private soldier, 1808–12. Present at Corunna in 1808–09 with Robert Craufurd's Light Division.
18. 95th (Rifle) Regiment, sergeant on campaign, 1808–09. This regiment distinguished itself at the retreat to Corunna, and it was during the withdrawal to Vigo that one of its crackshots, Tom Plunkett, killed General Colbert at Cacabelos.

The Emperor gave his orders: 'In a war of this kind, we must act with patience, with calm and according to well-established calculations. In civil wars, it is the important points that one defends. We must not go everywhere.'

Installed at Burgos, Bessières received the order to put the town in a state of defence, to send a body of troops against Saragossa and to watch over the insurgents of Old Castile and the Asturias. He sent General Lasalle to Torquemada and General Verdier to Logroño, where he beat the rebels on 5 June and took from them several ancient cannon.

Lefebvre-Desnouëttes, having successfully overcome Tudela, Mallen, Alagon and Epila, joined Verdier and arrived outside Saragossa on 28 June. The town, capital of Aragon, was built in a semi-circle on the right bank of the River Ebro. A stone bridge joined it to the suburb on the left bank. Surrounded by high walls, it was flanked by convents and public buildings whose stout construction formed so many carefully fortified strongholds. Since the end of May, the 60,000 inhabitants had refused to obey Guilheim, the Captain-General of Aragon, who was suspected of treachery. Instead, they had installed José Palafox as their leader. Presumptuous and of mediocre intelligence, he was well-supported by his two brothers and, most of all, by General Saint-March, a Belgian. Upon arrival, Lefebvre-Desnouëttes immediately stormed and carried Monte Torrero, one of the most important external points in the defence of the town. Palafox, enraged, had the officer in command tried and hanged in the public square so that 'all those who might be tempted to imitate him would be frightened by this example'. This sentence set the tone, and a fanatical populace left no stone unturned in order to drive away the French. All that self-sacrifice and patriotism could inspire was turned to the defence of the town. Outlying houses were burned, trees were cut down, and each dwelling was transformed into a bastion.

On the 30th, the French attack was launched against the Portillo, a gate in the fortifications flanked by the cloisters

Above: A setback during General Schwarz's expedition against Montserrat, 5–7 June 1808. After reaching Bruch, General Schwarz's French column, charged with the scouring of Montserrat, was attacked by the inhabitants of all the neighbouring villages and was obliged to turn back. In the course of their retreat the French soldiers had, at every step, to fight desperate battles; one of the bridges, so damaged that it would collapse under a heavy load, swept away in its fall an artillery piece and its team of horses. The losses were severe in dead and wounded. (Wood engraving)

Left: The monastery of Montserrat. (Bacler d'Albe, Musée de l'Armée)

Above: Augustina, heroine of the siege of Saragossa. Her name was to be changed to 'Augustina-Zaragoza' becoming thus the personification of the city. She was about 20 years old when, during the French assault, she was carrying refreshments to the defenders of the Porte du Portillo, when she found the battery defending the gate silent, with most of its crew out of action. She seized a lighted match and fired one of the guns, the grapeshot from which stopped dead the French assault column which had moved forward to within less than 100 metres of the guns.

of the barefoot Carmelite friars. The resistance was desperate. Despite an appalling carnage, the Spanish stood fast. A young peasant woman, Augustina, galvanized the hesitant fighting men, and herself set the match to a twenty-four pounder whose crew had been killed. During this time, Verdier broke through the Porte del Carmen and entered the town. At the cry of 'Viva Maria del Pilar' (the virgin protectress of Saragossa), the entire populace joined the fight and the French were obliged to retreat. After receiving reinforcements, Verdier began the assault again on 4 August. The French columns entered the town, and the street battles began anew, desperate and ruthless. Once more, women and children helped the Spanish soldiers, urged on by priests, who themselves led counterattacks. By 6 o'clock in the evening, half the town had been taken.

Verdier sent a messenger with a flag of truce to Palafox bearing a single word – 'Surrender'. Palafox replied straight away, 'Guerra a cuchillo' – war to the death. For several days the struggle continued without a break. Then, just as the Spanish were beginning to consider the possibility of a withdrawal to the suburb on the left bank, the French raised the siege and retreated along the road to Mallen; as a consequence of the disaster at Baylen, Verdier had received the order to make his way towards Miranda.

During this period, the beginning of June, Lasalle, the magnificent cavalryman, after having dispersed numerous gatherings near Torquemada, entered the town, which the exasperated French pillaged and burned. Pushing on towards Palencia, he beat several bands of insurgents at the Cabezon bridge on the Pisuerga and entered Valladolid.

Left: Rout of the Spanish on Cabezon bridge on 12 June 1808. (Drawing by Philippoteaux)

Below: The Battle of Medina del Rio Seco, 14 July 1808. General Lasalle prepares to lead the squadrons of the Guard in a decisive charge. (J. Girbal, taken from 'Le Général-Comte Lasalle', by F. G. Hourtoule)

Above: General Mouton (1770–1838). He commanded the 2nd Division of infantry, which took part in the victory of Medina del Rio Seco, 14 July 1808.

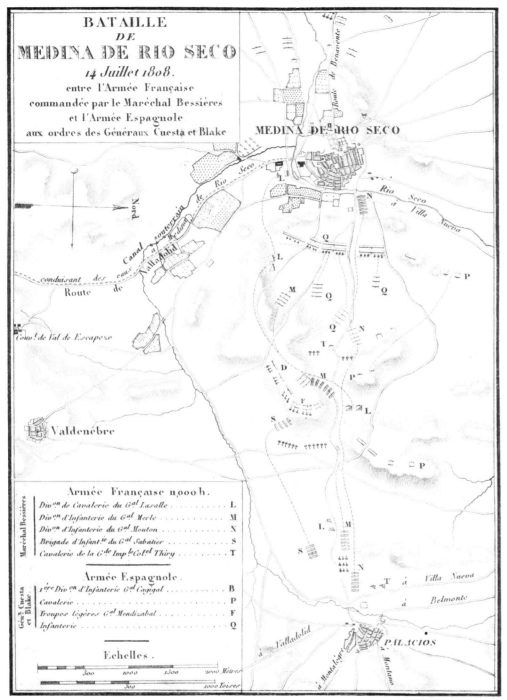

BATAILLE
DE
MEDINA DE RIO SECO
14 Juillet 1808.
entre l'Armée Française
commandée par le Maréchal Bessières
et l'Armée Espagnole
aux ordres des Généraux Cuesta et Blake

MEDINA DE RIO SECO

Armée Française 11000 h.

Maréchal Bessières	Div.on de Cavalerie du G.al Lasalle	L
	Div.on d'Infanterie du G.al Merle	M
	Div.on d'Infanterie du G.al Mouton	N
	Brigade d'Infant.ie du G.al Sabatier	S
	Cavalerie de la G.de Imp.le Col.el Thiry	T

Armée Espagnole.

Gén.x Cuesta et Blake.	1ère Div.on d'Infanterie G.al Cagigal	B
	Cavalerie	P
	Troupes légères G.al Mendizabal	F
	Infanterie	Q

Echelles.

Above: The Battle of Medina del Rio Seco, as depicted in General Foy's 'Histoire de la Guerre de la Peninsule sous Napoleon' (1827).

Right: Vice-Admiral Rosily (1748–1832). Appointed, with the title of Admiral, commander of the combined Franco-Spanish Fleet, he took command after Trafalgar and brought its remnants together at Cadiz. Attacked by insurgents and by the Spanish and British fleets on 9 and 10 June 1808, he was forced to surrender on the 14th. (Lithograph by Maurin, Musée de la Marine)

In Barcelona, Duhesme held firm, but the entire province of Catalonia was roused. To 'get a breath of fresh air' he left the town, defeated the insurgents at Llobregat and at Monga, pushed on as far as Gerona, which he attacked without success, and returned to Barcelona. Here he was surrounded again until Gouvion Saint-Cyr came to his rescue. In the south of Catalonia meanwhile, the Spanish General Caro had taken control of the resistance and showed great activity. Moncey crossed the poor province of Cuenca, beat the Spanish at Las Cabreras, flung them back to Valencia and besieged the town. After taking possession of the outskirts, however, his plan failed and he beat a retreat by the Almanza Pass on 3 July.

In the north, in the Asturias, Leon and Galicia, the junta of Oviedo had managed to assemble an army of about 40,000 men, commanded by the ageing Gregorio de la Cuesta. Advised by officers sent from Britain, he had established himself at Benavente on the Esla, threatening from there to descend upon Valladolid and Burgos to cut French communications. Bessières, with 14,000 men, marched to confront him. On the morning of 14 July, he found the Spaniards drawn up on the heights of the little-known town of Medina del Rio Seco. On his left he placed Mouton, the general of whom the Emperor had said, 'this "sheep" [mouton] is a lion'. Thrusting into the Spanish right flank, he took Medina del Rio Seco at the bayonet, while Lasalle's terrible charges decided the day. After six hours of fighting, de la Cuesta was in full flight towards Benavente, leaving behind about 900 dead, 6,000 prisoners and all his artillery, supplies and baggage.

Upon learning of this success, Napoleon cried, 'Bessières has put my brother Joseph on the throne of Spain'. He then announced the appointment of Jourdan as Chief of Staff in Spain.

While these events were being enacted, II Observation Corps of the Gironde, entrusted to Dupont, continued its march in the direction of Cadiz, where Admiral Rosily was in command of the remnants of the French Fleet that had been beaten at Trafalgar. Dupont de l'Etang, one of the most valued generals of division, an able administrator in Piedmont and Tuscany, successful commander at Ulm and Friedland, had returned from Germany with a high military reputation. No-one doubted that he would find his marshal's baton in Cadiz. On 24 May, he left Toledo with poorly trained troops, crossed the arid plains of La Mancha and arrived at Andujar on the Guadalquivir on 2 June. There he learnt that Rosily's squadron had been captured and that many bands of rebels were assembling around him under the command of General Castaños. Informing Murat of his perilous situation, he proceeded to Cordoba. On 7 June, at the bridge of Alcolea, he overcame 6,000 regular Spanish troops reinforced by partisans, and arrived outside the town. He called for its surrender, but meeting a show of resistance, he broke down the gates, shot the rebels and pillaged the town. On the 16th, however, fearing for the security of his lines of communication, he returned to Andujar, where he arrived on the 19th. There he received orders from general headquarters (Savary – replacement for Murat who was upset at not being made king); to stay where he was and await the arrival of the 2nd Division, that of Vedel, consisting of 6,000 men to which were to be added Gobert's 3,000. Reduced to inaction, he had the greatest difficulty in feeding his army, which was suffering from famine and the heat.

Meanwhile, the Seville junta had raised an army of 40,000 men, under the orders of Castaños. It was made up

Above: View of Cordoba in the nineteenth century. (Contemporary engraving)

Above right: General Don Francisco Xavier Castaños (1756–1852). In May 1808, he was appointed commander of all the Spanish troops concentrated in Andalusia. (Musée de l'Armée)

Above far right: Théodore de Reding de Schwyz (1755–1809). Swiss officer in the service of Spain; field marshal, appointed Commander-in-Chief of the Spanish forces in Granada, he rejoined Castaños's army and played a decisive rôle in the Battle of Baylen. Captain-General of Catalonia, he died at Tarragona as a result of wounds received at the Battle of Valls, 26 February 1809.

Right: The Baylen catastrophe, as mapped in General Foy's 'Histoire de la Guerre de la Peninsule sous Napoleon' (1827).

Above: General Count Dupont de l'Etang (1765–1840). Appointed Commander-in-Chief of the II Observation Corps of the Gironde on 3 November 1807, he was considered to be one of the best major-generals of the Grande Armée. His marshal's baton was awaiting him after his successful mission.

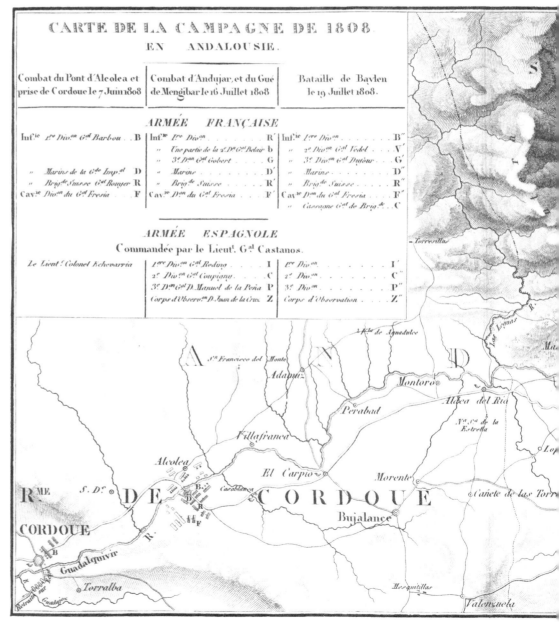

of four divisions: the first, commanded by Reding; the second, by Coupigny (a French emigré, formerly a marquis); the third, by Felix Jones, an Irishman; and the fourth by Juan Manuel de la Peña. After defeating the rebels at Despeñaperros, Vedel arrived on 16 July. He took up his position at Mengibar, a little above Andujar, leaving Gobert behind him at Baylen. On the same day, Castaños and Reding tried to force a crossing of the Guadalquivir, first at Andujar, then at Mengibar, but they were unsuccessful.

Believing that Vedel faced only a very small enemy force, Dupont asked for some of his troops. It was then that Vedel made a big mistake. He left his position and rallied to his chief, allowing Reding to occupy Mengibar and cross the Guadalquivir. The French left was outflanked. Gobert hurried from Baylen to stop Reding, but his division was overwhelmed and he was mortally wounded. Now Dupont

understood the danger. Reding must be dislodged and pushed back to Mengibar. Vedel, arriving at Baylen and finding no-one there, believed that Reding had gone northwards and so rushed off in pursuit, abandoning the Baylen hillside which was immediately occupied by the Spanish. The French army was cut in two. Communications with Vedel had to be re-established at all costs, and Dupont decided to attack Reding. On the evening of 18 July, preceded by a long line of 500 carts laden with booty and wounded, he left Andujar. At 4 am the advance guard ran into the Spanish outposts. The 15–16,000 men of Reding's and Coupigny's divisions held the heights. The French, only half their number, were engaged as they arrived. A confused action developed along the entire front-line. General Fresia's cavalry exhausted itself in useless charges, the artillery came into action piecemeal, and those guns that were put into action were successfully silenced. By

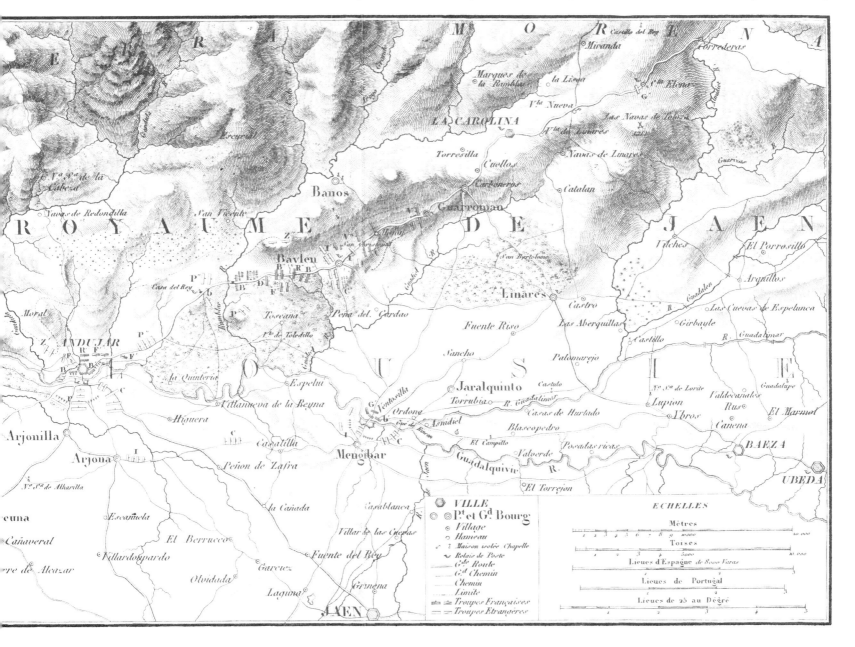

41

Above: Marines of the Guard at Baylen, 21 July 1808. (Painting by Brenet, Musée Napoléonien, Antibes)

Above: General Count Delaborde (1764–1833). He commanded the 1st Division of the Gironde Observation Corps.

Below: Marines of the Guard, colour party. In 1808 the five companies of the Marines of the Guard served in Spain and were present at the Madrid uprising on 2 May. A total of 444 marines under the command of Captain Daugier were assigned to General Dupont's corps, which was forced to surrender at Baylen. In 1811 Admiral Ganteaume was promoted Colonel-General of the Marines of the Guard. (Job)

Above: General Baron Pryvé (1762–1831). He commanded the advance guard of II Observation Corps of the Gironde on its march towards Cadiz.

Crest in the Musée de l'Empéri

midday, 2,000 Frenchmen were out of action and Dupont despaired of dispersing the enemy. Discouraged, he asked for a truce, which was accepted.

Meanwhile, Vedel, who could hear the guns, realized that Dupont was at grips with the enemy. He was separated from him by only 25–30 kilometres and so decided to turn back. The weary troops advanced slowly and he did not arrive at Baylen until 4 pm. Despite Reding's announcement of the truce, he attacked and scattered Coupigny's division, where one Irish regiment had already laid down their arms. Dupont sent an aide-de-camp accompanied by two Spanish officers to order him to cease-fire. Vedel obeyed, and it was from that moment that the indecisive day began to turn into a disaster. In fact, Dupont wanted to negotiate his retreat to Madrid and sent Generals

Chabert and Marescot to Castaños. The Spanish general, who knew that the French troops were worn out and desperate for supplies, was evasive. However, all was not lost. Vedel proposed a joint attack. Some generals suggested abandoning the wagons and artillery and storming their way through, but Dupont, had no energy left. He signed the surrender and with a stroke of his pen effaced all his former glory.

Vedel, who was not surrounded by the enemy, decided to elude the clauses of the treaty before they should reach him. During the night of 21/22 July he struck camp. Dupont did not wish this to happen and sent General Legendre to call on Vedel to halt and respect the clauses of the treaty (by which Vedel's troops were to be taken prisoner after laying down their arms). Vedel then made his final mistake:

Above: General Lepic (1765–1827). He commanded the section of the Guard present in Madrid in 1808.

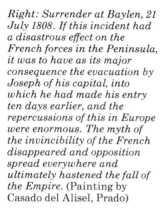

Right: Surrender at Baylen, 21 July 1808. If this incident had a disastrous effect on the French forces in the Peninsula, it was to have as its major consequence the evacuation by Joseph of his capital, into which he had made his entry ten days earlier, and the repercussions of this in Europe were enormous. The myth of the invincibility of the French disappeared and opposition spread everywhere and ultimately hastened the fall of the Empire. (Painting by Casado del Alisel, Prado)

Above: General Barbou d'Escouvrières (1761–1827). Commanded the 1st Division of II Observation Corps of the Gironde.

Right: Swiss prisoners aboard hulks. The 2nd Battalion of the 4th Swiss, the 1st Battalion of the 3rd and the 1st Battalion of the 2nd were all part of General Dupont's corps. The Convention of Andujar (the word capitulation was not used), which agreed that the French troops would be repatriated in Spanish vessels, was not dishonouring, but it was to be violated without scruple by the Seville Junta. General Dupont's soldiers, kept as prisoners-of-war, were put aboard hulks in Cadiz harbour with a complete absence of sanitation then escorted to the islet of Cabrera, where the majority perished of privation and misery. (From a painting by Dunki)

he obeyed. His 9,292 men handed over their weapons while, after marching past the troops of Castaños and Peña, Dupont's 8,242 men did the same. The clauses of the treaty were not respected. Crowded into hulks at Cadiz, then at Cabrera, the French prisoners were doomed to a wretched existence (which cannot help but call to mind that of the victims of the concentration camps).

Baylen weighed heavily in the Emperor's destiny. The invincible French had been beaten, and made prisoners. Everywhere, in Vienna, Berlin, London, there were outbursts of great joy. Castaños had flags made bearing the inscription, 'To the vanquishers of the victors of Marengo, Austerlitz and Jena'. But Dupont's soldiers were not the victors of Austerlitz; with those, Spain was soon to be acquainted.

When he learned of the disaster, the Emperor threw a memorable fit of anger. On their return to France, he had Dupont, Vedel and Marescot arrested and imprisoned at Vincennes. To Legendre, who was reporting to him, he said: 'On a battlefield, sir, one fights, and when instead of fighting one surrenders, one ought to be shot.' Then: 'I can see that I shall have to go myself to get things going again.'

The French Army, 1808–12

1. *Ist Provisional Regiment, cuirassier. This composite unit, based at Vitoria, was made up of detachments of the 1st, 2nd and 3rd Cuirassiers and the 1st and 2nd Carabiniers. At Baylen in* 1808 the 2nd Provisional Regiment of heavy cavalry formed part of Rigaud's Brigade.

2. 15th Light Infantry Regiment, grenadier in campaign dress. This was one of the white-uniformed regiments.

3. Imperial Guard, gendarme in campaign dress, 1808. In Madrid that year, there were 175 troopers with 18 officers under Colonel Jacquin.

4. Dragoon of the Guard in campaign dress, 1808. There were 219 troopers in Madrid in 1808, with a dozen officers under the command of Colonel Fiteau.

5. Line infantryman in greatcoat.

6. Fusilier-grenadier of the Middle Guard. The 1st and 2nd Battalions of fusilier-grenadiers formed part of the Guard Division at Madrid in 1808.

7 & 8. Marines of the Imperial Guard. At Madrid in 1808, the marines were commanded by Daugier. In July the battalion was captured at Baylen after a gallant resistance.

9 & 10. The Paris Guard. A first contingent arrived in Spain with Pannetier's brigade. A second detachment arrived with Major Daviet in 1808. After Burgos it was incorporated into the infantry of the line. (9) Fusilier of the 2nd Regiment. (10) Grenadier of the 1st Regiment.

11. Chasseur à Cheval of the Guard. At Madrid the chasseurs of the Guard formed part of the Guard division, with the Mamelukes. The squadron took part in the action at Benavente.

12. Mamelukes of the Imperial Guard, 1808. The company of Mamelukes rode with Murat at his entry into Madrid, and was involved in the rising of 'the 2nd May' (Dos de Mayo).

13. Chasseurs à Cheval, 1808. II Corps of the Gironde had a brigade of Chasseurs à Cheval composed of two provisional regiments. One consisted of detachments of the 1st, 2nd, 5th, 7th and 11th Regiments; the other of detachments from the 12th, 13th, 16th, 20th and 21st Regiments.

The charge of the Polish light horse at Somosierra, 30 November 1808. The countryside was stony, barren and uninhabited; the winding road that crossed the range was deeply sunken. However, it was the last obstacle before Madrid and the Emperor had decided to cross it with all speed. The Spanish, who thought the position impregnable, were confident, and their leader, Benito San Juan, had deployed his troops well on either side of the gorge. During the morning Ruffin's division tried without great success to outflank them via the ridge. Shortly after midday, the rising fog allowed the formidable position occupied by the Spanish to be seen. Colonel Piré, returning from reconnaissance, pointed out to an increasingly impatient Napoleon, 'Sire, it is impossible!' 'I do not know that word' replied the Emperor, and he turned to his escort: 'Storm that for me – at the gallop'. The squadron of Polish light horse on duty were the finest flower of Polish youth. These 150 horsemen looked magnificent in their crimson tchapskay and trousers and white aiguillettes. Their leader, Kozietulski, drew his sword and cried, 'At the trot!' Well seated, four abreast, the squadron sprang forward with drawn swords. The stones rolled, bullets and cannon balls thinned out their ranks and yet the insane charge continued. The irresistable whirlwind leapt over the batteries, cut down the artillerymen and did not stop until they had gained the summit, while the Spanish were fleeing on all sides. The feat of the Polish light horse at Somosierra passed into legend.
(Painting by J. Suchodolski)

The Portuguese Army, 1808–14

1. *19th Line, sapper. The Portuguese Army had 24 line regiments. The 19th was at Bussaco in 1810 (Coleman's brigade).*
2. *21st Line, grenadier, 1809–11. Also at Bussaco in 1810 (Champlemond's Portuguese brigade).*
3. *17th Line, musician.*
4. *19th Line, officer. At first attached to Champlemond's brigade, this regiment was present at the Battle of Bussaco, then as part of Power's brigade at the battles of Fuentes de Oñoro, Salamanca and Vitoria.*
5. *Battalion of Caçadores, drum major. In 1808 there were six battalions of these light infantry, with green or black plume according to company. They fought at Albuera in Collins's brigade.*
6. *11th Cavalry Regiment, 1808. The 11th was present at Vitoria in D'Urban's brigade.*
7. *6th Cavalry Regiment, officer, 1808–1813. This regiment fought at Vitoria in Campbell's brigade.*
8. *12th Battalion of Caçadores, officer, 1811. Present at Salamanca in Power's brigade.*
9. *3rd Artillery Regiment. At this time there were four regiments of artillery in the Portuguese Army.*
10. *12th Cavalry Regiment. Engaged at Vitoria in D'Urban's brigade.*
11. *11th Cavalry Regiment, trumpeter, 1811. The only distinguishing mark of the trumpeter was braid on the collar, facings and seams of the coat.*
12. *5th Battalion of Caçadores, rifleman in parade dress, 1808–11. Present at Albuera in Collins's brigade.*
13. *2nd Battalion of Caçadores, campaign dress, 1808–11. Fought at Bussaco in Coleman's brigade.*
14. *6th Line, corporal, 1812–14. In 1811 the Portuguese infantry adopted the British style of shako. This regiment fought at Vitoria in Ashworth's brigade.*
15. *24th Line, officer, 1814. The 24th was present with the 1st, 3rd, 4th, 15th and 16th at the blockade of Bayonne. The men wore white trousers.*
16. *4th Battalion of Caçadores, 1811–14. In 1811 a new uniform and a new organization: 12 battalions, each having five companies, including a company*

of skirmishers. The drums were replaced by horns. The 4th was present at Bayonne with the 5th and 8th Battalions.

17. *Corps of Engineers, officer, 1806. In 1812 a new organization with a general staff, a battalion of artificers, sappers and bridge-builders.*

Right: Horrifying scenes of the French retreat in 1808. 'In their flight French soldiers set fire to wagons full of wounded.' The scene, which is imaginary, depicts the retreat of General Duhesme's corps which, after having failed in its attempt to take Gerona, had to withdraw at the announcement of the Baylen surrender. Harried by the Milans del Bosch guerrillas, he had to abandon his baggage and return to Barcelona on 20 August. (Musée de l'Armée)

Right: Skirmish of Delaborde's division against the British at Roliça, 17 August 1808. The 2,500 men of the division victoriously contain the 15,000 British who are trying to envelop them. (Philippoteaux)

He gave the matter serious consideration and meanwhile brought the Guard back from Germany.

In Madrid, Joseph took fright and decided to leave his capital. After his ten-day reign, acting against the Emperor's directives, he left Madrid, followed by the army in confusion, neither attacked nor pursued. He rejoined Bessières at Burgos and withdrew towards Vitoria. He was to halt at the River Ebro. Behind the army, joy exploded. Married men, widowers, bachelors, priests and monks enlisted in groups for 'the war of the knife'.

The commotion at Baylen won over Portugal. On 1 August, Sir Arthur Wellesley, the future Duke of Wellington, disembarked with 15,000 men at the mouth of the Mondego, defeated at Vimeiro Junot's corps which, by the Convention of Cintra (30 August), was pledged to leave the country. His 20,000 men were to be repatriated. The British troops were now on the French flank as they withdrew from the peninsula, and British military and moral prestige were in the ascendancy. Of the 130,000 men who had crossed the Pyrenees, 30,000 were dead or prisoners, 20,000 languished in hospitals and 20,000 were being sent back to France under British colours.

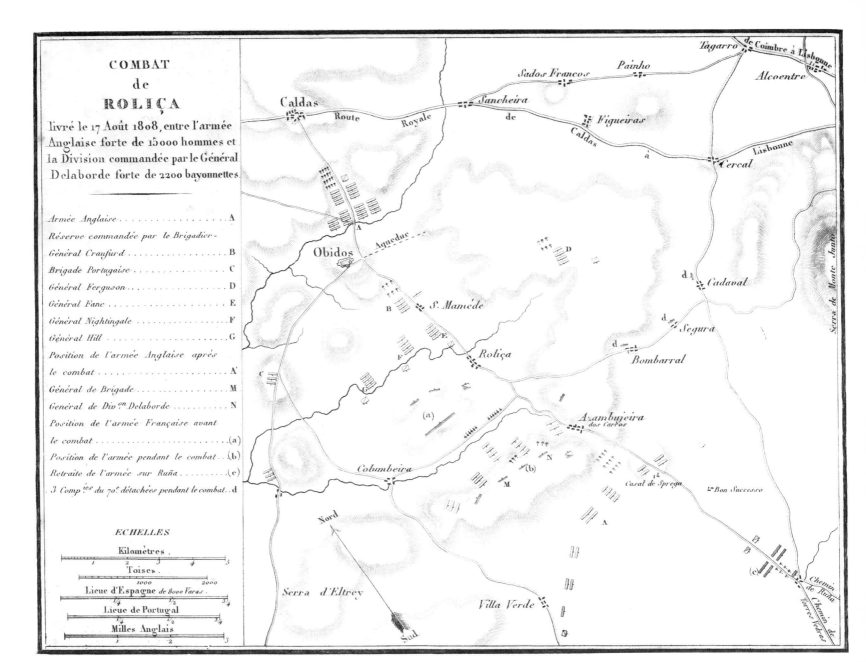

COMBAT
de
ROLIÇA

livré le 17 Août 1808, entre l'armée
Anglaise forte de 15000 hommes et
la Division commandée par le Général
Delaborde forte de 2200 bayonnettes.

Armée Anglaise . . . . A
Réserve commandée par le Brigadier-
Général Craufurd . . . . B
Brigade Portugaise C
Général Ferguson . . . . D
Général Fane . . . . E
Général Nightingale . . . . F
Général Hill . . . . G
Position de l'armée Anglaise après
le combat . . . . A'
Général de Brigade . . . . M
Général de Div.on Delaborde . . . . N
Position de l'armée Française avant
le combat . . . . (a)
Position de l'armée pendant le combat . . (b)
Retraite de l'armée sur Ruña . . . . (c)
3 Comp.ies du 70.e détachées pendant le combat . . d

ECHELLES

Kilomètres.

Toises.

Lieue d'Espagne de 8000 Varas.

Lieue de Portugal

Milles Anglais

Above: The Battle of Roliça as
depicted in General Foy's
'Histoire de la Guerre de la
Peninsule sous Napoleon'
(1827).

Right: Conscripts en route to
the Spanish frontier, August
1808. The levies intended for
the Army of Spain were set on
their way towards the Pyrenees
where, by order of the Emperor,
immense quantities of rations
and equipment had been
assembled. (Philippoteaux)

Above: Wellesley's headquarters on the eve of the Battle of
Vimeiro. (From a contemporary engraving)

Above: General Baron Margaron (1765–1824). He commanded the cavalry during the Battle of Vimeiro.

Right: The defence of the cemetery of Vimeiro on 21 August 1808 by the 43rd Foot. This plate illustrates the fruitless attack of Thomières's brigade (Delaborde's division) against the village of Vimeiro. (Caton Woodville)

Above: General Baron Prost (1764–1834). As Colonel, he was chief of the general staff of the artillery of I Observation Corps of the Gironde and was wounded at Vimeiro.

Right: The Battle of Vimeiro. General Brennier de Montmorand, wounded, is taken prisoner. Commanding fewer than 10,000 men, 1,200 of whom were cavalry, Junot gave battle to 18,000 British. The losses of the French army, which was tackling a solidly entrenched and well-ordered adversary, were severe. Brennier's brigade (70th and 86th of the Line) attempted to retake the guns of Solignac's brigade, which had just been seized by the 71st and 82nd Foot, but was in its turn overwhelmed. (Anonymous engraving after a painting by Lévêque)

Far left: The heroism of a piper of the 42nd Highlanders during the Battle of Vimeiro. (After Clark and Dubour)

Left: Cintra, on the road to Lisbon. (From a drawing by Bradford)

Left: Embarkation of the French army after the Convention of Cintra at the beginning of September 1808. The convention, signed at Cintra on 30 August by Generals Junot and Dalrymple, who had just taken command of the British army, accorded the honours of war to the French army and provided for its repatriation to French ports by the Royal Navy. (After a painting by Lévêque, National Army Museum)

Left: Erfurt. Faced with the turn of events in Spain, Napoleon, who needed security and peace in Europe to be able to intervene in person, met Alexander from 27 September to 14 October. Betraying Napoleon, Talley-rand urged Alexander to resist him and so the two sovereigns separated without any illusions about their alliance, which was renewed by the convention of 12 October. (Myrbach)

Finally, one more piece of bad news arrived: the 14,000 Spaniards that Napoleon had placed at the disposition of the King of Denmark had mutinied. Under the orders of the Marquis de la Romana, they had hurried to Nyborg, crossed to the isle of Langeland and boarded British ships. Despite the efforts of Bernadotte, who rushed to the rescue, nearly 10,000 men returned to Spain. The others were disarmed and taken prisoner. Something must be done. . . . all might be put aright with one great stroke. With his usual precision and speed, Napoleon dictated letters and memoranda for the organizing of the army in Spain.

The Pyrenees could be crossed only in the east and in the west; he therefore gave orders to Clarke, the Minister of War, to build-up supplies at Perpignan and Bayonne. He called for reinforcements: I Corps under Victor, V under Mortier, VI under Marchand. He had transports assembled, making the infantry travel by stages, to save fatigue and shoe-leather. He also organized rest facilities, officers in charge, gendarmes and shops. He was thinking too about morale. He ordered the Minister of the Interior to organize entertainments as the troops passed through the large towns and to allocate 3 francs per soldier to the local

Right: Fusilier-grenadiers of the Imperial Guard. Two regiments of fusiliers (six battalions) formed part of the infantry of the Guard that accompanied the Emperor in Spain. (M. Orange, Musée de l'Armée)

councils for this. He was not afraid to go into detail: 'you will have three kinds of songs prepared, so that the soldiers will not hear the same ones twice. . . .'

Now an entire army was on the march towards the Pyrenees. Units came from Italy, Holland, Germany and France. All the regiments entered Spain with three battalions. Cadres of the fourth were to stay at Bayonne to receive conscripts. On Sunday, 11 September there was a grand parade and a proclamation from the Emperor: 'Soldiers, after having triumphed on the banks of the Danube and the Vistula . . . let us carry our triumphant eagles as far as the very Pillars of Hercules. You have surpassed the fame of modern armies; but have you equalled the armies of Rome, which in a similar campaign triumphed on the Rhine and the Euphrates, in Illyria and on the Tagus?'

This inspired leader of men knew how to utter words that could ignite the fires of enthusiasm. Then, having regulated the order of march of wagons and supplies in minute detail, he left for Erfurt. He had to persuade the Tsar, whom he was to meet there, to leave him a free hand in Spain. In order to do that, he knew he might be obliged to take risks in the direction of Constantinople, and he did not wish this to happen.

Before an audience of kings and princes, the two emperors met from 27 September until 14 October. Each tried to convince the other with promises that did not bind them, but, they did agree to send a joint letter to King George III and to propose peace to him. Then, on 12 October on the site of the Battle of Jena, they signed a convention renewing their alliance. Napoleon had gained temporary security. In order to prove his good will, he disbanded the Grande Armée. The troops who remained in Germany took the less provocative name 'Army of the Rhine'. He reduced by 20 millions the contribution owed by Prussia, and on 14 October took his leave of Alexander on the Weimar road. The two emperors were never to meet again. . . .

Travelling fast, Napoleon arrived in Paris on the 18th, checked the last preparations, opened the session of the Legislative Council and, on the 29th at 11 pm, left the Tuileries for Spain. On 3 November, at about 1 am, he arrived at the Marracq Palace in Bayonne, which had seen the passing of the royal family and Godoy, and the successful issue of the politics that had placed Joseph on the Bourbon throne. Now he had his army near at hand. Formed from part of the Guard, reinforcements from the Elbe and the Rhine, Polish, German and Dutch contingents, and regiments from Italy, it consisted of six army corps.

I Corps (Marshal Victor): three divisions of infantry under Generals Villatte, Ruffin and Lapisse, and a division of cavalry.

II Corps (Marshal Soult): three infantry divisions under Generals Mouton, Merle and Bonnet, and a division of cavalry under Lasalle.

III Corps (Marshal Moncey): three infantry divisions under Generals Musnier, Morlot and Mathieu, and one of cavalry.

IV Corps (Marshal Lefebvre): three divisions under Generals Sebastiani, Leval and Valence who commanded the Polish Division, a Dutch division, a Westphalian division and three regiments of cavalry.

V Corps (General Gouvion Saint-Cyr): five divisions; three French under Generals Chabran, Souham and Chabot, two Italian (Pino and Lecchi) and a division of cavalry. To this corps was added Duhesme's division which was occupying Barcelona.

Above: Napoleon reviewing a regiment of light cavalry. On 4 November 1808 the Emperor at the head of 135,000 men, divided into six corps, entered Spain in order to restore his brother to the throne. (Myrbach)

Above: General Baron Mouton-Duvernet (1770–1815). He commanded the 63rd and 8th of the line, Pacthod's brigade, Villatte's division. (Engraving by Forestier)

Above: Imperial Foot Guards. From right to left: chasseur, fusilier, grenadier, tirailleur, cadet and voltigeur. 12,000 strong, the Imperial Guard accompanied the Emperor in Spain. (Philippoteaux)

Above: Polish lancers in Spain. (Philippoteaux)

Right: The Regiment of the Dragoons of the Imperial Guard (later the Dragoons of the Empress). It was part of the detachment of the Guard which accompanied the Emperor into Spain in 1808, rejoining the Grande Armée in 1809. After the Austrian campaign, the cavalry of the Guard present in Spain formed the 'mobile regiment of the Guard'. It was composed of chasseurs à cheval, Mamelukes and Polish light horse lancers. (Job)

French and Allied Armies, 1808–14

1. 65th Line, grenadier in campaign dress, 1812.
2. 16th Light Infantry, chasseur in campaign dress, 1812.
3. Gendarmerie of Spain, 1st Legion, sergeant, 1812.
4. Lancer-gendarme, 1810.
5. Marshal Soult's aide-de-camp.

6. Marshal Berthier's adjutant, 1808. Berthier, Prince of Neuchâtel, was present at Burgos, Toledo and Madrid.
7. 15th Regiment of Chasseurs à Cheval, cavalryman in campaign dress.
8. Neuchâtel Battalion, light infantryman, 1810. Raised in 1807 and arriving in Spain in 1810, this unit became famous, particularly in the struggle against the guerrillas. They became known as the 'canaries' because of their uniform.
9. 2nd Swiss Regiment, grenadier in campaign dress. The Observation Corps of the Gironde left Bayonne in 1808 with a majority of conscripts. Among them there were a few élite corps, including the Marines of the Guard, the Paris Guard and three Swiss battalions.
10. 3rd Swiss Regiment, fusilier officer in marching order. This was the first Swiss regiment to enter Spain, in 1807.
11. Regiment of Polish Light Horse of the Imperial Guard. This famous regiment, which distinguished itself at Somosierra, fought the campaign without the lance, which they did not receive until later.
12. Grand Duchy of Warsaw, 4th Line, grenadier. The

Grand Duchy furnished three infantry regiments (4th, 7th and 9th Line), a detachment of foot artillery and a detachment of sappers. The 4th Regiment distinguished itself at Talavera, at Albuera and at Sagunto.
13. Line infantry, light infantry corporal, carrying the company pennant, marching order, 1812–14.
14. 14th Line, grenadier, 1812. This regiment stayed in Catalonia and Aragon from 1809 to 1814, participating in the sieges of Saragossa and Tarragona, and in 1813 at the Battle of Villena. In 1812 they still wore the white hat and coat.
15. Line infantry, grenadier in marching order. Like many of the soldiers engaged in Spain, this grenadier has brown cloth trousers, which were very cheap, and therefore commonly worn throughout the Peninsula.
16. Spanish Gendarmerie, infantry company.
17. Marshal Suchet in dress uniform.
18. Marshal's aide-de-camp, 1809. Another example of the variety of aide-de-camps' uniforms.
19. General of Division, undress uniform, 1809.
20. 3rd Swiss Regiment, light infantryman.
21. Grand Duchy of Warsaw, 9th Line.
22. Grand Duchy of Warsaw, 7th Line, fusilier.

British and Allied Colours

1. *1st Foot Guards, King's colour. The battle honours were allotted in 1812.*
2. *Coldstream Guards, Royal standard. Battle honours allotted in 1814.*
3. *57th Foot (West Middlesex Regiment), regimental colour. This regiment distinguished itself particularly at the Battle of Albuera in 1811. Colonel Inglis, himself wounded, placed himself next to the colour, crying to his men who were reduced to a handful, 'Die hard, my men, die hard'. The regiment has kept the nickmane 'Diehards' ever since, and the battle honour 'Albuera' on their colour.*

4. *14th Light Dragoons (Duchess of York's Own), guidon.*
5. *5th Dragoon Guards (Princess Charlotte of Wales), pennant of the 3rd Squadron.*
6. *King's German Legion, 1st Regiment of Dragoons, pennant of 4th Squadron.*
7. *Colours of the Sicilian regiment 'Royal Bourbon', 1800-pattern.*
8. *Colour of 92nd Highland Foot. This colour, 1801 version, was changed at the time of the union of Ireland with the English crown and was carried during the Spanish campaigns. A new design was carried at the Battle of Waterloo.*

9. *Colour of the provisional Swiss battalion of Roll-Dillon. Yellow was the colour of Dillon's Swiss battalion and the emblems were those of Roll's battalion. These two units formed the provisional battalion of Roll-Dillon.*
10. *King's German Legion, 6th Line Battalion, regimental colour.*

Right: Napoleon's entry into Spain, 4 November 1808. (Philippoteaux)

Right: Shots having been fired from a convent, the cuirassiers storm the building which is looted, monks killed and nuns ravished . . . (Painting by Delaroche)

VI Corps (Marshal Ney): three infantry divisions under Generals Marchand, Lagrange and Mermet, a division of the Army of the Vistula and one of cavalry.

The general reserve, under the orders of Marshal Bessières, consisted of an infantry division (General Dessolle), six battalions of fusiliers, six battalions of grenadiers and chasseurs of the Guard and the divisions of dragoons.

This army numbered 120,000 men, which was very few in view of the vastness of Spain and the widely-scattered enemy.

The Spanish Army consisted of: the principal force, called the 'Army of the Centre', consisted of 40,000 men under Castaños, still basking in the glory of Baylen; the 'Army of the Right' was under the command of General Vives with Reding, the victor of Baylen, and Palafox, the defender of Saragossa; the 'Army of the Left' was commanded by Blake, who was born at Malaga of Irish parents, and who was considered to be an officer of great merit. In the rear, towards Burgos, were the reserves, commanded by the Marquis of Belvedere. The Spanish conceived a simple tactic – to surround the French Army by outflanking the two wings, cut it off from France . . . and destroy it.

Covered on the right by Victor and Lefebvre and on the left by Moncey, the Emperor arrived at Vitoria on 5 November. He regrouped his forces, and sent Bessières towards the plains to reconnoitre. On the 9th he learned that Lefebvre had beaten Blake at Zornoza (on 31 October) and occupied Bilbao. Giving Bessières's troops to Soult in order to leave Bessières in command of all the cavalry, Napoleon marched forward with the centre. On the 10th, Soult, who had set off with Mouton's division, found the Marquis of Belvedere's army ranged in battle order before the village of Gamonal. Its front was covered by 30 guns, and 7–8,000 armed peasants were drawn up behind 11,000 regular troops, the best in Spain, the Walloon guard, volunteers of good family, and several well-trained regiments. Soult still had only part of his command, but he gave the order to attack. Mouton's division stormed the village at the point of the bayonet, and broke through the enemy lines, while Bessières, arriving with his cavalry,

outflanked the wings, put the Spanish to rout and entered Burgos pell-mell with the fugitives. The Marquis of Belvedere withdrew, leaving behind 2,500 killed and wounded, 900 prisoners, 16 guns and 12 colours. The victors had lost only 200 men.

On the 11th, the Emperor entered Burgos – amidst cheering. However, the town was sacked, the houses (many of whose inhabitants had fled) were burned, convents were devastated and turned into stables. The *Bulletin de l'Armée*

Above: Marshal Lefebvre, Duke of Danzig (1755–1820). Commanding IV Corps, he opened the campaign by defeating General de la Romana at Zornoza (Durango) on 31 October 1808.

Right: Capture of the Spanish artillery at the Battle of Gamonal, 11 November 1808. (Philippoteaux)

Right: Occupation of Burgos by the French, 9 November 1808. Napoleon made his entry here on the 11th.

d'Espagne reported: 'Anarchy and disorder, that's what England is sowing in Spain. What will she reap from it?' Always the care to see in this resistance the gold of perfidious Albion . . . but . . . it was not only that which made the Spanish rise up against him. He would become aware of it later. . . .

For the moment, installed now between the two principal Spanish forces, which could no longer re-unite, Napoleon decided to destroy them in detail. He remained in Old Castile, watching for a chance to set up a 'manoeuvre capable of achieving great results with a single blow'. On the right, Victor and Lefebvre were at Espinosa de los Monteros, once more thrashing Blake's diminished army.

The Emperor sent Soult towards them and at Reinosa he cut off the Spaniards' retreat. On the left, Lannes, recently arrived from Naples, won a victory over Castaños at Tudela on 23 November. Unfortunately, Ney, coming from Soria, took the wrong road and his belated arrival prevented the destruction of the 40,000 men from Aragon, Valencia and Andalusia, who nevertheless lost 6,000 killed, wounded and prisoners, 26 guns and several colours.

The Spaniards' enveloping manoeuvre had failed. French communications were intact, and the neighbouring provinces had been evacuated by the regular Spanish forces. On 27 November, the Emperor decided to march on Madrid. On the 30th, Brigadier-General Benito San Juan, a worthy officer, took command of the remnants of Belvedere's army. Falling back to the Sierra de Guadarrama, he moved to defend the Somosierra Pass, which was the beginning of the road to Madrid. The position was well-chosen. With

Left: Mouton-Duvernet's infantry drive back the Spanish at the Battle of Espinosa de los Monteros, 10 and 11 November 1808. (Philippoteaux)

Left: The victory at Espinosa gained on 10 and 11 November 1808 by Marshal Victor over General Blake, who was driven back into the Asturias. (Musée de l'Armée)

10–12,000 men and 16 artillery pieces, he barred the route.

Napoleon sent some infantry onto the ridges to snipe at the Spanish, while the infantry of Ruffin's division attempted to advance. A thick fog covered the mountain and nothing could be seen at ten metres. Enemy bullets rolled at the Emperor's feet. At half-past eleven, the sun began to break through the mist and a barren, stony landscape appeared. Berthier's aide-de-camp, Colonel Piré, who had been sent forward, returned and declared, 'It is impossible.' 'I do not know that word', replied the Emperor and, turning to the three Polish squadrons, said, 'Storm that for me at the gallop.' Under a hail of grapeshot, Kozietulski, sabre high, led his 150 men off in columns of fours. At the second attempt they arrived at the batteries like a whirlwind, pinned the artillerymen to their guns

and put the infantry to flight. Eighty-three light horse remained on the road; all the officers were killed or wounded. The insanely heroic charge had lasted ten minutes. An extraordinary page of glory had been written. 'You are worthy of my Old Guard', said the Emperor ... and again they advanced on Madrid, while Benito San Juan payed the penalty for his defeat – tied to a tree, he was shot by his own soldiers.

On 2 December, the anniversary of his coronation and of Austerlitz, Napoleon arrived outside Madrid. In the distance, the tocsin was sounding in the 130 bell-towers of the town. At midday, Bessières brought the summons to surrender; the military junta replied with a refusal. At midnight a new summons; a new refusal. Now it was up to the guns. On 3 December at 9 am, breaches were made in the walls. The infantry entered the town, killing everyone encountered; the 'retiro' was taken. The Emperor had another summons taken to the junta. If it prolonged its resistance, he would crush the town. On the evening of the 3rd, Thomas de Morla, the perjurer of Baylen, signed the capitulation. During the night, the Marquis of Castellar, followed by his soldiers and some of the most compromised ringleaders, left the town. The French troops took possession the next day, in a dreary atmosphere, very unlike the triumphal entries into Vienna, Berlin or Warsaw.

Scorning the capital, the Emperor installed himself at Chamartin, situated two or three leagues distant, and undertook to 'regenerate' Spain. The Inquisition, feudal rights, the customs duties between provinces were abolished. The number of convents was reduced and their wealth confiscated. He formed the nucleus of an army for his brother and issued a proclamation: 'Spaniards, you have been led astray by wicked men. They have involved you in a senseless struggle and have caused you to take up arms. Is there anyone amongst you who, considering for a moment all that has happened, would not be convinced at once that you have been the plaything of the perpetual enemies of the Continent, who rejoiced to see French and Spanish blood shed? I told you in my proclamation of 2

Above: Kozietulski. He commanded the 3rd Squadron of the Regiment of Light Horse of the Guard and led the charge, during which he was wounded.

Above: General Krasinski (1782–1856). Colonel in 1808, he commanded the Polish light horse regiment (1st Light Horse Regiment of the Guard) which won fame at the battles of Medina del Rio Seco, Burgos and particularly in the charge at Somosierra, in the course of which his 3rd Squadron, serving close by the Emperor under the orders of Major Kozietulski, seized all the Spanish artillery (16 guns) and threw panic into an army of 13,000 men installed in a solid position, at the cost of 83 men, of whom 35 were killed, out of a total of 150.

Above: Napoleon's arrival at the summit of Somosierra, 'You are worthy of my Old Guard – I acknowledge you as my most brave cavalry.' (Painting by Kossak)

Left: The surrender of Madrid on the evening of 3 December 1808. (Painting by Gros, Musée de Versailles)

June that I wanted to be your regenerator. . . . Spaniards, is your destiny in your own hands? Reject the poisons that the English have strewn amongst you. . . . But, if all my efforts are in vain and if you do not return my trust, the only thing left for me to do will be to treat you as conquered territories and to place my brother on another throne. Then I should place the Spanish crown upon my own head and I would know how to deal with evil-doers. . . .' He dated this: 'In our Imperial camp at Madrid, 7 December of the year 1808.'

All the drama of the Spanish war was obvious in this proclamation. Certainly, as a son of the Revolution, the Emperor brought in reforms that at first gained him undeniable sympathies. But the Spanish were proud. They did not want a king imposed on them by a foreign army. The menacing tone of the last phrase and that expression 'in our Imperial camp', which seemed to make Madrid nothing but a halting-place in a victorious march – all of these were ill-fitted to persuade a tough and easily offended nation.

But, lo and behold, on 22 December, leaving his 'regenerating' activities, the Emperor departed to march against the British: 20,000 men under Sir John Moore. Moore had left Portugal during 1808 with the intention of crushing

Above: Philippe de Ségur (1780–1873), Napoleon's aide-de-camp. He participated in the charge of the Polish light horse at Somosierra and was gravely wounded during the action.

Right: Plasencia, important centre of communications at the time of the advance of the British army towards Salamanca. (From a drawing by Robert K. Porter)

Right: Convoy of British artillery in Portugal in 1808. (Atkinson)

Right: The crossing of the Tagus by Major-General Fraser's division at Vila Velna. (From a drawing by Major Saint-Clair)

Above: General Count Belliard (1769–1832). Murat's Chief of Staff, then Jourdan's Chief of General Staff. The Emperor appointed him military governor of Madrid on 5 December 1808, and he held this office until 24 December 1810. He was Chief of Staff of the Army of the Centre until 30 September 1811.

THE GUERRILLA WAR...

Above: French troops attack an insurgent stronghold. (M. Orange)

Left: Atrocities depicted in Goya's series 'The disasters of war'. (National Library, Madrid)

Above right: Assassination. (Bacler d'Albe, Musée de l'Armée) *More than 300,000 French soldiers or foreigners in French service fell in seven years of warfare on the soil of the Peninsula, most of them in obscure ambushes, victims of the guerrillas.*

the French on the banks of the Ebro. Meanwhile, he was to maintain the Spaniards' spirit of resistance and to establish a common plan of campaign with their generals. This was difficult to accomplish, since communications were bad and there was a lack of money. When he arrived at Salamanca on 13 November, to the announcement of French victories and the capture of Burgos, he made ready to do an about-face and return to Portugal. At the end of November Moore ordered General Baird, who was a little nearer to Benavente, to return to Astorga. He had set the withdrawal in motion when, on 3 December, the British delegate to the junta wrote to him: 'I cannot but point out to you most sharply the necessity of supporting the Spanish people's resolution by all the means that have been placed at your disposal to that end. I consider that the fate of Spain depends absolutely, for the moment, on the decision that you take.' Despite his lack of enthusiasm, Sir John Moore had to attempt something. He decided to try to cut off the French on the Ebro. In order to do this, he first had to crush Soult who, with 14,000 men, was occupying Asturias.

On 11 December, Moore left Salamanca, arriving at Mayorga on the 20th, at Sahagun on the 22nd, and there established his quarters, threatening Soult. But he was himself in danger of being cut off from Lisbon. Indeed, the Emperor was preparing his offensive against Portugal. At Talavera and beyond on the road to Badajoz, Napoleon was drawing up an advance guard with Lasalle, Milhaud, two divisions of dragoons with Bessières and IV Corps. He placed Victor and Latour-Maubourg at Toledo and Aranjuez. Ney and Lapisse's division he placed at Madrid, and asked Soult to cover Burgos and to occupy Santander. Then he concerned himself with the discipline of the 50,000 men he intended to take, gave orders for the security of communications and billets, and deliberated his plan of campaign. On the 19th, he learned that the British cavalry, followed by 5,000 infantry, had harassed the French at Rueda and Tordesillas. In panic, Valladolid was evacuated by Franceschi's cavalry. Napoleon would not go directly for Moore: he was going to cut him off, encircle him, destroy him. ... But not yet. The gods smiled upon the Englishman and brought before his eyes an intercepted letter that told of the Emperor's intentions and orders. Moore understood his danger, halted his advance, joined

On 28 December 1808 a decree by the Central Junta gave legal existence to a 'new kind of militia' under the names of 'partides', 'cuadrillas' and 'guerrillas', which, aided by the topography of the country, waged a merciless war of continual skirmishing against the French invaders.

'Not daring to attack the seasoned regiments in open country, the guerrilleros lay in ambush in the gorges, the woods, the difficult passages of their mountains in order to surprise the convoys and messengers coming and going from France. If the escorts were in force and had good scouts, the guerrilleros disappeared quickly into the mountains whose narrowest pathways were known to them. If the escorts were insufficient or composed of 'green' troops, they would attack boldly, would kill or disperse the defenders and make off with the convoy.' – Captain E. Martin, 'La gendarmerie française en Espagne et au Portugal'.

... In order to defend themselves from the Napoleonic invasion, the Spanish employed this means with an energy, an animosity and such constancy that only victory could crown. An excess of patriotic resistance, the system certainly contributed to the final success of the war of independence which would never have been achieved by regular armies. It was the unleashing of passion, the forgetting of the laws of humanity, the repudiation of military rules of discipline, the scorn for authority, the unbridled satisfaction of pride. Customs, the climate and fanaticism inspired the methods of a merciless resistance – ferocious in the mountains, more feeble on the plain. Yes, really a war to the death, for to kill the enemy became the general aspiration, the brutal goal pursued unceasingly wherever there was hope of its achievement; in the silence of the night, in the shelter of a house, in the repose of one's bed, in a corner of the woods, at the turning of a pathway, unexpectedly, through a hedge, behind a rock, on the highway, just as on the field of battle. ...' – Geoffroy de Grandmaison, 'Napoléon et l'Espagne'.

his forces with those of Baird, and decided to meet de la Romana in order to crush Soult with all his forces united.

Even so, Napoleon guessed Moore's plan, and decided to reach him with all speed. On the evening of the 22nd, with 50,000 of his best troops, he arrived at the foot of the Sierra de Guadarrama, on the road to Avila. The weather was dreadful. Eddies of snow blinded the men, the horses slipped on the ice, the troops were grumbling, troubles were coming to a head. Napoleon gave the cavalry orders to dismount. He himself dismounted, formed the staff into several groups, placed himself between Lannes and Duroc, around whom were ranged other generals. Then this heroic phalanx, led the army onwards. During the evening the ridge was crossed, but at what a price! On 23 December it rained, and the Duero valley became a sea of mud. Ney entered Medina del Campo.

One hundred kilometres to the north, Sir John Moore settled in at Sahagun, ready to attack Soult. It was then

Far left: The summit of the Sierra Guadarrama on 22 December 1808. Having learned on the 19th of the British army's movements, Napoleon intended to cut off its retreat to the sea by arriving before it at Benavente. On 22 December, in atrocious weather, the French army, 50,000 strong, crossed the Sierra Guadarrama at the price of much suffering. (From a watercolour by Eric Pape)

Left: The road to Corunna. No longer able to retreat into Portugal, the British army beat a retreat towards Galicia. (Robert K. Porter)

Right: Crossing of the Esla by the French cavalry. (Bacler d'Albe, Musée de l'Armée)

Right: Episode during the Battle of Benavente. The charge of the 10th and 18th Hussars (Lord Paget). On 29 December 1808 General Lefebvre-Desnouëttes at the head of four squadrons of the Chasseurs of the Guard forded the Esla near Benavente and attacked the British rearguard. Charged by more than 3,000 horsemen (the 18th, 7th, 10th Hussars, 3rd Hussars K G L, commanded by Generals Stewart and Paget), the chasseurs re-crossed the Esla still fighting. But in the course of this action, General Lefebvre-Desnouëttes was wounded and captured and about 30 of his men were disabled (nearly 200 according to British sources). (Painting by W. B. Wollen)

Left: Transport of the British army. (Atkinson)

that de la Romana sent him a piece of intelligence according to which the Emperor and his army had set off in pursuit of him. The Englishman decided to about-face, to fall back hurriedly across the Esla and to reach Corunna where a fleet was to await him.

Having impetuously set off in search of the British, Lefebvre-Desnouëttes with the chasseurs of the Guard came across General Paget's dragoons at Benavente. The whole of the British brigade turned to face them, drove them back across the Esla, through which they had just swum, put them to the sword and took Lefebvre-Desnouëttes prisoner. He, wounded by a pistol-shot, was to spend nearly four years in captivity before escaping. He was later to serve in Russia and at Waterloo. . . .

On 19 December, Marshal Moncey (III Corps) received the support of Marshal Mortier (V Corps). The Emperor's order – to besiege and take Saragossa. During the absence of the French, Palafox had not remained inactive. Various works had been constructed, and ditches and battlements now reinforced the buildings. In the streets, doors and windows were barricaded. Arms and munitions were abundant, and reinforcements had brought the garrison to about 40,000 men. Two hundred well supplied guns had been placed in position.

The French force was 30,000 strong: Moncey's corps with the divisions of Morlot, Grandjean and Musnier plus the Wathier brigade of cavalry; and Mortier's corps with the divisions of Gazan and Suchet. Six artillery companies, eight companies of sappers, three of miners and sixty guns were placed under the direction of Moncey. As in the first siege in June, it was the Monte Torrero that was attacked first. During the night of 21/22 December, it was occupied by Musnier. In the morning, Moncey, who had just learned of the capture of Madrid, sent Palafox a summons to surrender. The latter replied: 'To spill the blood of my subordinates is not my desire; but there is not one amongst them who would not give it with joy for his country. It does not follow from the capitulation of Madrid that other towns will also surrender.' So Saragossa must be taken by storm. Siege works were immediately begun.

Above: Lieutenant-General Sir John Moore, Commander-in-Chief of the British expeditionary force in the Peninsula in 1808. Well-liked by his soldiers, he was the author of a new method of instruction, and of modifications to equipment and tactics which gave the British infantry a strength and firepower which were to render abortive the French attacks. (From a portrait by Halls)

Top: The rearguard of the British army during the retreat to Corunna. (From a painting by J. B. Beadle)

Above: General Gouvion Saint-Cyr puts the Spanish to rout at Molinos del Rey on 21 December 1808. (F. Blanch)

1809

Napoleon enters Astorga and decides to return to France — Soult continues the pursuit towards Corunna — Embarkation of the British, death of Sir John Moore — Capture of Saragossa — Jourdan appointed Chief of Staff — Soult enters Portugal — Capture of Braga and Oporto — Soult halts — Arrival of Sir Arthur Wellesley, future Duke of Wellington — The French are attacked at Oporto and beat a retreat — Portugal is evacuated — Disagreement between Ney and Soult — Victor triumphant at Medellin and Sebastiani at Ciudad Real — Wellesley threatens Madrid — Battle of Talavera — Return of the British to Portugal — Siege of Gerona — The French victorious at Ocaña — Defeat of Marchand at Tamanès — Capture of Salamanca.

While the siege of Saragossa was getting under way, the Emperor, joined by Soult, entered Astorga on 1 January. He had with him 70,000 foot, 10,000 horse and 200 guns – an admirable effort considering how many obstacles had been overcome in only a few days. The road from Benavente was littered with the retreating British army's dead horses, and abandoned carts, equipment, artillery wagons and munitions of war. But on 2 January the 24th *Bulletin* reported: 'The Emperor has ordered the Duke of Dalmatia to go in hot pursuit of the British to the place of their embarkation, and to throw them into the sea.' Why not Napoleon himself? On that day a messenger had arrived from Paris, and the news was serious. Inevitable and impending war with Austria – perhaps before the spring! Russia uncertain; Prussian duplicity; Britain's growing activity in the chancelleries ... and, finally, a plot in Paris in which Talleyrand and Fouché were vying with each other in scheming and preparing the 'succession' – Murat, having forebodings, was being urged on by Caroline.... It was necessary to return to France, so Napoleon departed, leaving to his lieutenants the task of completing his work.

In the rain, along broken roads, Soult began the hunt for the redcoats. In the fogs of the winter days, the French searched for the British, who retreated via Bembibre, Ponferrada and Villafranca del Bierzo. On 3 January, their rearguard, which was posted on a vine-covered hillside at Cacabelos, fought an action in which the legendary French cavalryman General Auguste Colbert, was killed by a bullet in the forehead. His death aroused universal sorrow. Although their position was strong, the British abandoned it during the night and hastened towards Lugo. The pursuit continued, breathless and furious. On the 5th, Sir John Moore halted at Lugo to rally his army and give the transports in which they were to embark time to arrive. But Soult was soon on the scene and, fearing that he would not be able to hold out, Moore decided on the night of the 8th to retire to Corunna. By the time that the French realized he had gone, he had had a start of ten hours, travelling at a forced pace, killing horses, throwing into the ravine everything that might hold him up. After suffering unparalleled hardships, he gained Corunna with his vanguard and scanned the horizon. No fleet! He had to hold out. The remainder of the main army arrived. The bridge of El Burgo was destroyed, delaying Soult who did not reach Corunna until the 15th. The French arrived just in time to see the British fleet anchor calmly just out of range of the Imperial cannon.

Soult held back because he wanted to regroup his forces. Under pressure from his staff, however, he decided on the

Above: Death of General Auguste de Colbert at the Battle of Cacabelos in 3 January 1809. After taking part in the victory at Tudela on 22 November he participated in the pursuit of the retreating British army. In the advance on Astorga he captured 2,000 British troops, but on 3 January his chasseurs and hussars came up against the British rearguard, solidly entrenched in Cacabelos on the Guia. The horsemen cut their way to the approaches to the bridge; Colbert advanced as far as the line of skirmishers and saw his aide-de-camp fall. His men then saw him fall backwards. A bullet fired by a rifleman of the 95th had just hit him above the left eyebrow and had passed through his head. (After Louis Merllie, 'Notice bibliographique sur les frères Colbert'.

Above: Marshal Soult, Duke of Dalmatia (1769–1851). Commander of II Corps of the Army of Spain on 26 September 1809, Commander-in-Chief of the Army of the South in Spain on 14 July 1810. Lieutenant-General, Commander-in-Chief of the armies of Spain and the Pyrenees on 1 July 1813. (Painting by Ruddler, Musée de Versailles)

Left: General Baron Auguste de Colbert de Chabanais (1777–1809). Commander of the brigade of light cavalry of VI Corps (15th Chasseurs, 3rd Hussars).

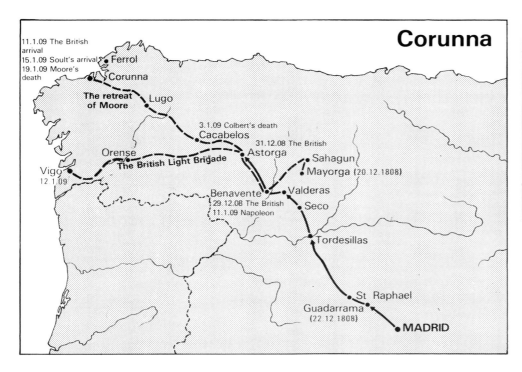

Corunna

11.1.09 The British arrival
15.1.09 Soult's arrival
19.1.09 Moore's death
Ferrol
Corunna
The retreat of Moore
Lugo
3.1.09 Colbert's death
Cacabelos
31.12.08 The British
Orense
The British Light Brigade
Astorga
Sahagun
Mayorga (20.12.1808)
Vigo
12.1.09
Benavente
Valderas
29.12.08 The British
11.1.09 Napoleon
Seco
Tordesillas
St Raphael
Guadarrama
(22.12.1808)
MADRID

Top: The road to Corunna by Bradford, 1809. (Library of R. and J. Brunon)

Right: Lieutenant-General Moore at the Battle of Corunna. (B. G. Backer)

Far right: The death of Sir John Moore. While personally leading his men in the battle, General Moore was hit by a bullet which shattered his collar-bone. Carried into Corunna, he died on arrival, to the sorrow of the entire army. (H. M. Paget)

16th to send an 'offensive reconnaissance'. Mermet's division, supported by a part of Merle's division, attacked the village of Elvina on the French left flank. They took it, destroying two British regiments and gravely wounding General Baird. Moore then brought forward his reserves and the terrible battle recommenced. Taken and retaken several times, the village was held in the end by the French. British losses were significant: Sir John Moore, mortally wounded, was carried into the town, but the embarkation continued under the command of General Hope, and, on the 19th, the fleet weighed anchor and disappeared. Some 8–9,000 British troops were killed or taken prisoner, but the bulk of the army escaped without Soult being able to intervene. Two days later, he entered Corunna, dislodged a small Spanish garrison that had installed itself there, and sent Mermet's division and a brigade of dragoons to take possession of Ferrol, where the French found considerable booty: eight ships, three frigates, 300 cannon and a not inconsiderable amount of equipment. The Emperor could only congratulate Soult on these results.

Above: Episode during the Battle of Corunna. The 42nd Highlanders recapture the village of Elvina from the 31st Light. This village was the scene of desperate battles between the soldiers of Baird's, Fraser's and Hope's divisions, and those of Generals Merle and Mermet. (Caton Woodville)

British Commanders:
Left: Major-General Alexander McKenzie Fraser, commander of Beresford's and Fane's brigades.

Centre: Sir David Baird. Gravely wounded in the Battle of Corunna. After the death of Sir John Moore he had been entrusted with command of the army. (Raeburn)

Right: Lieutenant-General John Hope. He had under his orders the Leith, Hill and Crawfurd brigades. He replaced the wounded Sir David Baird as commander of the army.

Above: Sir John Cradock (Lord Howolen). He commanded the 10,000 British troops left in the Peninsula after the re-embarkation at Corunna. (Painting by Sir T. Lawrence)

Right: Battle of Corunna. On 16 January 1809 a savage battle saw 7,000 French infantry, brought into action by Marshal Soult, opposing 10,000 British. Monte Mero, the key British position, was the scene of a desperate battle, as was the village of Elvina. The British, who had managed to hold their position on the summit of Monte Mero, evacuated it during the night. (Philippoteaux)

However, since the beginning of January, Junot, Duke of Abrantes, had replaced Moncey outside Saragossa, while Mortier received the order to attack Catalayud with Suchet's division. It was an army diminished by 9,000 men that was to storm the position, and the siege dragged on. The Emperor, losing patience, appointed Marshal Lannes to command the army outside the town and, while Mortier successfully attacked the Spanish relief army, Suchet returned with his division to drive back and keep at a distance the enemy outside. These tasks were actively pursued. On the 27th, after a violent preparation by the artillery, a general attack was launched. The surrounding wall, the convent of Santa Engracia, that of the Capuchins and the Porta del Carmen passed into French hands. Everywhere the fighting was desperate. Lannes wrote to the Emperor: 'The siege of Saragossa in no way resembles the war that we have waged until now. It is a craft for which we need great prudence and great strength. We are obliged to take one house at a time. The poor people defend themselves there with a desperate eagerness that one cannot imagine. In fact, Sire, it is a horrific war....'

The battle was now raging in the town itself. Food was short and an epidemic of typhoid was killing 4–5,000 people a day. Despite the methodical and constant progress of the French, no-one thought of surrender, though it must be said that gibbets set up in the street were always ready to welcome those who spoke of submission. On 20 February, at about 4 pm, Palafox, who was ill, realized that this time all was finished. He sent a deputation to Marshal Lannes to negotiate the capitulation. The latter demanded that 'the garrison taken prisoner-of-war will lay down its arms 200 paces from the gate of the Portillo. The civilians will surrender their arms and the officials will take the oath to King Joseph'. On the 24th, Lannes and Mortier made their official entry into the ravaged town. A total of 50,000 people of all ages had perished. A solemn Te Deum was sung in the

Above: Palafox y Melzi, defender of Saragossa (1776–1847). He was assisted in his action by four divisional leaders: Fernando Butron, Diego Fivaller, José Manson and Felipe Saint-March. According to Marbot's memoirs, it was this latter, a Belgian in the service of Spain, who played the principal rôle in the defence of the city, Palafox having fallen ill at the beginning of the siege. (Zuloaga Collection, Zumaya)

Left: View of Saragossa and the bridge over the Ebro. On the right, Our Lady of the Pillar, surmounted by its bulbous bell-towers. (Bacler d'Albe, Musée de l'Armée)

Far Left: Marshal Mortier, Duke of Treviso (1768–1835), commanding V Corps of the Army of Spain. He took part in the siege of Saragossa.

Left: Marshal Lannes, Duke of Montebello (1769–1809). Commanding III and V Corps, he took possession of Saragossa on 20 February 1809. He had assumed supreme command of the siege on 20 December 1808. (Painting by Gérard)

Top Right: The siege of Saragossa. (Library of R. and J. Brunon)

Above: Episode during the siege of Saragossa. A Spaniard, spared from the explosion of a mine, prefers to jump into space rather than be taken prisoner by the French. (Bacler d'Albe, Musée de l'Armée)

Right: Fighting in the church of San Augustino. (Painting by Alvarez Dumont, Saragossa Museum)

Above: Charles de la Bedoyère, aide-de-camp to Marshal Lannes during the siege of Saragossa. He had been appointed captain on 8 January 1809. (Guerin)

Above: The surrender of Saragossa on 20 February 1809. The survivors of the garrison, after surrendering their arms, were sent to Bayonne as prisoners-of-war. (M. Orange)

Left: Battle of Valls (Catalonia), 23 February 1809. In the foreground, General Reding at grips with a French dragoon. At the end of the battle, Souham's division, which had repulsed General Reding's army during six hours of fighting, was joined by Pino's Italian division commanded by General Gouvion Saint-Cyr. Routed, the Spanish were pursued by the 24th Dragoons, and in the course of this pursuit, General Reding received a sword-blow from a dragoon named Bouzon and died a few days later. The Spanish, pursued right up to the walls of Tarragona, lost 1,500 prisoners, their artillery and their baggage. (Lithograph by C. Motte)

church of Our Lady of the Pillar, and the 16,000 men who composed the remainder of the garrison filed before their conquerors.

With the British army gone, Joseph in Madrid and Catalonia conquered, submission was now but a matter of months away. So the Emperor thought. In any case, he intended to return himself and rapidly finish his conquest – this he had said to Soult when he left. But Austria was not to leave him the time. His presence had been enough to impart drive and unity to the campaign in the peninsula. After his departure, there was nothing but a mixture of successful operations and reversals, but always without any cohesion and without any follow-up. Their only result was uselessly to exhaust the French forces.

However, before his departure, Napoleon left his instructions with Berthier, his irreplaceable Chief of Staff. Soult was to march to Oporto with his divisions, less two regiments that were placed at the disposal of Ney to enable him to defend and organize Galicia. Ney had to undertake to ensure communications with Astorga and Benavente. The two marshals were to work together. Bessières, Duke of Istria, received command of upper Spain with its provinces of San Sebastian, Vitoria, Bilbao, Burgos, Valladolid where he was quartered, Palencia, Zamora, Leon and Santander. Soult's army, composed of seventeen infantry regiments and ten of cavalry, was destined for the expedition to Portugal. Victor was to unite his movements with him: 'Today, my lord Duke, is the 21st. It cannot be

Confederation of the Rhine

3rd Regiment of the Confederation of the Rhine.
3. *Grand Duchy of Baden, 4th Regiment of Infantry, skirmisher, 1808. This contingent consisted of a regiment of infantry and a battery of artillery.*
4. *Kingdom of Westphalia, 2nd Regiment, grenadier, 1808–09. Westphalia had sent to Spain three line regiments, a light regiment, a company of foot artillery and a regiment of light horse.*
5. *Hesse-Darmstadt, Regiment 'Prince Heritier' (Graf und Erbprinz), skirmisher.*
6. *Anhalt Regiment, 1809. The contingents of Anhalt-Dessau, Anhalt-Detmold and Anhalt-Köthen contributed to the formation of the 5th Regiment of the Confederation of the Rhine.*
7. *Kingdom of Westphalia, 4th Infantry Regiment, skirmisher.*
8. *Coburg-Saalfeld Battalion, fusilier, 1809. This battalion, integrated in the 5th Regiment of the Confederation of the Rhine, took part in the siege of Gerona.*
9. *Kingdom of Westphalia, 1st Battalion of light infantry, officer in campaign dress.*

10 & 11. *Kingdom of Westphalia, 1st Regiment of Light Horse, trooper and trumpeter in campaign dress, 1808.*
12, 13 & 14. *Principality of Lippe, officer and fusilier. The principalities of Lippe-Detmold and Lippe-Buckbourg were part of the Confederation of the Rhine the 1st and 2nd contingents formed, with the Anhalt Battalion, the 5th Regiment of the Confederation.*
15. *Nassau, 2nd Squadron of Chasseurs à Cheval, 1810.*
16. *Nassau, 1st Squadron of Chasseurs, 1807. When this squadron arrived in Spain, apparently the helmet was worn, but it was very soon replaced by the busby with red cockade.*
17. *Frankfurt-am-Main. Contingent of the Prince-Bishop of Frankfurt, grenadier, 1808–09.*
18. *Company of Schwarzburg-Sonderhausen, fusilier. This company, together with detachments from Schwarzburg-Rudolstadt, three companies from Waldeck and three from Reuss, formed the 6th Regiment of the Confederation of the Rhine.*

1. *Nassau contingent, 1st Regiment, 1st Company of Grenadiers. This contingent was part of the 2nd Regiment of the Confederation of the Rhine.*
2. *Nassau contingent, 2nd Regiment, company of grenadiers, sergeant-major. They formed part of the*

Spanish Colours, 1808–14

1. *Light Battalion of Barcelona, regimental colour. Around the royal arms a garland bears the inscription 'Batallon ligero de Barcelona'.*
2. *Cavalry Regiment 'El Principe', standard. The rules for colours and standards were laid down by decree in 1723.*
3. *2nd Regiment, 'Voluntarios de Barcelona', regimental colour. This regiment of light infantry belonged to de la Romana's army. Each regimental colour carried the cross of Burgundy, and at each extremity the arms of the province, or individual emblems, in this case the arms of Barcelona. The colonel's standard was white, with the arms of Spain in the centre and in the corners the arms of Barcelona.*
4. *Standard of a regiment of hussars. Crimson ground with the arms of Spain and on the other side the*

regimental device. For the 'Voluntarios de España' regiment: yellow ground with four gilded crowns. For the 'Maria-Luisa' regiment: yellow ground with the Queen's cipher and laurel wreaths in green. For the 'Husares españoles': yellow ground with two gilded columns, silver inscription and gilded crowns.
5. *Cavalry Regiment 'Cuenca', pennant. This unit was one of the numerous regiments of cavalry raised during the war. On the streamer 'Regimento de linea', the other side carried the image of the Virgin crowned with trophies and, above, 'Caballeria de Cuenca'. On both sides was embroidered the chalice and star, which were the arms of Cuenca.*
6. *Colour of the 'Real cuerpo de Artilleria'. Doubts exist as to the hues of these colours. For a long time dark crimson was attributed to this arm of service.*

According to the decree of 1710, the ground should have been white, but in the Military Museum in Madrid, there is an artillery colour indicated as having been carried during the war of independence. It is blue with a garland bearing its inscription 'Real artilleria'. The colour of the College of Artillery, founded in 1806, also has a blue ground. Moreover, the regulation of 1808 fixed the hues for each arm; blue is specified for the artillery and Walloon Guards.
7. *Regiment of 'Zapadores y Minadores', regimental colour.*
8. *Regiment 'El Rey', colonel's colour; conforms to the regulation.*
9. *Colour of Traxler's Swiss regiment.*

presumed that you could be in Oporto before 5 February and in Lisbon before the 16th . . .' he wrote to Soult. The orders followed with great precision. The march of II Corps was calculated by stages as if it were a manoeuvre. Communications with the other armies were provided for, their places in the system well prescribed.

Having thus made his dispositions for the campaign, Napoleon left the command of the armies to Joseph; but, having little confidence in the military qualities of his brother, Napoleon gave him Marshal Jourdan as Chief of Staff. Although he valued him little, the Emperor was not able to do other than to include the victor of Wattignies and Fleurus in his grand promotion of marshals. However, if he was lavish in giving noble titles to his companions in arms, the Emperor gave none to Jourdan. Of straightforward character, a little dull and morose, the marshal was obeyed by his equals with difficulty. Furthermore, the leaders of the corps were to correspond directly with the Minister of War and receive their operational orders from him. Thus they considered the authority of Madrid to be purely nominal. All this provoked many errors. Jourdan had no chance to adapt the master's orders, which often arrived late and in an inopportune manner. Napoleon, too much of a centralizer, was in a way chiefly responsible for the Spanish disaster. Later, at St. Helena, he was to point out that if he had not succeeded, it was because he had made a political error. However, he forgot to state that his military losses in Spain were caused by his desire to conduct the campaign from afar and, by leaving his generals and marshals without immediate central authority, he had allowed their rivalry to grow to the point where duty was forgotten.

Meanwhile, Soult began the execution of his orders. He mustered his army, handed over the conquered strongholds, and set off for Tuy. With his cavalry, Franceschi was ordered to take Vigo as he passed, to seize Tuy, and there to assemble all available boats. Unfortunately the Minho had flooded at Tuy. There was no bridge and the Portuguese had taken all the available craft to the left bank. Disappointment. An attempt to force a crossing with 300 men failed, and Soult was obliged to climb up again via Ribadavia as far as Orense to find a bridge. Crossing hostile country, he arrived at Allariz, where he noticed local excitement because of the presence in the neighbourhood of the Marquis de la Romana. On 6 March, Franceschi managed to reach his rearguard at Osoño. The Spanish met them, but soon had to flee leaving 200 dead on the field. This pretty business put la Romana's army out of action,

but the survivors regrouped and, aided by the population, began to harry the French troops again. On 9 March, nearly two months late according to the timetable laid down by the Emperor, Soult entered Portugal. The town of Chaves capitulated on the 12th. The French army marched towards Braga, fighting off the continual sallies of the fanatical populace. On the 17th it arrived at Carvalho. On the 20th it thrust aside the 15–18,000 men who barred its way and entered a totally deserted Braga. Before leaving, the inhabitants had murdered their 'corregidor' who was suspected of having a weakness for the French. Soult reported in his memoirs that the sight of this town, abandoned by all its inhabitants, remained one of the most moving experiences of his career.

Soult now had to make for Oporto as quickly as possible and, after having restored some order, repaired the cannons and provisioned the troops with munitions, the Duke of Dalmatia marched on the town which was held by nearly 60,000 men, who were resolved to defend it to the last round. Siege works were hastily built, and 200 cannon went into action. There was even a fervent hope that the British might arrive. Soult opened his attack on the 25th: his left flank occupied Guimarães and seized the bridges over the Ave. The centre, with General Foy, forced the bridge of Couchinha and fell upon the enemy artillery. Brigadier-General de Vallonga, commanding the Portuguese defenders, was killed by his own troops who blamed him for the defeat – his body was cut into pieces and buried in manure as a sign of derision. By the 27th, the French were occupying the heights that dominated the town.

On the 28th, Soult sent a summons to surrender to the Bishop of Oporto, who did not reply, and General Foy, sent to discuss terms, was seized, wounded and thrown into a dungeon. On the 29th the French mounted the assault. At the charge, with bayonets fixed, they entered the streets, murdering all whom they found in their way (apart from a few prisoners, including three British officers who had recently arrived from Lisbon). They released General Foy and, enraged by the sight of the tortured bodies of their comrades, they indulged in the greatest violence.

Soult, startled by the resistance he had met, hesitated to resume his march upon Lisbon; nor did he dare to return to Spain and thus contravene the Emperor's orders. He decided upon the worst solution – to establish himself in Oporto and declare himself Governor of Portugal. It is certain that Nicolas Jean de Dieu Soult, son of an insignificant notary from St. Amand-La-Bastide (Tarn), had his personal ambitions. The crown of 'Lusitania' would

Above: General Baron Foy (1775–1825). During the capture of Oporto on 29 March, he was stripped of his clothes and taken prisoner by the Portuguese who claimed they had come to discuss terms. He was gravely wounded at the Battle of Bussaco, 27 September 1810.

Right: View of Oporto in 1809. On 22 April Sir Arthur Wellesley disembarked at Lisbon and marched on Oporto at the head of 12,000 men. (Contemporary drawing)

Right: The populace crowd onto the only bridge connecting the town to the left bank. The bridge collapses and many drown in the Douro. (Philippoteaux)

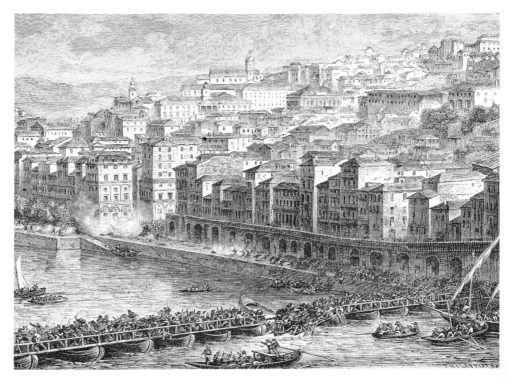

Right: From the heights of Mount Serra, which overlooks the town of Oporto, Sir Arthur Wellesley watches his infantry cross the Douro, to the surprise of the French. (After W. Paget)

Far right: The 4th Light and the 5th of the Line vainly attempt to dislodge Sherbrooke's brigade which had taken the centre of the town of Oporto by surprise. (G. Browne)

Right: Episode during the retreat from Portugal. The Miserere bridge, situated at the bottom of a gorge, was taken from the insurgents on 16 May, while the rearguard was being closely followed by Beresford's vanguard. Threatened with encirclement, the French army had to cross two Portuguese-held bridges, the Ponte Novo on the Cavado river and the Miserere bridge on one of its tributaries. The bridges were taken and the French reached Montalegre on the 17th. They were in Orense by the 19th. (From a painting by Lévêque)

Right: Battle of Oporto, 12 May 1809. (Beaume)

Right: The French rearguard attack at Salamonde, before the Ponte Novo. (From a painting by Lévêque)

Far right: Penamacor, a strategically important locality between the Douro and the Tagus. (From a drawing by Major Saint-Clair)

not have displeased him. Indeed, others had one – why not him? Supported by General Ricard, his Chief of Staff, like himself from the Tarn, he pursued active propaganda throughout the army. He circulated petitions among the populace which referred to him as the source of Portugal's happiness. He threw money to the people who would cry 'Long live Nicolas!' A clap of thunder was soon to rouse him from his torpor – the arrival of Sir Arthur Wellesley, the future Duke of Wellington.

Wellesley was born in Dublin. After an excellent education, he bought an ensign's commission and served his first campaign against the Empire in the Low Countries. He then went to India where his elder brother was Governor-General. As a lieutenant-general at the beginning of 1808, he was sent to Portugal against Junot. Although he had been serving under Dalrymple, he shared the blame for the

Convention of Cintra. However, when they had to find a successor to John Moore who had been killed at Corunna, the British cabinet thought of him. After some months of absence, he reappeared in Lisbon. Dry, cold, haughty and egoistic, he was above all a leader. Sober, with a profound sense of duty, he was a man of great talent who commanded respect. His tactics consisted of circumspection, to wait rather than to act, to draw back rather than advance. He did not know how to exploit his victories, but he did know how to choose the terrain upon which he wished to be attacked. Always the same: a reverse slope upon which he would dispose his lines, some distance from the crest, which would be manned by sharpshooters. When the French troops arrived out of breath at the crest, they would be received by violent fire which threw them into disorder. Then the British line would move forward and force the enemy back

down the slope they had just climbed. It is a pity that the Emperor did not study his future adversary better . . . it would certainly have served him at Waterloo.

On 5 May, Wellesley reviewed his troops at Coimbra, approximately 15,000 British, 3,000 Germans and 8,000 Portuguese. He hesitated. He could either march against Victor in the Tagus valley, but in so doing leave the Lisbon road open to Soult; or he could attack Soult. He took the latter course, because he thought he had time to beat Soult before turning to face Victor. He sent General Mackenzie with two British brigades and 12,000 Portuguese to Santarem and Abrantes to watch over the Tagus, and with his forces carried on towards the Douro, crossed it, and on 12 May, arrived opposite Oporto. General Foy was the first to glimpse the redcoats. With a handful of men he tried to stand, but this was pointless. The enemy emerged on all

sides. Soult who was about to eat, abandoned his lunch – which would come in handy for the British – jumped on his horse and forced his way out sword drawn, with an escort of chasseurs. The sick and wounded were abandoned as the French army fled down the road to Baltar.

Fortunately, the disorder did not last long. Horse and foot re-formed into column. The rearguard took up its position, and even before Valongo was reached order had been restored. However, the retreat proved difficult. The Braganza and Zamora route was closed because the Portuguese were occupying the port of Amarante on the Tamega, so the direct route from Oporto to Tuy had to be taken, on rough tracks through the mountains.

With the British at their heels, the army passed through Guimarães, Salamonde, Montalegre and Allariz, and crossed the frontier on 18 May. On the 19th it arrived at

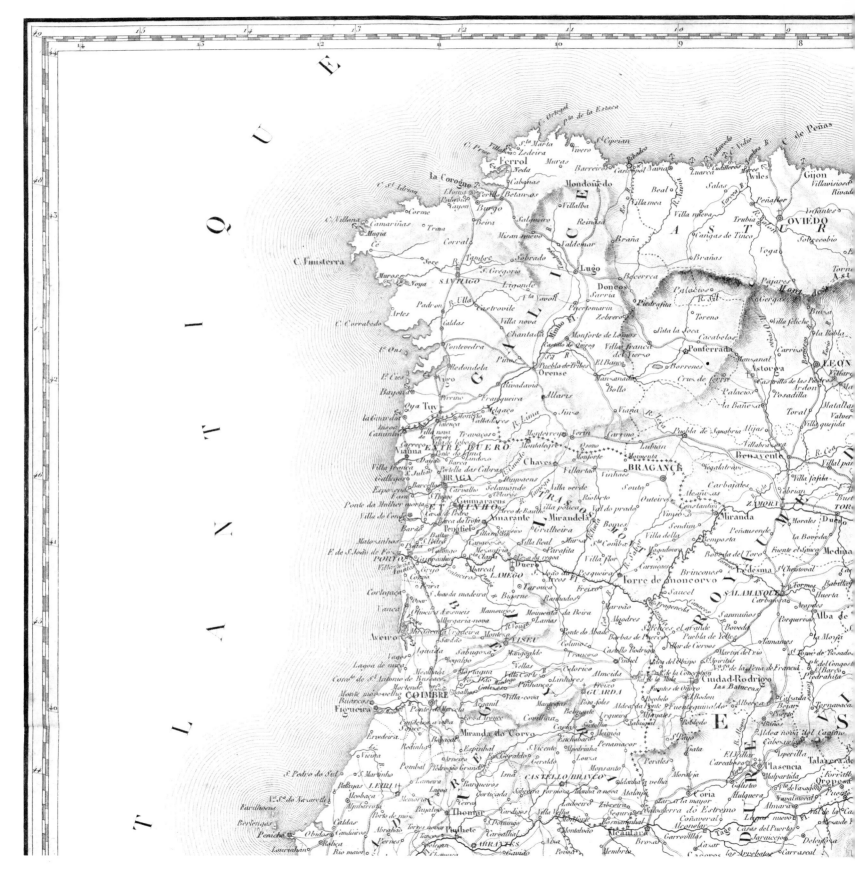

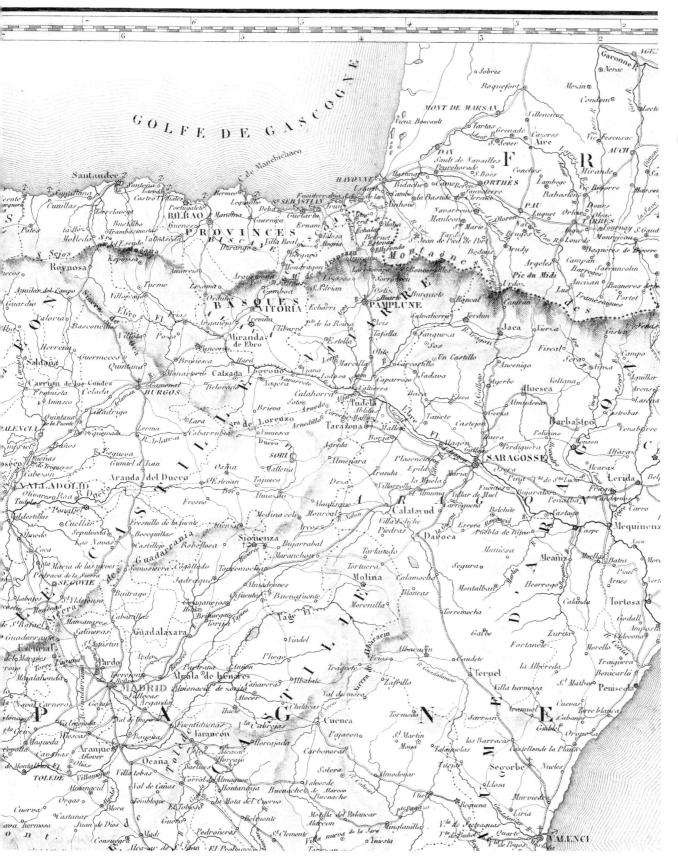

Marshal Jourdan (1762–1833). Chief of Staff of the Army of Spain.

Left: North-west section of the theatre of war map in General Foy's 'Histoire de la Guerre de la Peninsule sous Napoleon' (1827).

Right: Retreating along the roughest mountain tracks, the French army was harassed by Portuguese guerrillas and relentlessly pursued by the British. It reached Spain after having destroyed its baggage and artillery to prevent them from falling into enemy hands. The losses of this expedition were heavy, 5–6,000 men and 58 guns.

Right: The bridge of Alcantara on the Tagus. Marshal Victor was to have marched on Lisbon via the Tagus valley to support Marshal Soult's army. After capturing the bridge he remained there for more than a month. Learning of Soult's withdrawal into Spain, he, in his turn, beat a retreat after having destroyed the bridge, a magnificent monument dating from the time of Trajan. (From a drawing by R. K. Porter)

Right: On 21 March 1809 on the road to Miajades, a vanguard detachment of the 10th Chasseurs à Cheval fell into an ambush. Charged by horsemen of the Infante (line) and Almanza (dragoon) regiments, it lost 50 men who were savagely massacred. (J. Girbal)

Orense, took two days rest and left to relieve the town of Lugo, in which General Fournier-Sarlovèse was being besieged by the rebels. His 15th Dragoons and the two battalions of infantry wept with joy upon being reunited with their comrades. This was the end of the retreat, and the end too of an expedition that had been started too late and conducted too slowly. Portugal was lost and 7,000 men had been left there.

Jourdan was to write: 'The Duke of Dalmatia not having in any way sufficient forces to effect the conquest of Portugal, one could not, without injustice, blame him for having failed. But it seems to me that there is some little flattery when his retreat is placed amongst the most celebrated and when he is praised for not having concluded a convention similar to that of Cintra. It did not need a captain as great as the Marshal to conceive of the hope of avoiding this disgrace by destroying the artillery and baggage and by making his way towards Spain by the straightest route and along pathways barely negotiable by horses.'

Under the walls of Lugo, Soult was joined by Ney. Together, they decided to rescue Galicia from la Romana who was in Orense and had retaken Vigo. On 2 June Soult went down the Minho valley, halted at Monforte and gained Zamora. Ney, having left Corunna, made first for Santiago, then for Pontevedra. Arriving outside Vigo, he came up against unforeseen difficulties. The position, held by British and Spanish, was solidly built and furnished with redoubts. Ney hesitated, waited some time for Soult, then, furiously realizing that he had been abandoned, set off along the road to Santiago. Leaving a strong garrison in Ferrol, he returned to Astorga having lost not a man nor wagon. Here he vented his bad temper and wrote insulting letters about Soult to Joseph, but to no avail. Well aware of the intrigues in Oporto, Napoleon almost certainly made some comments to Soult, but appointed him 'Chief of Staff of the Army of Spain' . . . with command over II, III and VI Corps, the latter being that of Marshal Ney. This only made matters worse.

During Soult's action in Portugal, Victor, who was labouring to secure the left bank of the Tagus, encountered the ageing General de la Cuesta on 28 March 1809. De la Cuesta (the vanquished of Medina del Rio Seco) had no chance, but he was installed in a favourable position near Medellin, the birthplace of Hernando Cortez. Having put the River Guadiana behind him, Victor hesitated to attack and ordered a retreat. As luck would have it, an artillery wagon overturned and blocked the bridge. Lasalle, commanding the cavalry, took it upon himself to turn and face the Spanish. Assisted by the infantry, including Mouton-Duvernet (who was to die in a hail of royalist bullets), he attacked with vigour. Disconcerted, the enemy gave way. Exasperated by the sight of the mutilated corpses of their own soldiers, chasseurs, hussars and dragoons flung themselves upon the Spanish, cutting down with their swords all whom they met. The corpses of 12,000 men littered the ground. 7–8,000 prisoners remained in the hands of the Imperial troops, plus 19 cannon and a great number of colours.

At the same time (27 March), Sebastiani dispersed the corps of the Duke del Infantado at Ciudad Real. The honours of the day fell especially to the dragoons, the 'Cabazas de Oro' (Gold Heads) as they were called by the Spanish who admired and feared them.

But, lo and behold, having rid himself of Soult, Wellesley could now begin the second part of his plan – to attack, force back Victor and re-enter Madrid. On 27 June he left his camp at Abrantes. He climbed the Tagus valley and entered Spain to join the defeated Spanish at Plasencia. With him were four divisions of infantry and three brigades of cavalry – about 21,000 Anglo-Portuguese with 30 guns. Three new brigades joined him. He now had 30,000 men and, arriving in Oropesa, was met by la Cuesta, so that an army of nearly 100,000 men now threatened Madrid.

In the capital there was extreme agitation. More irresolute than ever, Joseph did not know what to do. Following Jourdan's advice he ordered Soult to descend from Zamora to Plasencia, to try and cut off the opposing troops. At the same time, Sebastiani, covering Madrid from the La Mancha side, proceeded towards Toledo, crossed the Tagus and came to support Victor who had prudently

fallen back before Wellesley's troops. On 23 July, King Joseph, escorted by his mentor, left Madrid to join Victor. With the few remaining battalions, General Belliard was instructed to restore order in the town, which the approach of the Spanish troops had rendered agitated and feverish.

Until now, the dispositions suggested by Jourdan had been judicious and if Joseph had only awaited Soult's arrival, the enemy army would have been cut off from its base, caught between two fires and easily destroyed. But the King was afraid that if he waited for Soult he would himself be cut off from Madrid if the British army were to make a turning movement, or if Venegas were to arrive at the Tagus, which was fordable at several places around Aranjuez, and take up a position midway between the

Left: The charge of the 2nd Hussars (Lasalle's division) at Medellin. Spurred on by their general, they surprised the Spanish cavalry as they were taking their positions. The victory was total, and Spanish losses were considerable. Miajades was avenged. (J. Girbal)

Above: General Count Sebastiani de la Porta (1772– 1851). Having returned from Constantinople where he was ambassador, he commanded successively, the 1st Division of IV Corps (September 1808), then IV Corps (February 1809).

Below: Victory at Medellin on 28 March 1809, gained by Marshal Victor over General Don Gregorio de la Cuesta. The dragoons of General Latour-Maubourg finish off the Spanish. (Philippoteaux).

Above: Marshal Victor, Duke of Belluno (1764–1841). He commanded I Corps (Lapisse, Villatte, Ruffin, Lasalle and Latour-Maubourg divisions). On 13 January at Ucles he gained a brilliant success over the 21,000 Spaniards of the Duke del Infantado.

Left: Salinas, 27 July 1809. The 87th and 88th Foot (Donkin's brigade), who were covering the retreat of the British forces towards Talavera, experienced heavy losses in the course of an engagement with General Lapisse's infantry.

Below left: On the evening of 27 July, during the retreat following the action at Salinas, four Spanish battalions were seized with panic and ran off in disorder. Don Gregorio de la Cuesta determined to decimate these battalions. Wellesley dissuaded him from this, but as an example the Spanish general ordered approximately thirty executions. (Caton Woodville)

Below: The Battle of Talavera. On the morning of 28 July, during a spontaneous cease-fire, French and British troops refreshed themselves from the same stream. (Wood engraving)

Right: Episode during the siege of Saragossa. The attack on the convent of Santa Engracia on 27 January 1809. The artist, who was aide-de-camp to Marshal Lannes, has represented himself wounded at the foot of the monument. Major Valazé of the engineers comes to his aid, while General Lacoste, commander of the engineers during the siege, leads his sappers and the Poles from the 1st Regiment of the Legion of the Vistula to the assault of the building. (Painting by Baron Lejeune, Musée de Versailles)

Above: Lord Henry Paget, later Marquis of Anglesey. He was gravely wounded during the battle.

French and the capital. So on arriving at the Guadarrama, where Victor and Sebastiani were already installed, a council was held. Faced with Jourdan's prudent views, Victor, fired by his unexpected victory at Medellin, was strongly in favour of an attack. As usual, Joseph hesitated for a long time, but fearing that Victor might write to the Emperor to complain of his faint-heartedness, he made his decision. Like most weak characters, once he had made up his mind, he acted immediately – which, in the present circumstances, was the worst thing to do.

To safeguard himself against Venegas's arrival, 3,000 men were left in Toledo to hold the bridges. The Spaniard would have to go back to Aranjuez if he wanted to cross and that would slow down his march considerably. A regiment of dragoons was sent to the right bank to keep open communications with Madrid, and on the 26th the entire French Army crossed the River Guadarrama. The dragoons of Latour-Maubourg came upon 6,000 Spaniards, charged them and soon put them to rout. A British division sent to their aid was obliged to cross back over the Alberche while the main army took up its positions behind. On the left, the British were established on steep hills, and on the right the Spanish rested on Talavera and the Tagus.

The Allied forces had an effective strength of about 60,000 men; the French had 45,000 men and 24 guns. The numerical inferiority of the French was compensated by the quality of the troops fashioned by several months of operations. It really was a pity that Joseph could not wait for Soult to arrive, for the battle of Talavera, which was about to begin, was to be yet another lost opportunity.

MISERERE
DOMINE
ET
DA VENIAM

Above: The 48th Foot (1st Brigade) at Talavera. Colonel Donnellan, seriously wounded, calls the nearest officer to him and, baring his head, tells him, 'Major Middlemore, you will have the honour of leading the 48th in the assault.' (extract from 'History of the Northamptonshire Regiment')

Left: After the Battle of Talavera and the joining into a single army of the corps of Soult, Ney and Mortier, Wellington retired towards Andalusia. During this retreat, on 12 August 1809, Marshal Ney's vanguard (General Lorcet) took the Banos Pass at the bayonet from General Wilson's troops. During the action, Private Tartre of the 59th Line captured a colour. (From an English print)

On the evening of 27 July, General Ruffin, with his 1st Division, attacked the hillock upon which rested the British left. Commanded by Lord Hill, the latter held. Only half of the 2nd Division, that of General Lapisse, which was instructed to support the 1st Division, was engaged. The French troops were reined in and darkness fell. During the night the British, having had their attention drawn to the strategic advantage of the hillside they were occupying, reinforced it and furnished it with artillery. At dawn the French troops resumed the attack, but in spite of their courage they were obliged to draw back before the terrible fire of the British. Here and there, overwhelmed by heat and fatigue, the combatants halted. Some of them even found themselves drinking from the very stream that separated their lines.

Joseph advanced to the ground occupied by I Corps and was startled by the solidity of the British positions. Once more he hesitated. Jourdan again suggested that they wait for Soult to arrive. Victor, who declared himself sure of success, demanded immediate action. Finally, his opinion prevailed and, at one o'clock in the afternoon, Joseph had the call to arms sounded and decided upon a general attack. This time, the entire front line came alight. Infantry and cavalry leapt forward, charges and attacks followed one upon the other. A British regiment of dragoons, launched at top speed, crossed the French lines, cutting down all in its path and came to a halt exhausted before the waters of the Alberche . . . where it was taken prisoner. The French wore themselves out trying to capture the northernmost knoll which was defended relentlessly by kilted Scotsmen. In the end, attackers and defenders were still in their original positions. When night came, 6,000 dead or wounded littered the ground. The two armies dressed their wounds

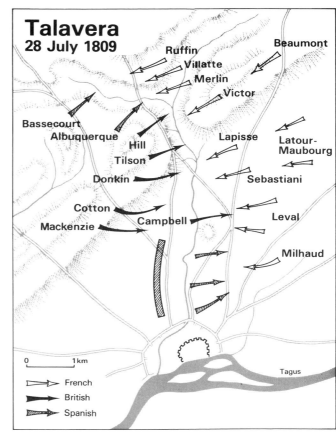

Above: General Hill, commanding the 2nd Division of infantry (Tilson and Stewart brigades).

Right: The charge of the 23rd Light Dragoons at Talavera, 27 July 1809. During the charge of Anson's Light Brigade, the regiment came upon a deep, concealed trench which scattered them and caused heavy losses of men and horses. The survivors vainly attacked the 27th Light who had formed square. Two squadrons which, in an insane charge, had attacked the French cavalry placed in support of the 27th Light, were surrounded by General Merlin's cavalry division (10th and 26th Chasseurs à Cheval, Westphalian Light Horse and Vistula Lancers). Only five riders regained the British lines (Colonel Sauzey). (Caton Woodville)

Above: General Baron Caulaincourt (1777–1812), younger brother of the Duke of Vicenza. He commanded the five brigades of dragoons which formed the cavalry of VIII Corps.

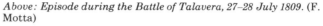

Left: Talavera. Hand to hand fighting between General Leval's infantry (German division) and the British of General Campbell. (G. Browne)

Above: Episode during the Battle of Talavera, 27–28 July 1809. (F. Motta)

Above: Sir Arthur Wellesley. Viscount Douro, he became Duke of Wellington and Talavera after the battle. His future successes were to win him also the titles of Marquis of Torres Vedras, Earl of Ciudad Rodrigo, and Grandee of Spain. (Portrait by W. Say)

Right: The Arzobispo bridge. On 4 August, Sir Arthur Wellesley having received intelligence of the new approach of several French corps, recrossed the Tagus by the bridge, while elements of the Spanish army held it. On 7 August it was captured by Marshal Mortier's troops who routed the Spaniards and captured thirty guns. (Bacler d'Albe, Musée de l'Armée)

Above: Colonel de Porbeck, commanding the contingent of the Grand Duchy of Baden (Leval German Division). He was killed during the battle. (Miniature by unknown artist)

Above: Colonel Torrens, Wellington's Military Secretary during the Peninsular War.

Above: Colonel Baron de Kruse, commanding the Nassau Regiment, was wounded at Medellin where he displayed the highest bravery. He attracted attention during the battle for his brilliant conduct. He continued to serve with distinction until December 1813, when he led the 2nd Nassau Regiment and the Frankfurt Battalion into the British lines. As a Major-General of the army of the Low Countries, he commanded the Nassau contingent at Waterloo.

Above: General Clarke, Duke of Feltre (1765–1818), French Minister of War 1807–14.

Above: General (later Field Marshal) Sir Stapleton Cotton, Viscount Combermere. He commanded a brigade of light cavalry (14th and 16th Light Dragoons) at the Battle of Talavera . (From a painting by Mrs C. Pearson)

and prepared for the next day's combat. If all the Anglo-Spanish troops had been deployed during the day, this was not the case with the French, for part of I and IV Corps and Dessolle's division had not been engaged. Under a good commander this could have changed the course of the battle, but Joseph was discouraged, and feared more than ever being cut off from his capital. He struck camp and, passing through Toledo and Illescas, returned to Madrid. Instead of pursuing the French, Wellesley rested on his laurels and congratulated himself for his prudence when he learned, on 2 August, of Soult's arrival. He left hurriedly, leaving behind 5,000 sick and wounded and part of his train. Victor, having retired to the Guadarrama, did not notice this stealthy withdrawal and did not return to Talavera until the 6th.

Soult, informed too late, had not been able to arrive in time, but he did try to cut off the Allies' retreat, and on 8 August he overtook the Spanish army at the bridge of Arzobispo. The troops of the rearguard had remained near the bridge, which was barricaded and defended by several cannon. Caulaincourt's dragoons found a ford, crossed the Tagus and, with drawn swords, fell upon the artillerymen who, taken from behind, were pinned to their guns. 600 prisoners and all the guns – it was a handsome success. . . . But Wellesley had gone and was on his way back to Portugal. During this time Joseph, well advised by Jourdan, turned towards Venegas who had pushed on to Aranjuez. Sebastiani thrust him back to the left bank of the Tagus, attacked him beneath the walls of Almonacid on 10 August 1809, and beat him roundly. That was the end of the campaign devised by Wellesley and the Junta, in which it had been intended to take Madrid after destroying the French army. Despite the indecisive Battle of Talavera, the British had returned to Portugal, and the Spanish armies had been vanquished and dispersed. If Talavera had been a better conducted battle, it would have assured the French of the Peninsula. But this was not to be, and, three months after this indecisive day, the Spanish resumed the offensive.

Top: Lancers of the Vistula. The 1st Regiment of Lancers of the Vistula entered Spain at the end of May 1808. The 2nd Regiment joined them in 1809. These two regiments became respectively the 7th and 8th Regiments of Light Horse Lancers in June 1811. (V. Huen)

Above: Skirmishers of the Legion of the Vistula in Spain. The Legion of the Vistula (Polish in the service of France) consisted of four regiments of infantry (1st, 2nd, 3rd and 4th) and two regiments of cavalry. The first three regiments of infantry and the 1st Lancers entered Spain at the end of May 1808, the 4th Regiment and the 2nd Lancers in 1809.

Left: Joseph Bonaparte, King of Spain. He returned to Madrid on 12 August 1809. (Painting by J. B. J. Wicar)

Above: General Count Gouvion Saint-Cyr (1764–1830), commanded the Army of Catalonia. After capturing Figueras he laid siege to Gerona.

In Catalonia during this time, Gouvion Saint-Cyr, future Marshal of the Empire, was at grips with Gerona. This fortified town, situated on the banks of the Ter, was being fanatically defended by about 7,000 men, commanded by Alvarez de Castro, a Spanish nobleman. Castro was to hold the French in check for nearly six months. Energetic and courageous, he knew how to fan the wind of resistance among his troops, just as well as among the population who were to hold out to the last extremity. From 4 June the town was invested by General Verdier, while Gouvion Saint-Cyr placed himself in a position to halt the aid that would certainly be sent to the besieged town. Sanson, the engineer general directing the siege works, had opened up trenches in front of the citadel of Monjuich – a strong-point of the defence system. On 7 July, after a solid preparation of artillery fire, 4,000 French and Germans launched the assault, but, despite their eagerness, they were repelled with heavy losses. The following month, the Spanish evacuated the fort which, having been subjected

Above: General Verdier (1767–1839). He commanded the troops which attacked Gerona on 19 September.

Left: View of Gerona. By 4 June, the town had been completely surrounded. (Bacler d'Albe, Musée de l'Armée)

Above: Struggle for one of the outer towers of Gerona. (From a nineteenth-century lithograph)

Below: Assault on the walls of Gerona repulsed by the Spanish. (Philippoteaux)

Above: General Don Mariano
Alvarez de Castro (1749–1810),
heroic defender of Gerona. The
garrison of nearly 10,000 men,
were actively assisted by the
inhabitants.

Above: Gerona's great day. Repulse of the French assault on 19 September 1809. (Painting by Alvarez Dumont)

Below: Capture of the great convoy of Gerona. On 26 September 1809 within sight of Gerona and despite the intervention of General
Blake's troops, a large convoy fell into the hands of the French, who also took 700 prisoners. (Langlois, Musée de l'Armée)

to intense bombardment, was nothing more than ruins. On 19 September a general assault was launched. Galvanized by their leader, the entire populace was behind the ramparts. As the tocsin rang, women and children mingled with the soldiers and offered a desperate resistance to their assailants who, caught under violent fire and crushed by masonry dropping on them from the walls, were obliged to withdraw after sustaining heavy losses. Realizing the impossibility of storming the place by main force, Gouvion Saint-Cyr decided to transform the siege into a blockade. Where French arms had failed, illness and famine would succeed. As expected, a column led by Blake arrived to assist the besieged. Thanks to fog that unexpectedly descended on Lecchi's division positioned outside the town, 4,000 men and some provisions got through, but Alvarez was short of ammunition. He sent urgent demands

to Blake begging for further aid. The latter, who could not refuse, set off accompanied by the prayers of the entire population of Catalonia. This time Gouvion Saint-Cyr was not to be deceived. The convoy of several thousand heavily-laden beasts of burden, was halted, broken up and the booty taken under the very eyes of the besieged.

Their situation was now becoming very grave. Typhoid, famine, scurvy and dysentery wrought havoc. A few deserters presented themselves at the French outposts, but the town as a whole continued its resistance, sustained by the great voice of Alvarez. But this was soon to be silenced because the heroic Spaniard was dying. On 9 December he was obliged to pass command to General Bolivar and, on the 10th, Marshal Augereau, who had replaced Gouvion Saint-Cyr, received the capitulation. Some 4,000 survivors, spectres rising from the ruins, surrendered, abandoning

Above: Marshal Augereau, Duke of Castiglione (1757–1816). Commander-in-chief in Catalonia (VII Corps) from 1 June 1809 to April 1811. He succeeded Generals Verdier and Gouvion Saint-Cyr in conducting this difficult siege. On 11 December he received the surrender of the town.

Above: The capitulation of Gerona on 11 December 1809. The town succumbed after a magnificent resistance lasting six months. (Painting by L. Barrau, Fine Arts Museum, Barcelona)

Right: The inhabitants of Figueras come to do homage to the mortal remains of General Alvarez de Castro. On 10 January 1810 he died of a fever contracted during the siege. (T. Muñoz Lucena)

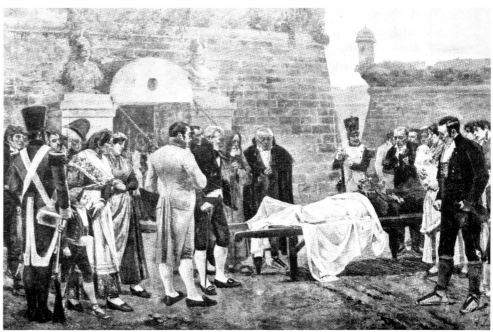

200 cannon and eight colours. Alvarez, only half-conscious, was sent to the fort of Figueras, where he died a few days later.

During this period, an army commanded by Venegas, the loser of Almonacid, had left Andalusia and was marching north. Areizaga, who had replaced de la Cuesta, accompanied him. King Joseph, Jourdan, Soult, Mortier and Sebastiani advanced against Venegas and attacked on 19 November at Ocaña, a short distance from Aranjuez and Almonacid, on the borders of the bleak plain of La Mancha. Nothing could resist the presence of such leaders, especially as their artilleryman, Senarmont, was one of the most able in the French Army. After a preliminary bombardment, which disorganized the Spanish positions, the cavalry divisions of Merlin, Milhaud and Latour-Maubourg charged with a terrifying din and put the enemy to rout. Areizaga, having quietly installed himself in the clock tower at Ocaña in order to see better, owed his salvation to a hasty flight, and only just escaped the French dragoons. Of 60,000 men, the Spanish army left half on the field – dead or prisoners. Fifty cannon and thirty colours were taken. This time the victory was total.

Above: General Count Kellermann (1770–1835). He temporarily commanded VI Corps, at the head of which he gained the victory of Alba de Tormes over the Duke del Parque.

Right: General Count Hugo (1773–1828). Sergeant of the King of Spain's Palace (November 1808), Majordomo of the Palace (January 1809), Field Marshal and Governor of Avila (August 1809). In November 1809, at the head of three battalions, he repulsed the fifteen battalions of General Ballesteros who were attempting to capture Avila. Chief-of-Staff to Jourdan (October 1811), he was to be King Joseph's senior aide-de-camp on 24 June 1813.

However, a second army under the Duke del Parque came from Portugal intending to capture Salamanca and thus menace Madrid. Ney, who was on leave, had left the command of VI Corps to Marchand, and he it was who advanced with his troops to meet the enemy. At Tamanes, between Ciudad Rodrigo and Salamanca, he attacked, although the choice of place was not a good one because the Spanish occupied the heights. The French clambered skilfully across rocks and brushwood, which very quickly caught fire and obliged them to turn back. Realizing the advantage of the enemy position, Marchand ordered the retreat, but the poorly transmitted orders provoked some confusion. A few units that were not informed continued to fight alone. Finally the French managed to disengage, having left 1,800 men on the field. The enemy made a great fuss of this defeat, especially as Marchand, who drew back to Salamanca and entered the town, thought he ought to evacuate it within two days to take up a position at Toro on the Duero. Master of Salamanca, where he permitted the murder of French wounded, the Duke del Parque hesitated, then established himself in Alba de Tormes, birthplace of the terrible Duke of Alba, King Philip II's best captain.

Kellermann, in command at Vitoria, now brought with him four regiments of dragoons, and took from Marchand command of VI Corps. On 28 November he arrived near Alba and found the Spanish encamped on both banks of the Tormes. He intended to take advantage of this mistake and, without waiting for his infantry and artillery, launched his cavalry in an attack. Hussars and chasseurs on the right, dragoons on the left, once more the terrible French cavalry issued forth at full gallop and routed the Spanish who left 3,000 of their men on the field. Pursuing the fugitives, Kellermann entered the town almost as soon as they, allowing some of them to be killed while the others took advantage of the shadows and ran off in all directions. This day's work, which cost the French 18 killed and 57 wounded, had seen the destruction of an entire army by eight regiments of cavalry. The French had re-entered Salamanca, and the Duke del Parque retired to Ciudad Rodrigo.

It was with this series of victories that the year of 1809 ended. Joseph in Madrid was able to reign without the painful uncertainty of the morrow. French troops held the major part of the country and communications with France were more or less secure. But the British were still in Portugal and their leader, Wellesley (now Viscount Wellington of Talavera), had no desire to re-embark ... which was tiresome. ...

1810

Joseph was in Madrid to be sure, but he was a penniless king. When he passed through, Napoleon had rightly confiscated the goods of a few powerful and hostile families. He had laid claim to the wool monopoly in the provinces where it belonged to the nobility. He had done all this, however, to the profit of the Imperial treasury alone, and the King of Spain was soon pleading poverty to his brother. Napoleon, however, listened only abstractedly and yet was particularly unsparing in his good advice. Joseph had the royal plate melted down, and decreed a sort of enforced loan, 'les cédules hypothécaires', destined for the purchase of national assets and which strangely resembled the 'assignats' (promissory notes issued by the French revolutionary government of 1790–96). Like them, they quickly became discredited. No one wanted to buy ecclesiastical goods. All this was very worrying. It was at this time that Joseph's advisers spoke to him of the merits of an expedition to Andalusia. The province was represented to him as being the richest of his states – a quality, in present circumstances, that was attractive. Furthermore, the French troops had not reappeared in this region since Baylen, and all the forces of independence, including the Junta, had withdrawn there. The decision was taken: they would go to Andalusia.

Upon being consulted, the Emperor disagreed. The enemy was Britain and she held Portugal – the devil take Andalusia! First drive the British out of Portugal, and it would be easy to fall back and finish off this irritating business. Joseph persisted, driven on by his entourage who represented the operation to him as a simple route march, and his brother, weary of family warfare, gave in.

With Soult as his Chief of Staff, Joseph had at his disposal three corps: I (Victor), IV (Sebastiani) and V (Mortier). II Corps with General Reynier, a native of Lucerne who had just arrived from Austria, remained on the banks of the Tagus in the Alcantara region, to watch over the British in case they suddenly took it into their heads to move. It was with enthusiasm that the 60,000 men of the three corps plunged into the Sierra Morena. Joseph, who wanted to appear well before his Andalusian subjects, did not hesitate to surround himself with a numerous and useless retinue of chamberlains, servants, courtiers and so on.

The pass was crossed without too much difficulty. The Spanish troops, taken by surprise, disengaged and abandoned their artillery. To the left, Sebastiani sent a column to capture the bridges over the Guadalquivir. This put the enemy into disarray, and 6,000 prisoners and 25 guns fell into French hands. Sebastiani issued to his troops an Order of the Day dated at Baylen, which was still surrounded by the débris of Dupont's army. IV Corps marched towards

Above: Granada at the beginning of the nineteenth century. The French army took the town on 20 January 1810.

Jaen and I Corps on Cordoba. These two towns opened their gates without resistance. Continuing its march, IV Corps took Granada on 28 January and pushed on to Malaga which surrendered on 5 February after a lively fight. During this time, Victor, who had set off in the direction of Cadiz with I Corps, saw his march arrested at Ecija by Joseph, who, wishing to capture wealthy Seville, ordered him to fall back. Soult and Joseph polemicized in their memoirs, accusing each other mutually of having taken this initiative. Whoever was responsible, the result cost the French dear. The Imperial armies were never again to enter Cadiz, which, with the irony of fate, was to be taken thirteen years later by the royal armies of the Duke of Angoulême.

Meanwhile the decision had been taken and, on 31 January, the army debouched outside the Andalusian capital. Here, a strange spectacle was presented. All the bells were ringing loudly. On the ramparts a furious crowd of people waved their fists and threatened the French. This was only a sham, since the Junta needed time to escape towards Cadiz, and the next day the town opened its gates. I Corps entered to the beat of drum and with colours flying.

Above: King Joseph's entry into Seville, 31 January 1810.

the guards and, with their retrieved weapons, prevented the approach of Spanish boats. There were not enough muskets, but what did that matter since they had to hand the iron ballast! They swung the bars at the enemy, breaking arms and legs . . . the hulk was drifting . . . but the capricious wind dropped and the hulk took an unlucky course. Under the direction of marine officers, who had been taken prisoner with Rosily's squadron, the fugitives fashioned makeshift sails from clothes and blankets, and regained their proper course, but too slowly. It was imperative that the French be informed before the Spanish could intervene. Courageously, Fauras, sergeant-major of dragoons, threw himself into the water and reached the French lines. The alert was given. Then, an unforgettable spectacle unfolded. Every available soldier of I Corps was determined to come to the aid of his comrades. Two thousand men under fire, swimming or in rowing boats, came to join in the rescue. The Spanish batteries redoubled their activity. Several times the hulk was set ablaze, only to be extinguished by the prisoners remaining on board. One last salvo sent the hulk to the bottom, but by this time it had been evacuated. 'It is impossible to recall the acts of generosity, bravery and humanity that took place in these circumstances. General Headquarters undertakes to set them down', said *Le Moniteur*. A total of 800 French prisoners had been liberated.

This example encouraged those aboard the other hulk, *Argonaut,* who repeated the exploit during the night of 26/27 May. Forewarned, the enemy was on guard. The British fired their artillery, causing dreadful havoc on the hulk, but, aided by miracles of ingenuity and bravery from the men of I Corps, numerous soldiers regained the French lines. This second escape infuriated the Spanish, who distributed the rest of their prisoners between the British hulks and, of grim reputation, the islet of Cabrera in the Balearic Islands.

Meanwhile, Joseph, who wanted to win over his Andalusian subjects, travelled about the country. He visited Xeres, Ronda, Malaga, Granada, Jaen and Cordoba. Everywhere he was received with curiosity and a certain sympathy on the part of the well-to-do classes. In other circumstances his natural benevolence could have gained him the hearts of his subjects, but for the people he remained the 'capitan vestuario' – that is to say, 'captain of clothes', an ironic allusion to the desertion of the Spanish troops whom he had previously kitted out. He was even to become known, unjustly, as 'Pepe Botella', because his enemies falsely attributed to him a love of the bottle. Nonchalant, but fundamentally honest, he was caught between the desire to render his subjects happy and fear of infringing the orders of his terrible brother. Joseph was an indecisive king, unfit to reign in such difficult circumstances. It was a pity for him that he could not have remained in his peaceful kingdom of Naples where he would have been spared many unpleasant occurrences. For the moment, followed by his glittering retinue, he received with favour what he thought were sincere manifestations of fidelity, and wished to know nothing of the widespread unruliness of the countryside.

A despatch from Paris quickly recalled him to reality. Napoleon, who treated Spain as a conquered territory, pointed out to Berthier: 'You will make known to the King of Spain that my finances are getting out of order, and that I have not sufficient means to sustain the enormous expenditure that Spain costs me . . . since nothing can depend upon the impossible, the King must maintain the

Then, replaced at once by V Corps, it set off again in the direction of Cadiz under the command of Victor, Duke of Bellune. The Duke of Albuquerque, who was ahead of the French, fell back very quickly towards the isle of Léon and was already in position when the French troops arrived. The isle of Léon was a vast triangular marsh, two sides of which were washed by the ocean and the third separated from terra firma by an arm of the sea called the canal of Santi Petri. At the summit of this triangle, Cadiz, built on a rock, raised its white houses above the waves. When Victor arrived, he was halted by the canal and as he had no boats, he could not cross it. He sent summonses which, naturally, were rejected, and had to content himself with establishing batteries in the most important positions, so as to secure the blockade.

He had opposite him not only the approximately 23,000-strong garrison, but also Admiral Parwis' squadron, and the Spanish squadron of Don Ignacio de Alava. The numbers of the besieged were superior to those of the besiegers. Victor endeavoured to secure his position, captured the fort of Matagorda, which allowed him to bombard the town, using the cannon received from Seville. He organized a series of redoubts, carefully linked one to another, and also tried to raise a flotilla of rowing boats to force a crossing of the Santi Petri.

During this time, the French prisoners who were aboard the Spanish hulks at Cadiz, regained their spirits. There were thousands of them there, mostly captives from Baylen, living in disastrously insanitary conditions with little or no food. These prison hulks oozed with vermin and decay. Until now nearly all attempts at escape had failed. Two fresh attempts, led with determination by the prisoners in the *Old Castile* and *Argonaut,* were to succeed. At 8 o'clock on the evening of 15 May, taking advantage of a strong wind, the prisoners in *Old Castile* cut the moorings, seized

Top: Hulks in the Cadiz roads. (Painting by W. F. Burger, 1810)

Above: The Old Castile *was reduced to a wreck by British and Spanish bombardment and ran aground. The survivors were picked up by the men of I Corps, 15 May 1810.*

Right: Ronda, the mountain retreat of the guerrillas in Andalusia. (From a contemporary engraving)

97

Army of Spain himself. All I can do is give two millions a month to supplement the balance and, if this proves impossible, there is only one means available – that is to administer the provinces' revenue to the account of France. ...' There followed a decree taking from Joseph the provinces of Biscay, Navarre, Aragon and Catalonia and transforming them into individually governed territories under Generals Thouvenot, Reille, Suchet and Marshal Macdonald, who had just been appointed Duke of Tarentum. The same decree remodelled the organization of the French forces in Spain into five armies – those of Catalonia, Aragon, Andalusia, Portugal, and the Centre. The Army of Catalonia was placed under the orders of Macdonald; that of Aragon under Suchet; that of Andalusia was left to Soult; while Masséna took command of the Army of Portugal. There remained for poor Joseph only the Army of the Centre, composed of a few depots and a single division – that of Dessolle. This was serious. Joseph was embittered, but the few valuable Spaniards he had gathered together (the afrancesados) were astounded. Many of them, artists like Goya, men of literature such as Moratin, Valdes or Minano, or distinguished and competent men like Hervas, Burgos, Muriel, O'Farrill or Azanza, had rallied to Joseph without really being Bonapartist supporters. They had done so because they had adopted the principles of the French Revolution and hoped to see their country transformed. This decree was going to make them seem party to the dismemberment of their country and deprive them of all credibility as far as the Spanish people were concerned.

Hurriedly Joseph returned to Madrid and sent his two best counsellors, Hervas and Azanza, to Paris. Their mission was to persuade the Emperor to reverse his decision. But it was a complete waste of time. Napoleon would do what he thought best, and to the first four military governments he added two others; that of Burgos, entrusted to General Dorsenne, and the other to General Kellermann. From now on, Napoleon was master of Spain. Joseph was king only in Castile.

Soult, himself, was master of Andalusia. He thought it possible that the Kingdom of Lusitania which had escaped him the previous year, might be transformed into another kingdom, of which Seville would be the capital. An officer who was close to him, the military pharmacist Fée, wrote: 'The Marshal really seemed to be more the King of Andalusia, rather than a simple lieutenant of the Emperor. Never did a monarch surround himself with more majesty. Never was a court more submissive than his. Like Homer's Jupiter, he made Olympus tremble with a movement of his hand. ... The Marshal was always accompanied by a splendid guard. On Sundays, the élite troops would form a guard of honour to the cathedral, awaiting the General-in-Chief. He would appear, followed by the civic authorities and a glittering retinue of staff. All this gilded entourage solicited a smile or a glance. He distributed the one or the other with a cold and studied dignity. Formed in the same school as the Emperor, he had the same gestures and moderation of speech.' He was very pleased with the manner in which Napoleon was conducting Spain's affairs, since it left him virtually independent of Joseph. In his memoirs he wrote: 'The Emperor was not so blinded by the real affection he bore for him that he could not acknowledge in him the military talents that were so useful in fulfilling such a rôle.' He seized all civil and military authority, well seconded in this by Sebastiani who was reigning over the Kingdom of Granada, and by Dessolle in Cordoba.

Above: Marshal MacDonald, Duke of Tarentum (1765–1840). Commander-in-Chief of the Army of Catalonia from 24 April 1810 to 20 September 1811.

Left: Devil's Bridge on the Segre. The road from Perpignan to Lerida ran along the Segre. This river passed through a succession of picturesque gorges crossed by small bridges, and the area was ideal for ambushes. (Captain Langlois, Musée de l'Armée)

Above: Battle of Vich (Catalonia), 20 February 1810. Fought by the troops of General Souham against the Spanish commanded by General O'Donnell. Here, at the decisive phase of the battle, General Souham, who has been wounded beneath the eye, takes his place at the head of his troops whose assault is to cause the rout of the Spanish. (Captain Langlois, Musée de l'Armée)

Above: General Dessolle (1767–1828). He served in Spain from July 1808 to February 1811. After having commanded the 4th Division of VI Corps (November 1808), he was assigned to the Army of the Centre (January 1809). During the Andalusian expedition he captured Cordoba (28 January 1810) of which he became governor. Later, he commanded Seville and the province of Jaen.

Above: General Baron Bigarre (1775–1838). He was appointed successively Commander of the Royal Guard of King Joseph (August 1809) and Lieutenant-General in the service of Spain (June 1813).

Above: The last cartridges of the 51st at Fuente Ovejuna, 7 September 1810. 2,000 Spaniards under General de la Romana attacked 96 men of the 51st of the Line entrenched in Fuente Ovejuna. For thirteen hours the Frenchmen kept up a desperate struggle, first at the threshold of the village, then in the church, and finally in the bell-tower. After putting more than 200 Spaniards out of action, it seemed that the detachment would perish in the tower which had been set alight by the enemy, when the arrival of reinforcements prompted the Spanish to take flight. 45 French soldiers died in this gallant defence. (Musée de l'Armée)

Shrewdly, he sought to minimize the weight of contributions levied by Joseph and, to the profit of the French treasury, he sold sequestered merchandise as being of enemy origin ... which fact was quite clear to Paris. The country was rich, life easy, the women pretty and less and less shy since the Spanish had discovered that the odious 'Gavachos', spurned by the clergy, were after all, quite often good, obliging courageous Frenchmen, even tempered and enterprising. Soon however, he was going to have to tear himself away from this agreeable existence.

The Emperor had accepted the Andalusian campaign against his better judgement, and was still thinking of the offensive he had set his heart upon, which would rid him of the British for good. Portugal, where Wellington had installed himself in force, must be conquered. Indeed, while Soult was playing at proconsuls in Seville, Wellington was going all out to make his position in Portugal impregnable. He had noticed the formidable barrier of steep and broken hills to the north of the Tagus, which covered the approaches to Lisbon, near Torres Vedras. Indefatigable, this haughty, precise, demanding man himself planned the details of the famous lines of Torres Vedras, which were to serve as a buffer to the last great French offensive, that which Napoleon was contemplating in the secrecy of his study.

Omnipresent, Wellington was thinking of the route the French might follow. Taking into account the natural obstacles, it did not need a great strategist to realize that only two itineraries were possible: the one to the north of the Tagus starting from Salamanca, the other following the Guadiana valley and starting from Merida. The northern route was barred by two fortresses, one Spanish at Ciudad Rodrigo and the other Portuguese at Almeida. As for the southern route, that was also barred by two fortresses: the Spanish Badajoz and the Portuguese Elvas. These four fortresses played a vital rôle in Wellington's strategy. They would enable him to delay the enemy's advance for some time, and the gigantic works he had undertaken at Torres Vedras had to be finished at any price before the French arrived. Meanwhile he had at his disposal 35,000 British, to which were added 20,000 regular Portuguese troops and 30,000 men of the provincial militia. All were well-equipped and he saw personally to their training. Under pressure from him, the Portuguese Government called to arms all able-bodied men between the ages of 16 and 60 to form the 'Ordenanca', an auxiliary force. Made up of bands of men with few weapons and without any real military training, these were to form elusive groups of partisans, familiar with all the muleteer tracks, prompt to act against isolated or weak detachments and quick also to melt into the hostile terrain, which was so difficult to scour.

While Wellington was preparing to stand up to him, the Emperor appointed the marshal who would take charge of the conquest. It would be Masséna, 'beloved child of victory'. Ship's boy at 13, smuggler at 30, general at 35 and marshal at 46, this tradesman's son from Nice was bedecked with laurels, the last of which he had brought back from the banks of the Danube and which had earned him the title 'Prince of Essling'. But now he was 52 years old and tired – indeed he looked 60 – worn out both by his campaigns and his rather troubled private life. Manoeuvres and protestations to the master were useless. Berthier's intervention was cut short and the marshal, heaped with praises, was obliged to forget his rheumatism and set off. He left Paris on 29 April with fourteen aides-de-camp, one

of whom, with a pretty figure, was none other than the piquant Henriette Lebreton, the wife of an officer and well-known in the army by the name of 'La Poule à Masséna' (Masséna's tart).

On 10 May he arrived at Valladolid, where he established his general headquarters and effectively took over command of the Army of Portugal: Ney's VI Corps, made up of the divisions of Marchand, Mermet, Loison and Lorcet; Junot's VIII Corps, composed of infantry divisions of Clausel and Solignac; and Reynier's II Corps, comprising two divisions of infantry and two of cavalry.

The instructions dictated via Berthier by Napoleon foresaw that: 'The Prince of Essling will have 40,000 infantrymen and 9–10,000 cavalrymen, giving him an army of 50,000 men with which he will first of all besiege Ciudad Rodrigo and then Almeida, and will prepare to march methodically towards Portugal, which I wish to enter only in September, after the hot weather and especially after the harvest ...', which in a country so difficult to supply was a useful precaution.

Thus the northern invasion route was chosen. It was now necessary to examine Ciudad Rodrigo, which was being covered by Craufurd's division. Masséna, escorted by Junot, observed the fortress and decided to reduce it by calling in his siege equipment. Ney was charged with the operation and, in June, after having driven Craufurd's troops beyond the Agueda, he began the siege. Well-equipped with arms and supplies, the town had a garrison of 5,500 men under the command of the courageous former marine officer, Don Andres Herrasti. On 24 June, Masséna himself came to direct operations, and subjected the town to a terrible bombardment that lasted sixteen days. On 6 July, Ney made the assault, captured the town and followed the Craufurd Division as far as Almeida. On the 24th, he attacked it outside the town and, after severe losses, forced the division to retreat beyond the Coa, thus uncovering the fortress of Almeida.

The position was invested on 15 August. The garrison, composed of Portuguese, was commanded by an Englishman, General William Cox. The town lacked neither artillery nor munitions. Its ramparts were solid, and Wellington hoped that it would hold out for at least two or three months, but the French needed only twenty-four hours to secure its surrender. The British retreated via the Mondego valley, while Masséna, who was in no hurry,

Above: Marshal Masséna, Duke of Rivoli, Prince of Essling (1758–1817). Commander-in-Chief of the Army of Portugal in May 1810. (Fontaine, Musée de Versailles)

Above left: Colonel Baron Pelet-Clozeau (1777–1858). He was Marshal Masséna's chief aide-de-camp.

Above right: Major Marbot, Marshal Masséna's second aide-de-camp during the Portuguese campaign.

Left: Entry of the French into Ciudad Rodrigo on 10 July 1810. Defended by 5,500 Spaniards under the command of the Governor, Rodrigo Andres Herrasti, the town had been besieged by Marshal Ney since 30 May. The capture of the fortresses of Astorga, Almeida and Ciudad Rodrigo opened the way to Portugal for Masséna. (Philippoteaux)

Above: Marshal Ney, Duke of Elchingen (1769–1815). He commanded VI Corps of the Army of Portugal (infantry divisions of Marchand, Mermet and Loison, Lorcet's cavalry division).

Above: General Dufriche de Valazé (1780–1838). As colonel he directed the siege of Ciudad Rodrigo in the course of which he was wounded. On 1 June 1811 he was appointed Commander-in-Chief of the engineers of the Army of Portugal.

Above: General Junot, Duke of Abrantes (1771–1813) commanding VIII Corps of the Army of Portugal (Clausel's and Solignac's infantry divisions, Trelliard's and Sainte-Croix's cavalry brigades). He opened the campaign by capturing Astorga on 6 May 1810.

Above: Dragoon of the Army of Spain (model). (Library of R. and J. Brunon)

101

Above: Episode during the Battle of Bussaco. General Craufurd leads the 52nd to the attack – 'Now 52nd, avenge Moore!' Loison's infantry, who had reached the British guns emplaced at the village of Sula, were shot down at point-blank range and thrust back with heavy losses to their original positions. (Caton Woodville)

Above: General of Division Merle (1766–1830) commanding the 1st Division of II Corps. He was wounded during the battle.

Above: General Count Marchand (1765–1851). He commanded the 1st Division of VI Corps. He was defeated by the Duke del Parque at Tamanes on 18 October 1809.

Above: General Reynier (1771–1814) commanding II Corps (Merle's and Heudelet's infantry divisions and two divisions of cavalry).

Above: General Sir Denis Pack (1772–1823). He had under his command an independent brigade composed of the 1st and 16th Portuguese Regiments of the Line and the 4th Caçadores.

Above: General Picton, commanding the 3rd Infantry Division. (Beechen)

Above: Lieutenant-General James Leith, commanding the 5th Division (brigades of Barnes, Spry and Eben). (From a portrait by John Wright)

crossed the frontier on 16 September with 50,000 men, 7,000 of whom were horsemen, and 80 cannon. He decided to pass through Celorico, which had just been abandoned by Wellington, through Viseu and the Sierra Alcoba in order to reach Coimbra.

On the rough roads, a great number of limbers and munitions wagons broke down. The troops advanced slowly and had to remain several days at Viseu for repairs. The delay, which was attributed maliciously by Marbot, the Marshal's aide-de-camp, to the fatigue of Henriette Lebreton, was turned to account by the British, who decided to await the French troops at the Bussaco ridge. Wellington assembled 50,000 men and 60 guns in this magnificent position, whose heights barred the route. On 26 September, as soon as the morning mist had dispersed, Reynier made contact with the enemy and informed Masséna, who came, inspected the position, and gave orders for the following day at dawn; 'II Corps will attack the right of the enemy army ... VI Corps will attack along the two pathways which lead to the Coimbra road ... VIII Corps will assemble behind ... and will make dispositions to support, at need, the attacking corps, and to march upon the enemy itself. ...'

Wellington had chosen a formidable position, and it was a matter of regret that Masséna, an experienced soldier, should fall into the trap of attacking when he could have skirted the position. However, at daybreak on the 27th, Reynier's infantrymen rushed forward and, under blazing fire, arrived at the summit, only to be dislodged by a counterattack from the flank led by General Leith. For his part, Ney, who was endeavouring to take the convent of Bussaco, saw his divisions (those of Loison and Marchand) halted by the troops of Craufurd and Pack. At the end of the day, Masséna abandoned the attempt and gave the order to break off the action. The next day he did what he should have done in the first place. He reconnoitred a practicable route that would allow him to skirt the Sierra Bussaco. Once found, contact was broken. During the

Portuguese Colours, 1806–14

1. Colour of the 9th Regiment of the Line. By Order of the Day, dated in Bordeaux, 13 March 1814, infantry regiment numbers 9, 11, 21 and 23, composing a brigade, with battalions of chasseurs numbers 7 and 11, received the right to inscribe their own particular device on their colours, as a reward for their action at the Battle of Vitoria.

2. 26th Regiment of Militia of Penafiel, regimental colour. This is an old-style colour which still bears the cipher of Queen Maria. This colour and that of the militia of Aveiro were captured by Colonel Damrémont of the chasseurs à cheval.

3. Colour of the 11th Caçadores Battalion. By decree of 13 November 1813, in honour of the Battle of Vitoria, the battalion received a special inscription on its colour.

4. Central motif of a regimental colour of one of the first six caçadores battalions.

5. 12th Regiment of Cavalry, standard of the 1st Squadron. The old Almeida regiment, this unit took part in the Battle of Vitoria within D'Urban's brigade.

6. 21st Infantry Regiment, regimental colour. This regiment was at Vitoria in Power's brigade and at Bussaco in Champlemond's brigade.

7. 7th Caçadores Battalion, regimental colour. By a decree of 27 July 1811, six new battalions of caçadores were created 7th, 8th, 9th, 10th, 11th and 12th. By a decision of the Prince-Regent these units received a new uniform and new colours.

8. 24th Infantry Regiment, regimental colour.

9. 19th Infantry Regiment, regimental colour. Statutory except for the word 'exemplo'.

The Spanish Army of King Joseph

Little is known about King Joseph's army. The best sources are the collection in three volumes of the 'Leyes y decretos', the correspondence of the embassies, some memoirs and often disputed engravings. In 1809, the following regiments were created: 1st Regiment of Grenadiers of the Guard; 1st Regiment of Tirailleurs of the Guard; a regiment of fusiliers (commanded by Colonel Clary, the King's nephew); an artillery corps of the Guard; the 'Joseph Napoleon' Regiment and the 'Royal Etranger' (Royal Irish) Regiment. In 1810, eight regiments of the line were raised and in 1812 a company of sappers. The infantry consisted of a regiment of chasseurs, six regiments of the line, two squadrons of lancers and of hussars. There were also the mountain chasseurs as well as the urban and civil militia.

1. 3rd Regiment of the Line, fusilier in greatcoat.
2. Hussar of the Guard in campaign dress.
3. Vélite (mounted grenadier) of the Guard.
4. Staff officer, 1812–13.
5. 5th Line, grenadier officer, 1809–14.
6. Captain-General in dress uniform (decree of 8 February 1809).
7. Aide-de-camp of a lieutenant-general or field marshal (decree of 8 February 1809).
8. 3rd Line, grenadier officer in marching order.
9. 3rd Line, skirmisher in campaign dress.
10. Catalan miquelet; Joseph Napoleon created various units to fight against the guerrillas.
11. Joseph Napoleon Regiment. This regiment was raised on 9th February 1809. The grenadiers had the bearskin and red epaulettes, the fusilier had shoulder straps.
12. Chasseur of light infantry, 1810–13.
13. Regiment of Catalonia. Raised in February 1812, the regiment had a short-lived existence.
14. Artillery of the Royal Guard, officer. The artillery was recruited from the French ranks.
15. Captain-general's aide-de-camp, 1809.

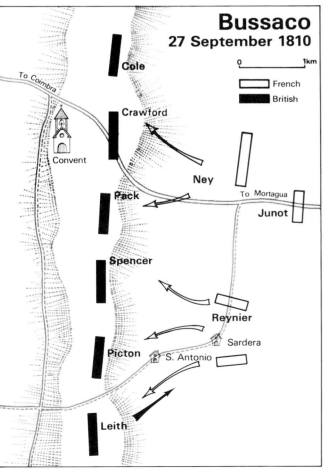

Bussaco
27 September 1810

0   1km

☐ French
■ British

To Coimbra

Cole

Crawford

Convent

Pack

Ney

To Mortagua

Junot

Spencer

Reynier

Sardera

Picton

S. Antonio

Leith

Top: The Battle of Bussaco, 27 September 1810. The French army, approximately 60,000 strong, and of whom only a part was engaged, vainly attacked more than 50,000 Anglo-Portuguese installed in a formidable position. French losses were considerable, four generals, 300 officers and 4,000 men out of action compared to less than 1,500 Anglo-Portuguese of whom 544 were British. (From a drawing by Major Saint-Clair)

Above: On 28 September, after the failure of the attack on the British positions at Bussaco, Masséna attempted to outflank the British army. General Montbrun, reconnoitring to the right of the army, found a route which would allow this manoeuvre and this was to cause the British to retreat hurriedly to Coimbra and thence to Lisbon.

Above: General of Brigade Marquis Nicolas Guye (1773–1845), aide-de-camp to King Joseph. In 1809 he commanded the skirmishers of the Royal Guard. In 1810 he was Field Marshal, Governor of the province of Seville, then Governor of the provinces of Guadalajara, Siguenza and Molina d'Aragon. Marquis of Rio Milanos, in 1812 he destroyed the gang of 'El Empecinado'. On 31 August 1813 he was wounded on the heights of Irun. (Goya)

Above: View north-west of the position of Torres Vedras (a triple line of fortifications covering Lisbon). From 12 October the British army was established in the shelter of these lines. (From a drawing by Bradford)

Above: General Poret de Morvan (1777–1834). As colonel he served in the Army of the North under General Dorsenne in 1810 and 1811, and took part in the defence of Soria of which he became governor in August 1812. He was wounded during this action.

Above: 'The Spanish Bullfight, or the Corsican toreador in danger', English satirical engraving by Gillray. (National Army Museum, London)

Above: General Foy explains to the Emperor the situation of the Army of Portugal, November 1810. (Philippoteaux)

night, leaving his camp fires ablaze, he marched towards Mortagua and on 1 October re-entered Coimbra, which had been abandoned by its inhabitants. Two days later he left again in the direction of Lisbon, leaving behind 3,000 wounded, some of whom were to be murdered by Colonel Trant's Portuguese troops – yet another example of the savagery of this war, in which the two sides vied with each other in cruelty.

Travelling across Redinha, Pombal, Leiria, Alemquer and Villafranca, Masséna now reached the Tagus. There, upon the heights of the town that dominated the right bank of the Tagus, he came up against the famous works of Torres Vedras. These were in the form of three parallel lines resting on the Tagus to the right and the sea to the left. The first of them, from Almandra to the mouth of the River Zizandro, stretched for 45 kilometres and was protected by 32 armed redoubts and 140 pieces of ordnance. The second line, from Alveira to Mafra, was six kilometres from the first, and was covered by 65 redoubts and 150 cannon. The third line, from Belem to Cascaes, was the strongest. Eight leagues from the first, it formed an independent line of defence, protected from behind by Fort St. Julian, armed with 94 guns, and by the mouth of the Tagus, where there was a flotilla of twenty ships of the line and 300 transports. All the resources of military engineering of the period had been used to enhance the natural obstacles of the terrain: roads blocked, bridges mined, rivers and watercourses made into lagoons and marshland, the ground cleared for firing, houses razed – all this gave the line maximum impenetrability. Communications were well taken care of, and the Royal Navy set up a system of signalling by semaphore, which allowed the movements of the French to be communicated very quickly. An army of 100,000 men, 30,000 of whom were British, 500 cannon and abundant supplies would halt Masséna's march in earnest ... which is in fact what happened.

Unable to advance, Masséna chose the worst solution and, with arms at the ready, he waited for Wellington to lose patience and leave his entrenchments to offer battle. Wellington, however, knowing that the French army was suffering bad conditions, took care not to do so. The persistent rains turned the French quarters into mud-pits, and provisions were cruelly lacking. Masséna was anxious. He decided that he needed the aid of Soult's army in order to do anything, so on 29 October he sent General Foy to the Emperor. Then, without waiting for him to return, he decided to withdraw to Santarem and fortify his position there, so as to spend the winter in less dreadful conditions. On 16 November, when the fog lifted, the British outposts discovered that the French lines were empty. With great skill, the Prince of Essling had broken contact. Henceforth, the two armies were well-entrenched and keeping watch over each other. As the French were so badly off for supplies, there grew up a veritable organization of marauders. If they often brought back grain and livestock, they also sometimes brought back women, who, although frightened at first, soon got used to the camp life in which they were passed from hand to hand. The deserters of both camps were roaming the countryside and even banded together in joint groups like that of the French sergeant, nicknamed ironically for his carousing, 'Marshal Cauldron', who led a joyous life installed in an abandoned abbey until a disagreeable encounter with some regular troops ended badly. Masséna had him shot as an example, together with most of his French followers; but, decent fellow that he was, he sent the British back to Wellington.

Above: On 16 October, during a reconnaissance of the enemy lines, Marshal Masséna, under fire from a British battery, was warned of his danger by the adversary himself. A single cannon shot knocked over the wall upon which he had been resting his telescope and caused him to withdraw. (Wood engraving)

However, back in Spain where no news was arriving, they began to worry. In warfare, the adage 'no news is good news' is rarely true. Gangs of Portuguese held the countryside and cut off communications. Count Drouet d'Erlon, in command of IX Corps, arrived from France and tried to make contact with Masséna on the Zézere. To do this, he sent a strong column of supplies from Ciudad Rodrigo, commanded by Gardanne. Entering Portugal without a guide, Gardanne got lost for several days in the midst of an arid and desolate terrain and, anxious about his retreat, decided to do an about turn when he was no more than three leagues from the outposts. On his return, he was relieved of his command. D'Erlon himself then decided to set off with a division of cavalry. He followed the route from Celorico to Coimbra via the left bank of the Mondego, joined up with Masséna at the end of December and installed himself around Leiria.

Meanwhile, in his Andalusian 'kingdom', Soult took a lot of coaxing to come to the aid of the Army of Portugal. True, he lacked troops, for Joseph had kept part of the reinforcements that had been destined for him. However, whether he liked it or not, he set off and slowly entered Estremadura with V Corps, about 12,000 infantry and 4,000 cavalry.

Before we finish with this year of 1810, we must recall that Suchet, Governor of Aragon by Imperial Decree of 8 February 1810, had well organized his III Corps, which had become the Army of Aragon. On 3 March, he entered the Kingdom of Valencia, but the capital was too well defended and he came back towards Lerida which had a garrison of 10,000 men. Having beaten O'Donnell, who came to the aid of the fortress, he energetically attacked the town, which capitulated on 14 May. Then, having taken Mequinenza on 8 June, he lay siege to Tortosa on the left bank of the Ebro. The siegeworks were skilfully supervised by General Rogniat, one of the best engineer officers, and in spite of the diversions sent out from Tarragona and Valencia, the fortress capitulated with its 9,000-man garrison in January 1811.

Above: Episode during the march on Valencia at the beginning of 1810. General Suchet was ordered by King Joseph and Marshal Berthier to march on Valencia with his III Corps, 20,000 strong, of whom 5,000 were detailed to guard the key-points. The Army of Andalusia was to support the movement by occupying Murcia. During the operation, General Boussard, sent off with two squadrons of cuirassiers and hussars and a few companies of élite infantry, captured Castellon de la Plana (March 1810). Despite the resistance of the rebels, the French seized the bridge. A cuirassier named Vinatier dismounted and, dashing forward alone, managed to cut his way through, despite the hail of bullets which the peasants fired at him. The army did not attempt to storm Valencia, but retired to Aragon. (Musée de l'Armée)

Right: The 114th of the Line at the siege of Lerida. (Musée de l'Armée)

Above: Marshal Suchet, Duke of Albufera (1770–1826) commanding the 1st Division of V Corps (Army of Spain, October 1808). In April 1809 he commanded III Corps which was to become the Army of Aragon on 8 July 1811; Commander of the Army of Aragon and Catalonia, April 1813, Colonel-General of the Imperial Guard on 18 November 1813, Commander-in-Chief of the Army of the South on 22 April 1814.

Right: Episode during the siege of Lerida. Assault and capture of the Carmen bastion. The fortress surrendered after having lost 1,200 men. (Philippoteaux)

Above: Baron de Saint-Joseph (1787–1866), Marshal Suchet's aide-de-camp. (Painting by Etienne Louis Advinent, Musée de l'Armée)

Right: The Siege of Tortosa. Sortie of the garrison repulsed. After having secured Lerida on 14 May 1810, Mequinenza on 8 June and Morella on 14 June, Suchet with the support of Frère's division of VII Corps (Army of Catalonia) and after six months of blockade, seized Tortosa on 2 January 1811. (Philippoteaux)

THE GUERRILLA WAR...

Right: On 17 April 1809 a decision of the Seville Junta decreed a mass uprising and a merciless guerrilla war against the invader. The insurgents ranged over all the territory occupied by the French since June 1808, led by men who have remained famous: Francisco Mina and Xavier Mina, 'El Empecinado' (Diaz), the curate Merino, Renovales, Sarasa, 'El Capuchino' (Delica), Julian Sanchez, brother Rafael, 'El Marquesito' (Porlier), Isidoro Mir, Jimenez, Camilo Gomez, Milans del Bosch, Claros, Barrid, Rovisas, Bagets, José Mansa, Antonio Franch, 'El Pastor' (Jauregui), 'El Medico' (Palarea), 'Papel' (Longa), Etcheverria, 'El Manco' (Albuir). A French convoy attacked by guerrillas while crossing a bridge on the Burgos road, near Miranda de Ebro. (Bacler d'Albe, Musée de l'Armée)

Below: Scenes of action against the guerrillas in the Aoiz valley. Surprised by guerrillas of Navarre, who shower large stones down on them, French infantry scale the cliff and hurl their aggressors from the top. (Bacler d'Albe, Musée de l'Armée)

*Right: General
Franceschi-Delonne,
entrusted by Marshal
Soult with a mission to
King Joseph, was
captured by 'El
Capuchino's' gang near
Toro on 12 May 1809.
Taken to Granada, then
to Seville, treated
without respect, he was
transferred to Cartagena
where he died of yellow
fever in 1810.
(Philippoteaux)*

*Left: A detachment of the
2nd Dutch Infantry
Regiment (1st Brigade of
the Division of the Rhine)
in action against the
guerrillas in the province
of La Mancha (1810).*

Above: General Count Claparède (1770–1842). He commanded the 2nd Division of IX Corps which, 8,000 strong, at the begining of 1811 was charged with maintaining communications between the Army of Portugal and Spain. He achieved several successes against the Anglo-Portuguese and took part in the Battle of Fuentes de Oñoro.

Right: South-east section of the theatre of war map in General Foy's 'Histoire de la Guerre de la Peninsule sous Napoleon' (1827).

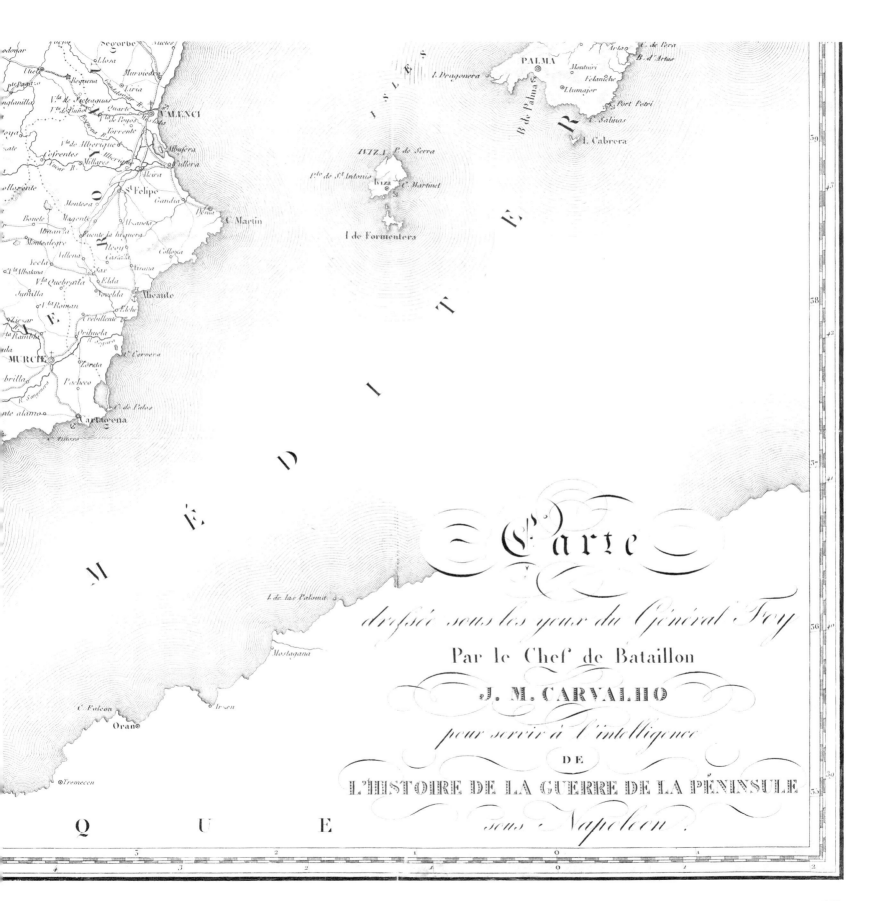

THE GUERRILLA WAR...

Right: Fighting against the guerrillas. For the duration of the campaign a sizeable portion of the French army was absorbed by the struggle against the guerrillas and was to be absent from the principal battlefields where it was sorely needed.

Left: Gendarmes of the Army of Spain. (J. Girbal)

Right: General Buquet, Commander of the Gendarmerie of Spain, inspecting his troops. Twenty squadrons of gendarmerie were assigned to assure communications. Sixteen of these squadrons guarded the main road from Bayonne to Madrid, divided into the following posts: Irun, Hernani and Tolosa, between Tolosa and Vitoria; Vitoria, Miranda de Ebro, Briviesca, Burgos, Lerma and Aranda, between Aranda and Somosierra, Buitrago, Cabanillas, Alcobendas and Madrid. 'This line', wrote Napoleon, 'will henceforth be the line of operations of the Army of Spain.' Four other squadrons were in reserve, destined to be sent wherever their presence might be needed. When the Gendarmerie of Spain was dissolved at Tarbes on 27 August 1814, from an effective strength of 4,000 men, 2,000 had been killed or wounded. (J. Girbal)

'Comparing the occupation of its country to the Moslem invasion, the mass of the people, urged on by the clergy, waged a merciless war against our soldiers. In a nightmare country, surrounded by hostile nature, faced by the passionate and cunning hatred of the inhabitants, stirred up by the first national war sustained by a people for its legitimate defence, the French soldiers were to fight valiantly, enduring constant privations and hardship.'— R. and J. Brunon. (After Maurice Orange)

Left: Block-house on the road between Hernani and Tolosa. The French built these block-houses of wood, and posted infantry in them to escort couriers and protect convoys. (Bacler d'Albe, Musée de l'Armée)

115

GUERRILLA LEADERS...

Left: Formidable gang leader Don Juan Palarea, 'El Medico'. At the head of his hussars and chasseurs, he extended his activities from upper La Mancha to Toledo and around Madrid. On 6 April 1811 near Madrid, his band of guerrillas, after having wiped out his escort, captured Colonel Lejeune, who was on an errand for King Joseph.

Left: Juan Diaz Porlier, called 'El Marquesito' (1783–1815). A former marine, he took part in the Battle of Trafalgar. He led the struggle in the Asturias and in Galicia. His guerrilla band numbered 1,500 men in 1809 and grew to more than 4,000 in 1811.

Left: Francisco Espoz y Mina, considered to be the most cunning of the guerrilla leaders. He succeeded his nephew, Xavier Mina, who was captured by General Harispe's soldiers in March 1810, as head of a band, which he reformed. A former peasant, he avoided holding the villages to ransom and maintained strict discipline. He was active in Navarre, rendering more than precarious the route between Madrid and France. He waged a veritable 'war to the death' against the French and everywhere his atrocities followed one upon the other. Pursued by General Abbé,
who had put a price on his head, he continually eluded him and won two major successes against the French by attacking strongly escorted convoys, to which he caused heavy losses, in May 1811 and April 1812. In 1813 he was wounded and almost captured in his lair at Ronda.

Left: Don Juan-Martin Diaz, 'El Empecinado'. A former soldier turned farmer, he became one of the most famous of the guerrillas. He organized his first band after the Battle of Medina del Rio Seco. He provided his men with a semblance of uniform, and rapidly became a celebrated leader whose exploits remain famous. Pursued by General Hugo's troops, then by General Guye, he was beaten several times and his band dispersed. However, he continued the fight until the end of the war, operating in Castile between Aranda, Segovia and Guadalajara. (Anonymous, Lazaro Galdiano Museum, Madrid)

The year 1810 was crucial for Spain. All her regular armies had been vanquished and dispersed. Napoleon, victor at Wagram, had been able to send fresh reinforcements and the British army was immobilized in Portugal. But the guerrilla bands continued to create a feeling of insecurity for the occupying army, requiring them to mobilize at any moment. In the long run, the guerrillas demoralized the French army, which was used to conquering princes and regular armies on the battlefield according to the rules, and not to fighting an entire nation. Proud and easily offended, and spurred on by the clergy, the Spanish were obsessed with the idea that the French were instruments of the Devil. Masters of half the country, in reality the French controlled only 'the ground upon which the soles of their shoes rested'.

Soult's capture of Badajoz — Masséna's retreat — Incident with Ney who is relieved of his command — Battle of Fuentes de Oñoro — Masséna's disgrace — Soult's problems in Andalusia — Battle of the Chiclana (Barossa) — Beresford besieges Badajoz — Battle of Albuera — Marmont's manoeuvre and meeting with Soult — Relief of Badajoz — Return of Soult to Andalusia — Defeat of Godinot at Tarifa — Suchet — Siege of Tarragona — Attack on Montserrat — Suchet appointed Marshal — Siege and capture of Sagunto — Siege of Valencia.

Above: Captain Gillet's devotion to duty at the siege of Badajoz, March 1811. (Drawing by Philippoteaux). *The fortress of Badajoz had been invested since 27 January by the troops of Marshal Soult. In March, Soult, alarmed by the news from Andalusia and Portugal, decided to try a surprise attack. An argument ensued between the officers of the engineers and those of the artillery concerning where the breach should be made. Eventually, it was decided that a detachment of twenty-five sappers would demolish the crest of the counterscarp. The sappers, led by Captain Gillet, were discovered as they prepared to carry out the work. In a matter of moments, sixteen sappers were killed or wounded and the rest scattered. Captain Gillet returned alone, having proved at the risk of his life that his section had been right in the controversy.*

Above: General Baron Eblé (1758–1812). He commanded the artillery of the Army of Portugal.

Above: Masséna's retreat. The crossing of the Mondego by the British Light Division. The retreat of the French army began on 5 March 1811. (From a drawing by Major Saint-Clair)

At last Soult decided to strike camp. On 2 January he set off in the direction of Badajoz. With him he had Mortier's V Corps, formed of the infantry divisions of Girard and Gazan and Latour-Maubourg's cavalry division. He gathered together as much artillery and as many engineers as he could. On the 3rd, the Spanish troops of Ballesteros were beaten near Monasterio, and in dreadful weather, along impracticable tracks, he arrived on 13 January outside Olivenza and took the position after a siege of ten days. Instead of going at once to Masséna's aid, he decided to lay siege to Badajoz, which was defended by a garrison of 8,000 men. This little town of 20,000 inhabitants was the capital of Estremadura. Established on the left bank of the Guadiana, it was joined to the right bank by a stone bridge, the head of which was defended by the fort of San Christobal, at whose feet ran the River Gebora. These tumultuous waters made the attack difficult, and Soult held back, waiting for materials with which to build pontoons to come from Seville. During the night of 18/19 February he at last decided to attack the two Spanish divisions encamped on the Gebora, covering the town. Thanks to the skilful manoeuvres for which Latour-Maubourg's cavalry won renown, the Spanish were put to rout, leaving on the field 6,000 dead and prisoners and 17 guns. Pushing his advantage, yet without undue haste, Soult completed his siegeworks and sent a final summons on 10 March. That was enough for the Spanish, who, having no longer any hope of further aid, surrendered and handed over to the French 8,000 prisoners and 170 guns.

Masséna, still at Torres Novos hoping for Soult's arrival, had by now almost completely run out of food and munitions. General Foy, having arrived in Paris, spoke to the Emperor, telling him that there was no way of avoiding a movement to the north. 'If he is obliged to retire for lack of supplies, let him come towards the Mondego', conveyed Berthier. To re-cross the Tagus would signify the abandonment of the north of Portugal to the British, and the Marshal made his decision only after consulting his subordinates, especially Ney with whom his relations were difficult.

During the night of 5/6 March the retreat began. Reynier's corps reached Espinhal and Junot's went to Pombal. The Duke of Elchingen commanded the rearguard. Eblé, who was to win fame at the Beresina, destroyed all the bridge-building materials so laboriously assembled on the Zêzere. In the first hours of the morning of 11 March, Montbrun, at the head of his dragoons, reached the left bank of the Mondego, but was unable to cross it. At that same moment, the English advance-guard of General Erskine attacked Pombal which was held by the French rearguard. Having fired the town, the rearguard withdrew

117

Above: General Baron Charbonnel (1775–1846) commanded the artillery of VI Corps. He particularly distinguished himself during the Battle of Redinha.

Left: Skirmish during the retreat of the Army of Portugal, March 1811. (From a contemporary drawing)

in good order while Wellington, continuing the pressure, attacked Ney with two divisions (one of which was General Picton's 4th) at Redinha. After an admirable defence, the Marshal, who had only Marchand's division at his disposal, retired during the night.

There was no longer any question of passing through Coimbra, for the route was difficult and the enemy was there in force. Masséna decided to change the route of his withdrawal and made for Miranda de Corvo, then, still protected from behind by Ney, he continued along the Ceira valley and reached Celorico on the 21st. He was now 56 kilometres from the Spanish frontier. Although but feebly pursued at the end, the exploit was remarkable. Across a mountainous and devastated region, the French accomplished 20 kilometres a day in the worst of conditions.

Almost all their equipment had been lost, but the men were there, ready to fight. Wellington had not been able to annihilate this army which he believed he could hold in check. Better still, communications had been re-opened with Spain. However it was impossible to stay long in Celorico because of the lack of food. Masséna contemplated marching on Almeida and Ciudad Rodrigo, but the country was exhausted and fresh supplies were impossible to obtain; so, contrary to all expectations, he decided to descend towards Coria on the Alagon and re-open operations in the Tagus valley. At midday on the 22nd he issued his orders. If Reynier was in agreement, Ney was furious. He flew into a violent rage and pointed out that Wellington would certainly invade Spain along the Almeida and Ciudad Rodrigo routes if the French abandoned them. Then, at 6

118

o'clock in the evening, he sent a letter to Masséna indicating his intention to continue on the morrow his march towards Almeida. The Prince of Essling's reaction was immediate: 'Be so good as to advise me whether you are to persist in your disobedience and in your failure to recognize the authority which the Emperor has entrusted to me. In that case, I shall know what to do to maintain it. I await your reply by return of my aide-de-camp.' By 9 o'clock, the aide had brought the reply to his leader. It was a pure and simple refusal to obey. Ney wrote: 'I persist in not allowing VI Corps to march on Coria and Plasencia as your Excellency has ordered me by letter of the day . . .' By 10 o'clock 'the red-head' had been relieved of his command and replaced by Loison. That was the end of a collaboration that had never gone well.

On 24 March, Masséna's three corps set off in a southerly direction, but the roads were atrocious, the guns were unable to follow, and in the desolate mountain villages food was not to be found. On the 29th, he regrouped his army behind the Coa and decided to turn back to Almeida and Ciudad Rodrigo. However, Wellington, who had regained contact with the French troops, thought that the moment had come to destroy Reynier's IV Corps, which was at Sabugal, 15 kilometres from Masséna. The Englishman carried out his outflanking manoeuvre. Beckwith's cavalry brigade and the Light Division were to attack the French position from behind while the 3rd and 5th Divisions were to engage Reynier's front-line. The manoeuvre failed. The French fought like lions and the British abandoned the attempt. The retreat continued in good order.

On the 4th, the French army crossed the Spanish frontier. Masséna pushed on to Salamanca, established himself there, and set about putting everything in order. Reinforcements were shared out among the battalions, which once again reached full strength. Munitions were distributed, supplies organized. 'We have arrived in this town with as much joy as if we had returned to France', reported Captain Marcel of the 69th of the Line. It was true that Salamanca, where General Thiébault commanded, was a well-ordered and calm town. The Spanish had an excellent opinion of their governor. He was a cultivated man (and had undertaken a translation of *Don Quixote*), thought to be intelligent and, in the eyes of the people, was a man of integrity. A little court of Frenchmen, inspired by the Duchess of Abrantes, set the tone, and many distinguished 'afrancesados' frequented the salons where the 'bel esprit' reigned.

Within a few weeks Masséna had refitted the French army. The horses, decimated during the retreat, had been replaced, the lines of supply were assured. All this was not accomplished without friction with Bessières, who remained Chief of Staff of the northern army of Spain. Masséna wrote to him: 'My dear Marshal, the Army of Portugal is without bread and without artillery harnesses. In waiting for you it has not only consumed the food it brought with it, but also part of the supplies of Rodrigo . . .' Bessières was a man of quality and, despite his own problems in Navarre, he himself came to the assistance of the Duke of Rivoli. This was important to the latter who had left behind him the fortress of Almeida with General Brennier in command, and who wished to relieve the town, which the British were besieging. Indeed, Napoleon was urging him to action from Paris. Berthier conveyed the message: 'His Majesty hopes that you will soon have the opportunity to extract a most brilliant revenge. The Emperor has not forgotten your fifteen successful years and has the greatest confidence in you. You will be victorious in order to leave to your descendents that military reputation acquired by so many glorious labours . . .' Such an appeal was not to be resisted, and on 2 May the army set off, 35,000 men and 52 guns – II Corps with Reynier, VI with Loison, VIII with Junot and IX with Drouet d'Erlon. The left flank was covered by Montbrun's cavalry. Morale was excellent. The presence of the two marshals was felt to be an assurance of victory. The army had decided to take revenge for Torres Vedras. Masséna issued a proclamation: 'Soldiers of the Army of Portugal, after six months of glorious labours you have returned to the field of your first triumphs. But the enemies of the great Napoleon dare to blockade a place that a short while ago they did not have the courage to defend. . . . Soldiers, you need a victory to enable you to enjoy to the full the repose that your privations and fatigues have long since demanded. You will achieve this, and comfortable quarters will be your prize.' Fond of glory and good living, the Frenchman understood this language only too well.

On 3 May the army crossed the Agueda and debouched on to the plain. Opposite was the British army, ranged along the Coa, with the village of Fuentes de Oñoro at its back. Following his custom, Wellington had chosen his terrain. The sloping position was strong and could be outflanked only from the right, which is to say, from the south. The only serious disadvantage was that eight kilometres behind the lines the plain was dissected by the gorge of the River Coa, the edges of which were as much as 120 metres high. This obstacle might make a precipitate retreat very dangerous. The British disposed of 37,000 men and 48 guns, being six infantry divisions and one of cavalry.

Above: General Baron Thiébault (1769–1846), Chief of Staff to Junot in the Army of Portugal (1808). In 1811 he was Governor of Old Castile, then Toro, Zamora, Almeida and Ciudad Rodrigo, which he managed to supply despite the blockade.

Right: On 4 April Masséna's army recrossed the Spanish frontier after six months of occupation in Portugal. (Wood engraving)

Right: Episode during the Battle of Fuentes de Oñoro, 5 May 1811. At the beginning of the battle, while Houston's division (7th) with the support of Cotton's cavalry and Major Bull's horse artillery held off the charges of Montbrun's cavalry and began to withdraw to the main positions of their army, Lieutenant Norman Ramsay managed to save his section of two pieces by cutting straight through the French cavalry. (W. B. Wollen)

Above: General Count Montbrun (1770–1812) commanded the cavalry of the Army of Portugal.

Right: The charge of General Fournier-Sarlovèse's cavalry at Fuentes de Oñoro. They broke through two squares, formed by Craufurd's brigade, while the dragoons dispersed the third.

Spain: Regiments, Militia and Guerrillas raised from 1808 to 1814

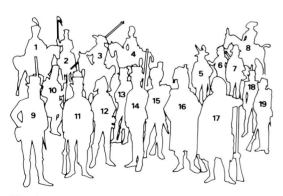

Nearly 200 infantry regiments of the line and 100 of light infantry, plus cavalry units, were raised in Spain between May 1808 and March 1814. Guerrillas and irregular troops were also very numerous. Each province (sometimes even each village) had its 'guerrilleros', led by men who were often nothing more than bandits.

1. Cazadore de Iberia, officer 1809–14. This unit was raised in 1808 by Palarea, a guerrilla from Toledo, head of the 'Corsarios terrestres' and of a 'numantino' squadron.
2. Lancer of Don Julian Sanchez, 1814. A native of Salamanca, Sanchez formed a guerrilla band of 200 lancers or 'Garrocheros'. He ended the war as a brigadier-general.
3. Garrochista de Baylen.
4. Dragoon of Granada, 1808–14.
5. Guerrilla of the Kingdom of Granada.
6. Guerrilla of Andalusia, 1808.
7. Guerrilla of the Basque provinces, 1813.
8. Guerrilla of the Asturias.
9. Volunteers of Navarre, 1808. Commanded by Mina, they were part of a real infantry division, well-organized and clothed.
10. Volunteer of the Kingdom of Valencia, light infantry.
11. Tercio of Miqueletes of Gerona. It was in 1808 that the supreme junta of Catalonia organized its regiments in 'Tercios de Miqueletes de Cataluña'.
12. Somaten or Catalan volunteer. Part of the irregular units, but well disciplined, these Catalan volunteers always refused regulation and military dress. Nevertheless they were integrated into the ranks of the San Fernando Regiment.
13. Regiment of Baza, 1808. Raised at Granada, this regiment took part in the defence of Gerona.
14. Tercio de Voluntarios Barceloneses Expatriados.
15. 3rd Guipuzcoano Battalion, 1812.
16. Battalion of light infantry of chasseurs of Catalonia. Raised in 1811, this unit was one of the most famous in Catalonia. It was known as the 'Cazadores de Manso'.
17. Guerrilla of the Kingdom of Leon.
18. Corregimiento de Cerbere, 1811. This was one of the 14 regiments of the reserve army, organized by General Lacy.
19. Legion of Catalonia, 1809–12.

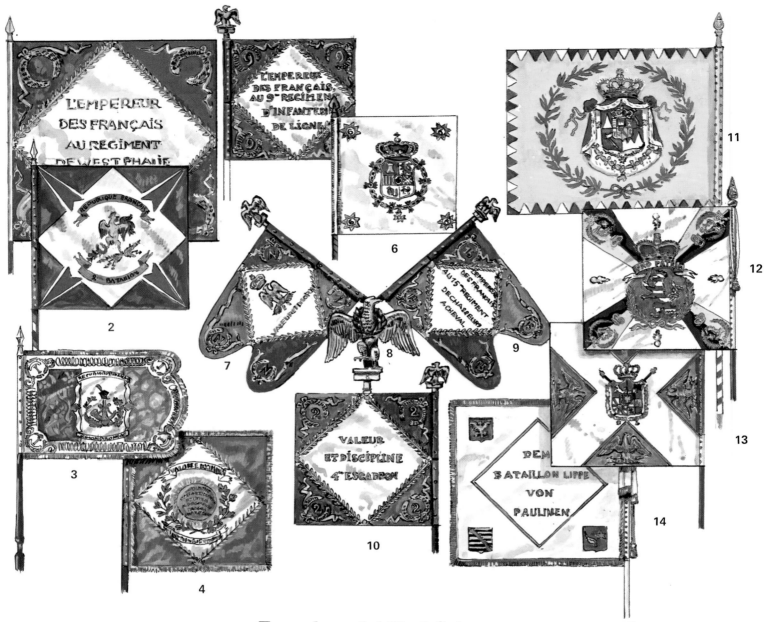

French and Allied Colours

1. Colour of the Westphalia Regiment, 1807–15. This regiment, not to be confused with the units of the Kingdom of Westphalia, was raised in 1806, recruited from former Prussian and Brunswick soldiers. Arriving in Spain in 1808, it took part in the siege of Gerona in 1809.
2. Legion of the Vistula. Colour of the 2nd Regiment of infantry, 1800–13. Four regiments served in Spain until 1812. This colour, under which the legion fought in the Peninsula, was of an old design dating from 1800.
3. Pennon of the 1st Regiment of Lancers of the Vistula. Like the infantry, the lancers never used the eagles to which they were entitled. This regiment fought all its campaigns until 1814 with republican emblems.
4. Italian Regiment 'Napoleon Dragoons', standard

of the 1st Squadron, 1805–13.
5. 9th Regiment of the Line, colour of the 1st Battalion.
6. Army of Joseph Napoleon, colour of the 6th Battalion of the Line 'Malaga', 1809. It was by a decree dated at Madrid on 24 May 1809, that Joseph drew up rules for the style of his flags.
7. Guidon of the Mamelukes of the Guard.
8. Crowned eagle of the 8th Regiment of the Line. This eagle was lost at Barossa on 5 March 1811.
9. Guidon of the 15th Regiment of Chasseurs à Cheval, 1804–14. This regiment remained in Spain from 1808 (Madrid) to 1814 (Toulouse).
10. Standard (reverse) of the 2nd Regiment of Hussars, 1804–09. This regiment went to Spain in 1808. On the obverse of the standard was inscribed: L'Empereur des Français au 2ème Régiment de

Hussards.
11. Colour of the Würzburg infantry regiment. This regiment was integrated into the 1st Regiment of the Confederation of the Rhine.
12. Colour of the Erbprinz Regiment, 1804 model. This regiment took part in the Spanish campaign from 1808 to 1812. In 1812, it surrendered at Badajoz where two of its colours were captured by the British.
13. Kingdom of Westphalia, standard of the 1st Regiment of Light Horse, 1808–14.
14. 5th Regiment of the Confederation of the Rhine, colour of the 2nd Battalion, 1812–14. The battalion was formed of four companies of Lippe and two companies of chasseurs of Schaumburg-Lippe. The 1st Battalion was formed by a battalion of fusiliers from Anhalt.

Above: General Fournier-Sarlovèse (1773–1827). He commanded the 7th, 13th and 20th Regiments of Chasseurs à Cheval. On 3 May, in a headlong charge, his brigade had overthrown 2,000 enemy horsemen.

The 5th was on the left under Erskine, a courageous officer who was to become insane within a year; the 6th on the right of the 5th with Campbell; the 3rd in the centre with Picton; the 1st also in the centre with Spencer; and the 7th on the right with Houston. The cavalry division was under Cotton's orders and was also on the right.

Masséna made the same mistake as at Bussaco. Instead of trying to outflank the British, he launched Ferey's division of Loison's corps into a frontal attack on the village of Fuentes de Oñoro. Taken and re-taken several times, by nightfall the village remained for the most part in British hands. The morning of the next day allowed Masséna to reconnoitre the British positions and to realize that the only possibility of victory lay in outflanking Wellington's right wing. But the British had anticipated this manoeuvre, and Spencer's and Picton's divisions moved southwards. At daybreak on the 5th the battle resumed. Beneath Montbrun's furious charges, Wellington's right wing gave way, while the Fournier-Sarlovèse's brigade covered itself in glory. Meanwhile, the French IX Corps was capturing the village of Fuentes de Oñoro. Victory was within reach and Masséna, sensing this, gave the order to General Lepic, kept in reserve with the cavalry of the Guard, to come to the support of Montbrun. Young Oudinot who carried the message, was told to reply that 'the Guard only recognizes the Duke of Istria and cannot unsheath their swords without his order'. Bessières was nowhere to be found, and the exasperated Masséna could do nothing. The British took advantage of this and pulled back their right wing. This was the end. Montbrun was unable to renew his attacks and Picton's division even recaptured most of the village of Fuentes de Oñoro. Night fell, operations were halted and though the armies remained face to face for two more days, the indecisive battle was over. However, Masséna was now concerned with saving Almeida and asked for volunteers to cross the British lines and carry the order to General Brennier to destroy all his equipment and rejoin the army. A great number of men came forward, lots were drawn and three were chosen. Of these, only Tillet, a chasseur with the 6th Light, managed to get through, showing astonishing skill and courage. Having blown up the ramparts, Brennier fought his way through the British siege lines and rejoined the main army.

But now Marmont had arrived from Paris and Bessières informed Masséna of a letter from Berthier: 'Marshal, Prince of Essling, the Emperor having deemed it advisable to give command of his Army of Portugal to the Marshal, Duke of Ragusa, His Majesty's wish is that as soon as you have handed over your command you are to return to Paris. . . .' Masséna had so nearly been victorious, and his disgrace was very hard to take. His military career was almost at an end. Wellington had the last word when he wrote to his brother William, 'This was the most difficult battle in which I have ever taken part. It carried the gravest risks, and if Boney had been there we would have been beaten.'

Soult had not effectively intervened and that was one of the causes of the Prince of Essling's defeat. It must be said that since the end of February the Duke of Dalmatia had been having a few worries in his own kingdom. An Anglo–Spanish army of 22,000 had disembarked at Tarifa. The Spaniards were commanded by Count de la Peña, the British by Sir Thomas Graham, a vain but talented man. Soult was worried. He had been manoeuvring slowly since the beginning of the campaign, and he now decided to

Above: Marshal Masséna, Duke of Rivoli, assembled II, VI, VIII and IX Corps, Montbrun's cavalry and 1,500 cavalry of the Guard under the command of Bessières, to relieve Almeida which was being blockaded by the Anglo-Portuguese. (Painting by Fontaine, after Gros)

Below: General Doyle. He commanded the Portuguese brigade of the 7th Division (7th and 19th Line, 2nd Caçadores).

Right: On 3 March 1811 part of the Cadiz garrison, led by General Zayas, attempted a sortie in support of the action of the Anglo-Spanish army which had approached from Gibraltar. It was repulsed on the Isle of Léon by Villatte's division. In the course of the action the 63rd Line seized a Spanish colour. (Musée de l'Armée)

Left: Cadiz at the beginning of the nineteenth century. The town's garrison was reinforced by the 9,000 men of the Duke of Albuquerque, all that was left of the Army of Estremadura, and supported by a British squadron.

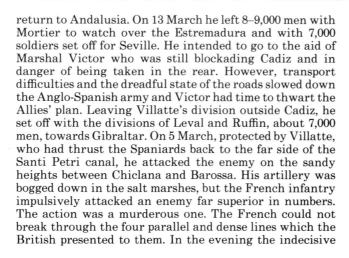

Above: The Duke of Orleans, future King Louis Philippe (1773–1850). Disembarking at Cadiz on 20 June 1810, he offered to serve in the Spanish ranks. Although he was received with consideration his proposition was refused and on 3 October he returned to Britain, disappointed and dissatisfied.

return to Andalusia. On 13 March he left 8–9,000 men with Mortier to watch over the Estremadura and with 7,000 soldiers set off for Seville. He intended to go to the aid of Marshal Victor who was still blockading Cadiz and in danger of being taken in the rear. However, transport difficulties and the dreadful state of the roads slowed down the Anglo-Spanish army and Victor had time to thwart the Allies' plan. Leaving Villatte's division outside Cadiz, he set off with the divisions of Leval and Ruffin, about 7,000 men, towards Gibraltar. On 5 March, protected by Villatte, who had thrust the Spaniards back to the far side of the Santi Petri canal, he attacked the enemy on the sandy heights between Chiclana and Barossa. His artillery was bogged down in the salt marshes, but the French infantry impulsively attacked an enemy far superior in numbers. The action was a murderous one. The French could not break through the four parallel and dense lines which the British presented to them. In the evening the indecisive

battle ceased and Victor took up his dispositions to recommence the battle. However, the British were afraid of being forced into the sea if reinforcements arrived, either from Granada or Badajoz, and they withdrew. If Sebastiani, commanding IV Corps in the Kingdom of Granada, had intervened, the destruction of the enemy would have been assured. Thus, when Soult arrived the threat had been averted. The siege of Cadiz could be renewed with vigour and Soult himself was available to give assistance to Marmont.

Meanwhile back in Estremadura, Mortier was endeavouring to pacify the province and attempting to capture the fortresses still held by the Spanish. On 15 March, Latour-Maubourg took Albuquerque and dismantled it. On the 21st, it was Campo Mayor which suffered the same fate, but this time Beresford arrived at the head of an Anglo-Portuguese army and the French withdrew. General Philippon, an energetic man who had remained in Badajoz,

Above: Marshal Victor, Duke of Belluno (1764–1841). Commanding I Corps, he lay siege to Cadiz in February 1810. The town, whose governor was Francisco-Javier Venega de Saavedra, was to be besieged for two years. (Philippoteaux)

Left: Episode during the Battle of Chiclana-Barossa, 5 March 1811. Charge of the hussars of the King's German Legion. (General Whitingham)

Above: Capture of the eagle of the 8th Line by the 87th Foot at the Battle of Barossa. This was the first French eagle to be captured by the British. After a furious mêlée during which seven Frenchmen were killed, Lieutenant Gazan, severely wounded, had to abandon the emblem of a crowned eagle to Sergeant Masterton. (Source: 'Les aigles impériales et le drapeau Tricolore' by General Regnault)

Above right: The arrival in London of the crowned eagle taken at Barossa gave occasion on 18 May 1811 for a dazzling ceremony. A carefully arranged procession, with detachments of the British Foot Guards in dress uniform, paraded the French trophies along a lengthy route among an enormous crowd, before presenting them to the highest authorities and to the Spanish and Portuguese Ambassadors. The other trophies were old ones: five eagles captured in the Antilles, a flag captured in Egypt, a fortress standard taken in Spain, a pennon of the 2nd Battalion of the 5th Line, two flags without eagles of the 2nd and 3rd Prussian regiments (captured at Walcheren), a colour of a provisional regiment. The main part of the ceremony was the 'formal act of obeisance and humiliation of the vanquished'. Eagles and colours, lined up opposite the colours of the King's Grenadier Regiment, 'were dipped and lowered to the ground as a sign of submission' (General Regnault 'Les aigles impériales et le drapeau tricolore'). It is interesting in this context to recall that in seven years of campaigning in the Spanish war, the French army had captured 387 trophies, among which were 320 Spanish colours, 45 Portuguese colours and 22 British colours. The French army had lost only 11 eagles, 8 of which had fallen to the British. (R. and J. Brunon, after a sketch by Dighton)

Above: General Baron de Latour-Maubourg (1768–1850). He served brilliantly in Spain from November 1808 to the end of 1811. During the Battle of Albuera his cavalry, supporting the attack by the infantry of Girard's division, overthrew Colborne's brigade, taking 1,000 prisoners and several colours.

Above: Lieutenant-General William Carr Beresford, Marshal of the Portuguese Army. (Painting by Sir W. Beechy)

Right: The British army build a bridge over the Guadiana on 3 April 1811. (G. Browne)

Above: General Baron Chamorin (1773–1811), killed on 25 March 1811 at the Battle of Campo Mayor.

Left: On 21 March General Latour-Maubourg received the order to evacuate Campo Mayor and to transfer its armaments to Badajoz. The 13th Light Dragoons, supported by the heavy dragoons, attacked the convoy and, despite desperate resistance by the escort (100th Line and 26th Dragoons), managed to capture several cannon and some baggage. During the action General Chamorin, recently promoted, was killed at the head of his old regiment, the 26th Dragoons. (S. L. Wood)

organized the town's defences. He had the old French trenches filled in, repaired the fortifications and had extensive mine galleries dug out. When the enemy arrived, he vigorously defended the approaches to the fortress, and his sorties afforded the besiegers little chance of progress. On 14 May, Beresford raised the siege and left to confront Soult, who was coming to Philippon's aid with 18,000 men and 40 guns. The Englishman, who had joined up with Blake's corps, disposed of 31,000 men, whom he deployed behind the River Albuera with its muddy bottom and steep sides.

On the 16th the battle commenced with great violence. Soult, holding the enemy centre with furious bayonet charges, attempted to outflank the enemy right, but the British resisted and even counterattacked. Two French generals were killed and some regiments gave way. Luckily, Latour-Maubourg's cavalry arrived at the gallop, deployed on the French left and halted the enemy. In the centre, the artillery, commanded by General Ruty, intervened with staggering precision. The advancing British masses were scythed down, and darkness fell on an unchanged scenario, the two armies, both extremely sorely tried, resting face to face. Fearing the British superiority of numbers, Soult decided during the night to withdraw to Solana and thence to Llerena. This last position was easy to defend, and seemed to the Marshal well-chosen both to prevent access to Andalusia and to await necessary reinforcements.

Meanwhile, Marmont, replacing Masséna, was not inactive. On 3 June he left Alba de Tormes and made for

Above: The colour at Albuera. On 16 May 1811 Colborne's brigade, having advanced in support of General Zayas's Spaniards who were in difficulty, was charged by the 1st Lancers of the Vistula and the 2nd Hussars. Within a few minutes, three out of four battalions had lost two-thirds of their effective strength. At the beginning of the battle, the French cavalry, about 4,000 men under General Latour-Maubourg, made several brilliant charges against the British front line and captured several colours (six according to General Regnault) and approximately 1,000 prisoners.

Above: General Baron Brayer (1769–1840) distinguished himself at Corunna and Ocaña. His left leg was shattered during the battle.

Above: General Lowry Cole, commanding the 4th Division. His rôle determined the outcome of the battle.

Above: General Blake (of Irish origin). With General Castaños he commanded the Spanish troops that took part in the battle. (From a nineteenth-century engraving)

Above: General Baron Quiot (1775–1849). He was wounded by a bayonet thrust during the battle.

127

Left: The British 57th Foot at the Battle of Albuera on 16 May 1811. During the battle, Colonel Inglis, commanding the regiment, was killed and the regiment lost 1,054 men from a total of 1,600. (Caton Woodville)

Above: The 48th Foot at the Battle of Albuera; heavily engaged, their colonel was killed during the action.

the Guadiana and Badajoz, passing through upper Estremadura. He crossed the Tagus at Almaraz and continued his march towards Merida, while sending Clausel's division in the direction of Medellin. This manoeuvre renewed Soult's courage, and by another route he received a reinforcement of 6,000 men brought by Drouet d'Erlon. On 18 June the two marshals met at Merida and descended the Guadiana as far as Badajoz where they arrived on the 20th. The garrison, whose conduct had been heroic, were overjoyed to be reunited with comrades they had never thought to see again. Wellington, who had raised the siege on the 11th, had retired some little distance to the slopes of Portalegre and had deployed in his usual well-chosen defensive position.

Fearing another Talavera, the two marshals, neither of whom wanted to help the other, agreed to separate. Marmont regained the Tagus valley, Soult went to Andalusia and Wellington, who had lost a lot of equipment in this affair, struck camp and returned to Portugal. This refusal to join battle can be considered a grave error. Jourdan wrote: 'It seems that, the Armies of the South and of Portugal being united, the chance to do battle with Lord Wellington, encamped two steps from Badajoz, was favourable. We do not know the motives that determined the marshals not to take it. Perhaps they gave in to that spirit of rivalry and disagreement that has preserved the British army from defeat more than once. However that may be, the Duke of Dalmatia hastened to return to Andalusia where his presence was growing daily more necessary.' This last phrase reflected reality very accurately. Profiting from the absence of French troops, the Spanish, commanded by a French emigré, Count de Penne-Villemur, were agitating and threatening Seville. General Darricau, commanding the position, withdrew into La Cartuja, a vast Carthusian monastery that had been fortified, and with the few available depot troops prepared to defend himself. The first elements of the enemy to reach the western heights of the town were repulsed, but very soon the arrival of Soult obliged the Spanish troops to decamp. As soon as he returned, the Duke of Dalmatia applied himself to restoring order, for which there was a great need. Victor was still marking time outside Cadiz. At Granada and Jaen uprisings broke out, and the elusive Ballesteros was running about the countryside between the mouth of the Guadiana and Gibraltar.

Little by little, a series of successful actions restored a certain tranquility. Blake was banished from Granada, and Ballesteros was defeated by Drouet d'Erlon at Ayamonte. One setback was that of General Godinot, defeated outside Tarifa. Obliged to follow the coast road, the general was caught by cannon-fire and was forced to give up the attempt. A few days later, a violent altercation set him against Soult and he committed suicide, reputedly from despair.

Whilst Soult was attempting to pacify his fief, Suchet in Aragon continued to organize his kingdom methodically. The fall of Tortosa on 2 January 1811 brought the surrender of 9,000 men, who were sent to France; then on the 8th the St. Philip fortress at the summit of the Balaguer Pass was captured, and the Tarragona route was now open. Situated at the mouth of the River Ebro, this town served the Spanish as a base of operations. Defeated armies often found refuge there, and its port welcomed British ships

Above: General of Division Baron Girard (1775–1815) commanding the 1st Division of V Corps. He had a series of successes during the campaigns of Marshals Mortier and Suchet in 1809, 1810 and 1811. However, he allowed himself to be taken by surprise at Arroyo de Molinos on 28 October 1811.

Top: Captain Fawcett of the 57th, although mortally wounded, continues to command his company. All French efforts to push back the enemy were in vain and Soult was forced to give up the attempt to relieve Badajoz. Losses were heavy on both sides; 7,000 French and 6,000 Allies, of whom 3,500 were British.

Above: Skirmish at Arroyo de Molinos, 28 October 1811. At the end of October, General Hill, at the head of 10,000 Anglo-Portuguese and Spanish, penetrated into Estremadura by a circuitous route. He surprised and surrounded Briche's brigade (Girard's division) which managed to escape by sacrificing a battalion composed of élite companies. (From a contemporary drawing)

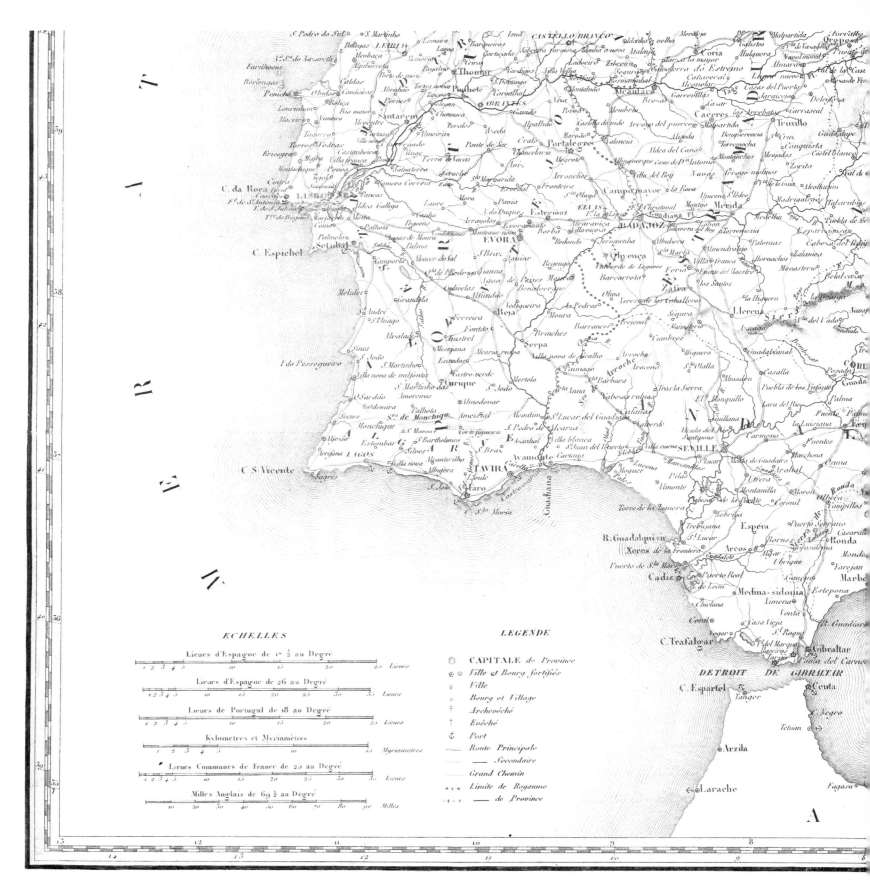

ECHELLES

Lieues d'Espagne de 17 ½ au Degré
1 2 3 4 5   10   15   20   25 Lieues

Lieues d'Espagne de 26 au Degré
1 2 3 4 5   10   15   20   25   30   35 Lieues

Lieues de Portugal de 18 au Degré
1 2 3 4 5   10   15   20   25 Lieues

Kylomètres et Myriamètres
1 2 3 4 5   10   15 Myriamètres

Lieues Communes de France de 25 au Degré
1 2 3 4 5   10   15   20   25   30   35 Lieues

Milles Anglais de 69 ½ au Degré
10   20   30   40   50   60   70   80   90 Milles

LEGENDE

◎   CAPITALE de Province
⚜   Ville et Bourg fortifiés
◉   Ville
○   Bourg et Village
‡   Archevêché
†   Evêché
⚓   Port
—   Route Principale
—   Secondaire
—   Grand Chemin
+++   Limite de Royaume
-+-+   de Province

A

Above: General Alava,
Spanish liaison officer with
Wellington.

Left: South-west section of the
theatre of war map in General
Foy's 'Histoire de la Guerre de
la Peninsule sous Napoleon'
(1827).

that supplied the guerrillas. Built on a rock, the town was divided into two parts: the upper town, protected by the old Roman walls, and the lower, defended by a bastioned 'enceinte'. A short distance away, dominating the surrounding area, was the port of Olivo, defended by 12,000 men and 50 guns. Brigadier-General Contreras was in command of the garrison of 18,000 men and 400 guns, while the British ships anchored outside the harbour of the lower town were ready to intervene in support of their allies.

The approach march of the French was slow, for Suchet advanced only when communications were well assured. He made for the town in two columns, one coming down from Lerida with General Harispe – a future marshal, but in the Second Empire – the other from Tortosa with General Habert, who was a very large man and a magnificent trainer of troops. In all, about 20,000 men of disparate origins, Frenchmen, Italians, Germans, Poles, were strung along together with one common denominator – they were hardened and disciplined soldiers. During the night of 4/5 May, General Salme, at the head of his brigade, attacked the fortress of Olivo. Despite the Spaniards' stubborn resistance, he occupied the outer entrenchments,

Above: Lieutenant-General Baron Habert (1773–1825) commanding the 3rd Division of the Army of Aragon.

Right: Death of General of Brigade Salme. He was killed leading the 7th and 16th Line in the assault on the fortress of Olivo.

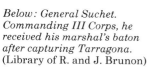

Below: General Suchet. Commanding III Corps, he received his marshal's baton after capturing Tarragona. (Library of R. and J. Brunon)

but it needed more than three weeks of bitter fighting before the fortress could be taken. On the 24th, Salme fell mortally wounded while leading the 7th Regiment of the Line, and it was General Ficatier who, on the 29th, took the fortress and made prisoner the 900 surviving defenders. This success spread consternation in the town of Tarragona and a relief column left the town the next day to try and dislodge the French. The counterattack failed, and Suchet wished to take advantage of his troops' enthusiasm to attack the fort of Francoli, situated by the sea at the entrance to the lower town. On 7 June, three columns under Colonel Saint Cyr-Nugues attacked the fort; at the head, the sappers with ladders opened the way and soon the overwhelmed Spaniards were retiring in disorder towards the town. At 7 o'clock on 21 June, with the cry of 'Vive l'Empereur', five columns rushed to the assault of the lower town. The Spanish, supported by the British, defended themselves desperately, but were unable to hold out.

Early next morning the lower town, its bastions and considerable equipment were all in the hands of the asssailants. In spite of this defeat the upper town still held out, however, and the Governor had no intention of surrendering. Suchet wanted to finish with the business, for he was afraid that an outside attack, combined with a sortie by the 12,000 men still in the town, would put everything back where it had started. He positioned Harispe on the Barcelona road with General Palombini's Italian division and Boussard's cavalry brigade and, at the end of the afternoon of the 28th, the assault was launched. General Habert, at the head of 1,500 men, scaled the breach. He was followed by General Ficatier's column, while General Montmarie forced the Rosaire Gate and joined up with them. The Spanish resistance was stubborn. The long road leading up to the cathedral was the site of bloody

scenes. The houses were taken one by one, and the fighting continued mercilessly to the precincts of – and even inside – the cathedral, which was crowded with wounded. Provoked beyond measure, the French murdered all who crossed their path. The gutters ran with blood, and the officers were often unable to prevent the carnage. Panic-stricken, the Spaniards fled and the inhabitants and soldiers threw themselves from the ramparts. Contreras took advantage of the night to try to escape along the Barcelona road, but he came upon General Harispe's troops. It was the end. Driven towards the sea, cut down by the French horse and decimated by British grapeshot which rained down at random along the coast, the Spaniards surrendered. To Contreras, who complained of the 'cruelties' of the French soldiers, Suchet replied that he, Contreras, alone, by prolonging a useless resistance, had incurred the responsibility for such excesses. Nearly 10,000 men remained in French hands.

Having shown proof of his skill and energy, Suchet received by decree of 8 July, the envied title of Marshal of the Empire – the only one to be bestowed by the Emperor for the Spanish campaigns. The newly-promoted Suchet described the siege in these terms: 'The divisions of Harispe, Habert, Frère and Palombini showed admirable devotion to duty, constancy and ability. We had, as it were, five successive sieges, or rather we gave the assault five times and assailed nine breaches. The infantry had 3,750 men out of action; 142 officers, 13 of them staff officers, were killed or wounded. We fired 42,000 artillery rounds, 30,000 of them with balls, bombs and shells from the fortress thrown back after our soldiers had paid for them.' This last remark lacks nothing in flavour!

The capture of Tarragona dismayed the Catalans, and Suchet wanted to take quick advantage of the situation. He decided to attack Montserrat, a monastery turned fortress that served as a lair for gangs of Spanish terrorists. Situated amid wild mountains dissected by ravines, this formidable Benedictine edifice now bristled with redoubts and embrasures. The monks had left, but they had been replaced by 4,000 regular and irregular Spanish troops under Baron d'Eroles. Suchet had the roads leading to the monastery blocked. On 24 July, at the head of the élite companies of the 1st Light and 114th Line, General Abbé entered the pass, preceded by a company of sappers. Caught under fire from the 'miquelets' posted on each side, bombarded by rocks pushed down on them by the peasants, the French clung to the hillside, climbing upwards until, with incredible courage and agility, they reached the monastery. Supported by six other élite companies under General Maurice Mathieu, the assailants hurled themselves against the defences and successively secured the three batteries that constituted the defence. Eroles managed to escape with the remnants of his troops by flinging himself into ravines and pathways which could be reached only with difficulty. 3,000 prisoners remained in French hands.

Suchet returned to Saragossa and learned of his elevation to the Marshalate as well as a series of promotions for his subordinates. He signed a proclamation beginning, 'Soldiers, the Emperor is well pleased with you . . .' but which continued, '. . . soon a new campaign will begin . . .'. He did not wish to let the Frenchmen's enthusiasm wane, and intended to take advantage of the Spanish confusion to pacify the region and take Valencia. It must be quickly done. The Junta had learned with dismay of the fall of Tarragona and the recapture of Figueras in Catalonia by

Right and below right: Capture and sack of Montserrat by the French. Defended by Brigadier d'Eroles, this, the only arms depot remaining to the Catalan insurgents, was captured on 24 July 1811 by Marshal Suchet leading the brigades of Abbé and Montmarie, and a detachment from the Barcelona garrison under General Maurice Mathieu.

Baraguay d'Hilliers, serving under Macdonald. They sent General Blake into the Kingdom of Valencia with full authority. Blake mustered an army, fortified Peniscola, Oropesa and Sagunto, and assembled arms and munitions which had been landed by the British at Graõ, the port of Valencia. A second-rate general, but a skilful psychologist, Blake exalted patriotism and the enthusiasm of the inhabitants and, confident in the dispositions he had taken, calmly awaited in Valencia the possibility of French attacks. These were about to begin.

On 15 September, Suchet set off at the head of three columns; the first under General Habert, the second under Palombini's Italian Division and the third under Harispe. On the 27th, the Marshal entered Murviedro. On the 28th, the enemy was pushed back into the fortress overlooking the town of Sagunto. The assault that followed failed, and the French were obliged to mount a formal siege. The houses were fortified with passages built to link those in the shelter of the fort together. Generals Valée and Rogniat were directing operations, while Suchet awaited Blake, who could not fail to come to the aid of Sagunto. Indeed, Blake left Valencia on the night of 24/25 October. On the morning of the 25th, the action began when the enemy advanced to less than half a league from the walls of

Above: The amphitheatre of Sagunto in 1811. The ruins are dominated by the fortress. (Bacler d'Albe, Musée de l'Armée)

Below: The 114th Line at the Battle of Sagunto, 25 October 1811.

Sagunto, but the charges of Boussard's brigade, then that of General Delort at the head of the 2nd Dragoons, broke through the Spanish lines. While the troops of Generals Harispe, Habert, Palombini and Montmarie endeavoured to encircle and trap the Spanish army, Blake escaped, leaving behind 2,000 killed or wounded and 4,000 prisoners. The defenders of Sagunto, who had thought for a moment that they were to be relieved, were discouraged and capitulated the following day.

Master of Sagunto, Suchet went immediately to the walls of Valencia. Transformed into a fortified camp, the town sheltered a garrison of 20,000 men commanded by Blake, with lieutenants better than their leader, such as Zayas, Lardizabal, O'Donnell and Velasco. Moreover, the irrigation canals, which so enriched the Huerta of Valencia, made access difficult. So Suchet, fearing a defeat, appealed to the Emperor for reinforcements. The Emperor ordered the armies in Spain to aid the new marshal. Reille came from the north of Spain, and Montbrun from the Army of Portugal. Only Soult sent nothing from Andalusia, and Suchet was to remember this later when the Duke of Dalmatia required assistance. The reinforcements were all that was necessary to break the town's resistance, but it did not fall until the beginning of the following year.

So ended 1811. Wellington had gone back to Portugal. Marmont was reorganizing his troops and was settling down in Talavera. Despite his defeat at Tarifa, Soult was enjoying a relative calm in his fief. The provinces of the Asturias, Biscay and Navarre were more or less quiet, and the famous guerrilla leader Mina was only successful in minor skirmishes. Still king in Madrid, Joseph might have thought that his brother was about to desist from the dismemberment of Spain and provide him with some real assistance.

However, the year 1812 was going to be quite different. It would see the Emperor undertake the Russian campaign and his main preoccupations diverted from Spain. But in spite of everything, it began with a success, the capture of Valencia.

Above: General Count Dorsenne (1773–1812) commanding the infantry detachment of the Guard, November 1808. He was Commander-in-Chief of the Army of the North from 8 July 1811 to 5 May 1812. (R. and J. Brunon)

Right: View of the interior of an inn in the kingdom of Valencia. (R. and J. Brunon)

Crest in the Musée de l'Empéri.

1812

Capture of Valencia by Suchet — Capture of Ciudad Rodrigo and Badajoz by Wellington — Soult's manoeuvring — Wellington's capture of Salamanca — Battle of Los Arapiles (Salamanca) — Marmont wounded — Clausel's retreat — The Army of Portugal retires to the Ebro — Suchet in Aragon — Raising of the siege of Cadiz — Evacuation of Andalusia — Wellington enters Madrid — The Fuente de Higuera interview — Wellington checked outside Burgos — Recapture of Madrid — Wellington's disengagement.

Right: The Grao Gate at Valencia. This well-fortified town had a garrison of about 20,000 men. (Bacler d'Albe, Musée de l'Armée)

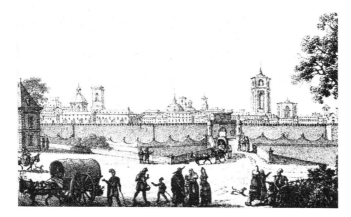

At Valencia, Suchet, conscious that victory was within his grasp, actively pursued his siegeworks. The outer defences were taken and, on 6 January, a terrible bombardment ravaged the town. A first summons was declined but, on the 9th, at the moment when the French attack was imminent, Blake agreed to surrender and, together with the entire garrison of about 18,000 men, was taken prisoner and sent to join Palafox at the fortress of Vincennes. His vanquisher was made Duke of Albufera by the Emperor, who regarded him highly.

But already the first serious cracks were making themselves felt in Spain. Well-equipped and supplied, Wellington arrived from Portugal and laid siege to Ciudad Rodrigo. Informed of the French dispositions, he wished to take advantage of them. Indeed, having set off to aid Suchet and arrived too late, Montbrun was wasting time

Right: Suchet's entry into Valencia on 9 January 1812. After only seven days of siege the town surrendered, handing over to the French 18,000 prisoners including the Commander-in-Chief Blake and 23 other generals, 21 flags and 393 guns. (Philippoteaux)

outside Alicante, while Dorsenne had taken the greater part of his available forces back to the north-east, so the town, with its 2,000-strong garrison, was isolated. General Berrié was in charge, having succeeded General Reynaud, who had been taken prisoner during an ambush by Don Julian's band. Berrié was courageous but lacked firmness. Fearing Marmont's intervention, Wellington rushed his attack, and, on 19 January, the town was captured and the garrison made prisoner.

Having secured his supply lines and put troops into the fortress, the British general retired to his fortified position at Fuente Guinaldo. Then, at the beginning of March, with a rapidity unusual for him, he decided to take Badajoz. Though the capture of Ciudad Rodrigo had left Salamanca exposed and had opened the Old Castile road to the British, the continued presence of the French in Badajoz was a strong threat to the southern provinces of Portugal. On the 16th, with 25,000 men, Wellington presented himself before the town, which was defended by 4–5,000 French, Germans and Spaniards. There were not enough of them to hold all the redoubts and defences effectively, but their commander, Philippon, was an energetic man. By means of

Right: View of Alicante in the nineteenth century. To ward off the threat posed by the enemy concentrated at Alicante, on 4 February Marshal Suchet occupied Peniscola, and Denia – a fortress situated about 100 kilometres to the north of Alicante.

Right: Lieutenant-General Craufurd directs the advance of his division's assault columns. He was killed during the action. Since 13 January two breaches had been made and, during the night of the 19th, the 3rd Division (Picton) attacked the main one, while the Light Division attacked the lesser breach. The capture of the two breaches, at a price of severe losses, brought with it the surrender of the garrison.

Far right: Wellington gives his instructions before the attack on Ciudad Rodrigo. (From a drawing by W. B. Wollen)

The 30th Foot at the siege of Badajoz, 6 April 1812. (Watercolour by Simkin)

Above: Marshal Marmont, Duke of Ragusa (1774–1852). He replaced the Prince of Essling as Commander of the Army of Portugal on 7 May 1811, with the twofold task of closing Spain to the British around Ciudad Rodrigo and collaborating with Soult in Estremadura.

Above: Colonel Colborne, commanding the 52nd Regiment (Drummond's brigade) during the Peninsula campaign. (From a painting by Pickersgill)

Opposite page: the defence of Burgos. (Painting by Heim, Musée de Versailles)

Burgos, the last of the Army of Portugal's depots of arms, munitions and supplies. Defended by 1,800 men under General Dubreton, the castle of Burgos was besieged on 16 September. On 22 October after 35 days, the British abandoned the siege, having lost 2,500 men.

Left: Wellington in 1812. The capture of Ciudad Rodrigo resulted in his appointment as a Grandee of Spain and 'Knight of the Golden Fleece' by the Regency, while Portugal made him Marquis of Torres Vedras and later Duke of Vitoria. The English parliament accorded him the title of Earl, then Marquis of Wellington. (Philippoteaux)

Top and above: The capture of Ciudad Rodrigo. Led by 300 volunteers, the Light Division secured the lesser breach at the cost of heavy losses, which included its Commander, General Craufurd, who was mortally wounded. Scenes of drunkenness and indiscipline took place after the capture of the town. The Allies' losses amounted to approximately 1,700, 195 of whom were killed. (H. Payne)

vigorous sorties he demolished the British siegeworks and maintained high morale among his troops, who were outnumbered by five to one.

At the beginning of April, Wellington learned that Soult was preparing to come to the aid of the besieged town, and decided to attack in force on the evening of the 6th. The French opened fire with dreadful determination, and soon nearly 3,000 of the assailants littered the ground. Unfortunately for the defenders, the castle was not well guarded and was surprised by General Picton's troops. After a desperate struggle, Philippon withdrew into the fortress of San Christobal. In the town, horrific scenes now began. Napier, the British historian, said in his *History of the Peninsula War*: 'There now developed a scene of hideous crimes which tarnished our soldiers' shining heroism. It is true they did not all show themselves the same, for hundreds of them risked – and a few even lost – their lives in trying to halt such unbridled violence. But madness

Above: General Colville commanded the two divisions which attacked the breaches made by the assailants (3rd and Light Divisions) and suffered heavy losses (30 per cent of their effective strength). (Painting by Raeburn)

Above right: Badajoz. (From a painting by Henry Smith)

Right: The 4,000-strong garrison of Badajoz, under General Philippon, swear to die, sword in hand, rather than surrender. (Philippoteaux)

prevailed generally, it must be said, and as in such cases, the worst species of men lead the others. All the most detestable passions of human nature gorged themselves in broad daylight: a rapaciousness without shame, a brutal intemperance, a savage lewdness, cruelty, murder . . . that was the spectacle offered by the streets of Badajoz for two days and nights.'

By early morning on the 7th, Philippon, wounded and without supplies or munitions, was obliged to surrender, (but he was to escape a few months later). Meanwhile, he had lost a third of his effectiveness, about 1,300 men killed or wounded. The British had lost 5,000 and Napier wrote: 'When Lord Wellington had learned of the full extent of the night's disaster, his manly steadfastness and his vanquisher's pride gave way for a moment, and the pain which he felt at the loss of so many valiant soldiers, burst out with distressing emotion.' This was certainly not a customary view of the man who would later be dubbed the

Above: The Light Division at the capture of Badajoz on 6 April 1812. It was to lose 1,000 men in the attack on the breach. A detachment of the Light Division, which had managed to scale the St. Vincent bastion, was flung back outside the enceinte. (W. B. Wollen)

Above right: Wellington in the breach at Badajoz. The official estimates of British losses during the siege were 317 officers and 3,344 men killed or wounded, while the garrison had 1,300 men put out of action. (J. T. Jones, after Caton Woodville)

Right: After the capture of Badajoz, Wellington was greatly moved on learning of the extent of the losses sustained during the assault. (Caton Woodville)

'Iron Duke'. No similar occasion has been recorded, and, in any case, the tears observed by witnesses did not alter the fact that his victory was a very important one.

Soult had hastily mustered all his available troops and had just joined with d'Erlon's V Corps. But it was too late. He was two days' march from Badajoz when horsemen sent out at the last moment by Philippon told him that all resistance had ceased. There was no question of his confronting the British alone, particularly as the news from Seville was bad. The Spanish Generals Morillo and Ballesteros had appeared outside the town. General Rignoux, who was in command, mustered all his able-bodied men and sent out several detachments to attempt an escape. Luckily Soult arrived, having left V Corps in Estremadura to cover the Andalusian frontier, and calm was restored.

Because of his previous successes, Wellington now controlled the corridors into both northern and southern Spain, but with his usual prudence he considered this to be almost worthless while the two French marshals, Soult and Marmont, were still in communication. Their line of contact passed through Almaraz, where a pontoon bridge had been thrown across the Tagus. This was the only means of crossing upstream from Toledo, because the other bridges had all been destroyed. The Duke of Ragusa was aware of this and had had the pontoon fortified. Wellington instructed General Hill to capture it. Hill executed the order to perfection and, on 18 May, despite the desperate resistance of the French who were defending the left bank, he took the bridge, burned it and rejoined the British Army with his division.

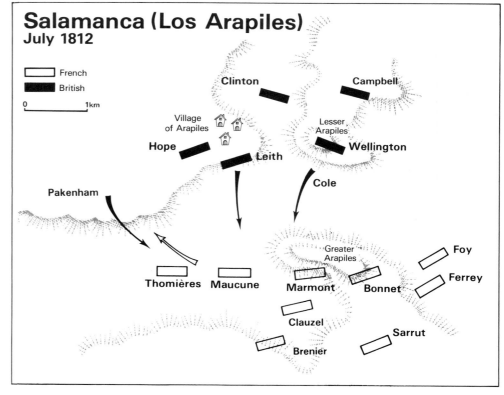

Salamanca (Los Arapiles)
July 1812

☐ French
■ British

0   1km

Village of Arapiles

Clinton

Campbell

Lesser Arapiles

Hope

Leith

Wellington

Cole

Pakenham

Greater Arapiles

Foy

Thomières   Maucune   Marmont   Bonnet   Ferrey

Clauzel   Sarrut

Brenier

Above: Major-General Sir Edward Pakenham, commanding the 3rd Division (brigades of Wallace, Power and Campbell). (Painting by T. Heaphie)

Above: General Sir Colin Halkett (1774–1856). At the Battle of Salamanca, his brigade (7th Division) consisted of the 1st and 2nd Light Battalions of the K.G.L. and Brunswick-Oels chasseurs.

Wellington, who had received reinforcements, was now ready for his offensive on Salamanca. The moment was particularly favourable for him. Napoleon's Russian campaign was under way, and the Grande Armée needed troops. Spain was to furnish them. Indeed, the Emperor had thought for a moment to withdraw to the Ebro in order to tighten up his dispositions, but the capture of Valencia, with its destruction of Blake's Spanish army, had dissuaded him. The whole situation was much to be regretted, since his altercation with the Tsar called for many troops, and was to deprive Spain of soldiers of the first order who knew the country perfectly. The Young Guard, the Red Lancers and a large number of dragoons had to recross the Pyrenees. With them went prestigious leaders such as Eblé and Montbrun, who would not return from this adventure. Napoleon evidently realized that the directing of operations, which he had already managed so poorly from Paris, would be impossible from the depths of Russia, and so he gave the command of the armies of Spain to Joseph and assigned Marshal Jourdan as Chief of the General Staff—the same partnership as at Talavera: an irresolute leader, not made for the military life, and a prudent and far-seeing assistant who lacked the strength of character to enforce his own decisions. The result was not long in manifesting itself.

On 12 June the Anglo-Portuguese army set off. By the 16th, it had arrived outside Salamanca which had been evacuated by Marmont. The 700 men he had left behind were distributed between three monasteries, which had been converted into small forts, whose firepower commanded the bridge over the Tormes. By means of a desperate defence, they held up the British for twelve days and inflicted losses of nearly double their own strength. However, on the 28th, a salvo of red-hot shot set Fort San Vincente ablaze, and all the French surrendered. Marmont crossed the Duero at Tordesillas, set up camp there and received reinforcements, chiefly the 8,000 men of Bonnet's division. Stationed in the Asturias, Bonnet had found himself completely cut off after Wellington's attack. But he knew the terrain well, and was able to thwart the manoeuvres of the Spanish troops who were on their way to meet him. Crossing the Pajares ridge, he reached Reinosa and rejoined Marmont.

Now, Marmont had an army of 42,000 men with eight divisions of infantry, a handsome cavalry force and 75 guns. On 17 July he recrossed the Duero a little downstream of Tordesillas, which was threatening the British flank.

Rapidly, Wellington concentrated his army and withdrew towards Salamanca. The adversaries were marching in the same direction, Marmont still hoping to outflank the British. This skilful manoeuvre on the part of the Duke of Ragusa should have been maintained until the arrival of Joseph, who was hurrying to reinforce him. But, once again, Spain was a battlefield that inspired more rivalry than a spirit of co-operation in the French leaders, and the fear of sharing a success which he thought ought to be his alone, led the marshal to attack immediately. On 21 July, he crossed the Tormes and encamped on the left bank close to Salamanca. The next morning, the armies were face to face, each occupying one of the two steep hillocks called Los Arapiles. These were to become the pivot of the battle. Bonnet's division held the Greater Arapiles, which they had taken after a fight with Portuguese troops who had been attempting to capture it from their own side. Marmont repaired thence with his staff, while Wellington with his own occupied the Lesser Arapiles. The higher French position was a good one: in the event of a retreat, the British would be obliged to pass under the French guns. The French right was composed of the divisions of Foy (1st) and Ferey (2nd); in the centre were Clausel (2nd), Sarrut (4th), Maucune (5th) and Brennier (6th). On the left was Thomières's division (7th) and in reserve was a division of dragoons under Boyer.

At about 1 o'clock the Duke of Ragusa opened fire with a dreadful cannonade on the Portuguese front-line, which pulled back, and began his manoeuvre to occupy the plateau directly in front of the one upon which the French artillery was positioned. General Thomières carried out his orders badly and allowed his left to advance too far, while Maucune followed suit with the 5th Division. The British general, who was on watch from the Lesser Arapiles, noticed the gap left by the French between the centre and the left. 'My dear chap,' he said to Alava, his Spanish aide-de-camp, 'Marmont is lost.' He personally took the head of a column of infantry and attacked violently in order to cut the French in two. Seeing the advantage that the British might draw from the blunder of his left wing, the Duke of Ragusa had just given the order to pull back towards the hillock when he was badly wounded. Indecision threatened to paralyze the French troops. It was at this moment that Thomières was killed. His division was cut to pieces by the British cavalry, and the divisions of Maucune and Clausel coming to the rescue were soon obliged to fall back upon the centre, which in

Right: The charge of the heavy dragoons at Salamanca. The 66th and 22nd Line were cut off, charged by the British horse and totally routed. During the action the eagle of the 22nd was captured by the British.

Above: Major-General MacKinnon, who commanded a brigade of Picton's division (3rd Division). During an assault on the most important breach, he was killed by an exploding mine, which caused heavy losses to the assailants. (From a contemporary painting)

Right: The charge of Pakenham's division at Salamanca. Surprised in mid-movement, Thomières's division (7th) hastily reformed, faced the British attack, but were unable to prevent their artillery from being captured by the infantry of Wallace's brigade. General Thomières was killed during the battle. (Caton Woodville)

Right: Charge of the 12th Light Dragoons at Salamanca. At the end of the day, the 12th Light Dragoons, supported by the Light Division, twice charged General Foy's division which was withdrawing to the Tormes. (H. Granville Baker)

Above: Major-General Le Marchant, commanding the 3rd and 4th Dragoons and 5th Dragoon Guards. He was mortally wounded leading his men in the charge.

Above: Wellington and Pakenham at Salamanca. On 22 July, Wellington, who had fallen back before Marmont's army, took up his position outside Salamanca. The French army consisted of about 40,000 infantry and 3,000 cavalry, supported by 78 guns. The Anglo-Portuguese army had 43,000 infantry, 4,000 cavalry and 60 guns. Attacked by Wellington in a full outflanking manoeuvre by the British right, the French army was disordered and forced to retreat with heavy losses. In June 1812, at the moment when the Russian campaign was about to begin, and after the departure of contingents of the Imperial Guard to rejoin the Grande Armée, the army in Spain still numbered 210,000 – an imposing strength, but unevenly distributed on Spanish territory.

Above right: After Marshal Marmont, and then General Bonnet had been wounded, General Clausel, who commanded the 2nd Division of the Army of Portugal, directed the retreat, although he too was wounded. (Philippoteaux)

147

turn bore the brunt of the British attack. General Bonnet, who had succeeded Marmont, was also gravely wounded. The battle was lost. It was Clausel who, although himself wounded, was to avert total disaster. He succeeded in reforming the lines and rallied the centre and left upon the right, which had not suffered, and held his ground until nightfall. At 9 o'clock, leaving behind General Foy's rearguard, he withdrew and crossed the Tormes without difficulty. Behind him, 5,000 French dead or wounded

remained on the battlefield. Three generals—Thomières, Ferey and Desgraviers—had died on the field of honour.

Henceforward, the French dispositions in Spain were completely disorganized. The Army of Portugal was to evacuate Valladolid and even Burgos, and draw back to the Ebro. Having arrived too late, Joseph had to flee Madrid, as he did after Baylen, and take refuge with a sorry company near Suchet. It was at this time that Napoleon, having set off with his Grande Armée, decided, after a long conference with Berthier, Poniatowski and Lefebvre-Desnouëttes, to march on Moscow. In a few months, Europe would be shaken by the first rumbles of the fall of colossus, the first cracks of which were already becoming perceptible in Spain.

However, despite the defeat at Salamanca, all was not yet lost. Catalonia with Decaen, Aragon and the Kingdom of Valencia with Suchet, were more or less tranquil. The French held firm before the Spanish forces of Lacy and O'Donnell. Moreover, O'Donnell had been severely defeated on 21 July at Castalla by General Delort, and since then had remained circumspect.

This privileged situation, which Suchet knew how to exploit, was due to the richness of the country, which rendered the problems of food supplies less acute. Elsewhere marauding was an institution; here order and discipline reigned. The inhabitants were well aware of this, so they stayed quietly at home and did not feed the bands of guerrillas. The Kingdom was divided into fourteen subdivisions, in which the levying of taxes was left to the 'corregidors', and the French administration saw to it that the apportionment of contributions was fair. Enormous military depots were set up and, when villages sent requisitions, the provisions deposited were valued at market prices and the surplus was paid to the villagers. Elsewhere, Suchet himself saw to it that no extortion took

Top: The 65th Line during the retreat from Salamanca. The retreating French army was continually harassed by guerrillas. (Musée de l'Armée)

Above: The Battle of Castalla, 21 July 1812. 9,000 Spaniards commanded by General O'Donnell were totally routed by the 1,500 men of the vanguard of the Army of Aragon commanded by General Delort. During the charge of the 24th Dragoons and a squadron of the 13th Cuirassiers, the cuirassier Bécheret captured a colour. (Ch. Langlois, Musée de Versailles)

Right: Cuirassier Bécheret, holding the colour he has captured from the enemy, drinks to victory. (Ch. Langlois)

Right: Wellington's triumphal entry into Madrid on 12 August 1812. The victor of Salamanca is welcomed by the delighted Madrilenes. He was warmly received by the Madrid authorities together with the principal guerrilla leaders of the region, including 'El Empecinado' and 'El Medico'. Very quickly 'his distant attitude and air of scornful superiority' made him unpopular with the capital's inhabitants. He was to have to evacuate the city on 30 October at the approach of the re-united armies of the Centre, Andalusia and Portugal. Madrid was re-occupied by the French on 3 November.
(Bromley)

place, and did not hesitate to penalize all breaches of discipline severely.

It was in this context that the news of the defeat at Salamanca and the imminent arrival of King Joseph came to Valencia. Joseph was, in fact, being driven out of Madrid by the arrival of the British. Since his victory, Wellington had been convinced that Clausel was not in a position to resume the offensive, and so he was marching towards Madrid. On 6 August he left a strong detachment at Cuellar to watch over the line of the Duero; next day he entered Segovia; and by the 12th was at Madrid, where he was given a rapturous welcome. But the Spaniards were soon to tire of the drunken and badly-behaved British. Clausel was saved by this diversion in which, for once, British pride had sacrificed efficiency for ostentation.

Meanwhile, the great convoy from Madrid was making its way towards the Kingdom of Valencia, escorted at the outset by the troops of General Hugo. In this immense caravan, 20,000 people crowded together in an ill-assorted collection of vehicles of varying ages. French families, 'afrancesados', courtiers – all those who, for one reason or another, feared the arrival of the British – were there. Witnesses who saw these refugees pass by could not believe their eyes. 'Two or three thousand vehicles trailed behind the King – magistrates, counsellors of state, chamberlains, generals, ministers, ambassadors and their families. A large number of foot soldiers turned cavalrymen were mounted on all kinds and all sizes of quadruped, and were wearing the most bizarre clothes.' Although neither the British nor the guerrillas worried the convoy, the journey was particularly hard; heat and dust beat down upon these unfortunate people who were dying of thirst.

Joseph and his equipage finally arrived in the Kingdom of Valencia at the moment when Soult was beginning the evacuation of Andalusia. It was not without regret that the Duke of Dalmatia had decided to do so. For a moment he wavered, hoping that Joseph might come with his troops. 'As a loyal subject of the Emperor', he wrote, 'I must make known to Your Majesty that I cannot believe that the affairs of Spain are so hopeless as to call for such violent measures. I can still see a remedy, if Your Majesty will only take the dispositions I have proposed, and while preparing to execute my orders, I venture to ask him for new instructions.' Annoyed, Joseph confirmed the orders and Soult, sick at heart, complied. After having destroyed equipment and munitions, Semelé, who had replaced Victor outside Cadiz, raised the siege. All detachments scattered about the province were ordered to return to Seville, Antequera, Cordoba or Granada. The marshal wrote: 'I had to withdraw a vast network from every part of a huge territory and reassemble it in one place without losing any of its parts, and I had to co-ordinate all the troops marching from opposing directions, sometimes by divisions, sometimes by mere detachments . . .' The operation was a success, however, and he even managed to evacuate without mishap the Spaniards compromised by association with the French. At Huescar, he joined d'Erlon's army, which had come from Estremadura, avoided Murcia where yellow fever was raging, and on 30 September the vanguard reached Tobarra and the outposts of Joseph's Army of the Centre.

On 3 October, a council took place at Fuente de Higuera at which the King and the three marshals, Jourdan, Soult and Suchet were present. The news was not very encouraging. Having been sent back to the Army of Portugal by the Emperor, Masséna was detained at Bayonne because of the state of his health. Commanding in his place, Clausel made it known that the British army, inactive for several

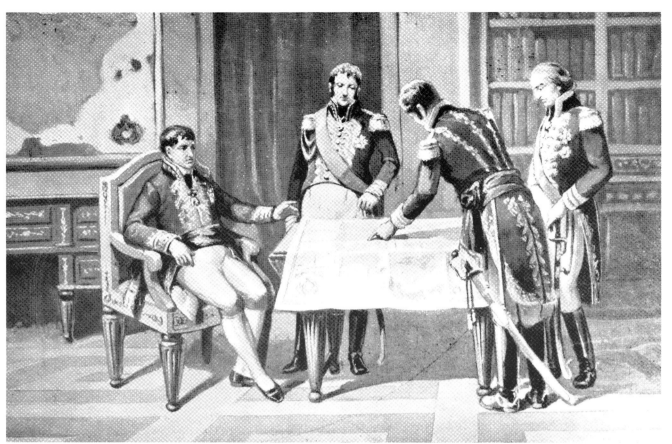

weeks, was now moving to meet him and this obliged him to withdraw to Burgos. As for the Army of the North with its scattered troops, it could do nothing: General Caffarelli, in command, was in fact only to assure communications. Finally, Suchet feared invasion of the Kingdom of Valencia by the British who were entrenched near Alicante. The movements of the Armies of the Centre and the South, therefore, had to be combined in order to force the enemy to abandon the north of Spain and thereby disengage the Army of Portugal. This done, the Army of Portugal, moving forward, would be able to unite with the two other armies and form a sufficiently large mass to manoeuvre effectively. This would be the plan. On the 20th, d'Erlon, appointed to the command of the Army of the Centre, took Cuenca; on the 31st, Soult overthrew Hill's men at Valdemoro; and on 2 November Joseph re-entered his capital.

In Old Castile, the Army of the North was soon to resume the offensive. At the beginning of September Clausel halted his retreat at Burgos after having been forced to evacuate Valladolid. Then, suffering from the wound received at Salamanca, he handed over command to General Souham, who withdrew to Briviesca, leaving General Dubreton and 1,800 men entrenched in the castle at Burgos. Knowing how important the town was, Wellington hurried from Madrid to capture it. By 18 September he was outside the Castillian city. On the 19th, he attacked the castle in force, but it resisted and was to hold out for more than a month, allowing time for the Armies of the Centre and the South to effect their strategy and for Souham to take up the offensive. In fact, after re-occupying Monasterio, Souham arrived at Burgos, which Wellington had left, not wanting to risk a battle before being able to regroup his forces together with Hill. During the retreat, the British were closely followed by Generals Maucune and Foy, and lost more than 3,000 men killed or taken prisoner during many engagements, such as those at Celada, Villadrigo and Villamuriel. On 28 October Souham entered Valladolid. Having crossed the Duero at Tordesillas, the French army arrived outside Zamora and halted to await orders from Joseph's general headquarters. Following the advice of his

Above: General Count Souham (1760–1837). He replaced the wounded General Clausel at the head of the reinforced Army of Portugal.

Left: At the head of 45,000 men, General Souham marched to the aid of the Burgos garrison. During one of the rearguard actions fought by the British at Villadrigo on 23 October, the 1st Legion of the Gendarmerie, called 'Burgos', overthrew General Anson's dragoons and caused them heavy losses. The action, led by ten squadrons (15th Chasseurs, Berg Lancers, the Commander-in-Chief's escort and four squadrons of mounted gendarmerie), a total of 1,350 horse, lasted less than ten minutes, during which time more than 300 British horsemen were put out of action at the cost of 7 killed and 132 wounded. (Musée de l'Armée)

Left: The pursuit of the Anglo-Portuguese army at the Tordesillas bridge on 27 October 1812. After the raising of the siege of Burgos, the British rearguard, smartly pursued by General Maucune's troops, destroyed all the existing bridges, including the one at Tordesillas. This was surmounted by a tower occupied by the enemy, which made any attempt to repair the bridge hazardous. Eleven officers and 40 NCOs from Foy's division, infantrymen and sappers of the engineers, led by Captain Guingret, demanded permission to swim across the Douro. They placed their arms and cartridge pouches on a raft and swam through a volley of bullets. Fighting naked, they stormed the tower and took eleven prisoners. (Lithograph by Motte, after Grenier)

Chief of Staff, Marshal Jourdan, Joseph did not want a general action before the various French armies had been re-united. This took place on 7 November at Medina del Campo and, on the 10th, Soult arrived at Alba de Tormes. Wellington's British, installed at San Christobal, numbered 68,000 men. Opposing them were nearly 80,000 excellent French troops. Everything seemed set for the avenging of Salamanca, which was nearby.

Joseph had little confidence in his own military talents, passed the Command to Soult. The French army drew up in battle lines: on the left, the Army of the South; in the centre, Drouet d'Erlon with Joseph and Jourdan; on the right, the Army of Portugal under Souham, resting on the River Alba. On the morning of the 15th, the French began to move, with abnormal slowness. The morning passed in manoeuvring and deployment. This gave Wellington time to notice that he was in danger of being outflanked on his left, and he began to retire. A few hours of daylight remained, in which a victory might be snatched, especially now that the British were presenting their flank to the French. But it was too late. The rain, which had been falling since morning became heavier, and the terrain was transformed into a vast bog. It was impossible to man-oeuvre, and men and horses were in danger of being engulfed by the torrents. Wellington, who was marching off on the higher ground, took advantage of this to slip away towards Ciudad Rodrigo. The pursuit by Soult brought some rewards including the capture of Sir Edward Paget, Second-in-Command of the British army. But, on the 18th, Wellington crossed the Agueda and installed himself in Ciudad Rodrigo. The exhausted French troops halted. Anxious, Joseph left for Madrid, and the French

armies took up their winter quarters between the Duero and the Tagus. The British were saved.

In his Kingdom of Valencia, Suchet was holding an Anglo-Sicilian expeditionary force in check. On 8 October he made a show of force outside Alicante, but the garrison refused to join battle and only one squadron of British light horse was overthrown by the 4th Hussars which had been brought up by General Delort. Suchet's foray did, however, restore calm and, on 20 November at Yecla, the British General Elio, who had replaced O'Donnell, saved himself by fleeing, his cavalry having been surprised in the middle of the night and put to the sword by the French. Meanwhile, in a series of fortunate, minor actions, General Decaen in Catalonia and General Caffarelli in Biscay held their ground. So the year ended apparently less badly than its disastrous beginnings had promised.

Nevertheless, at the other extremity of Europe, in the terrible cold of Russia, the Grande Armée had died in the snow, and the Emperor had returned to Paris where a soldier of fortune named Malet had very nearly seized his throne.

Situation in Spain at the beginning of 1813 — Wellington leaves Portugal — The French retreat — Battle of Vitoria — Spain lost to the French except for Suchet's provinces — Suchet forced to pull back — Napoleon's anger — Soult appointed Commander-in-Chief — Joseph disgraced — Reorganization of the French army — Soult's attempt to relieve Pamplona — French attack towards San Sebastian — Surrender of San Sebastian — Battle of the Nive — Battle of St. Pierre d'Irrube — Withdrawal of the French — Suchet in Catalonia — Defence of Monzon — Relief of Tarragona — The Valençay interview.

Under the blow of these dreadful events, part of the army was recalled, and each regiment had to send a complete batallion or squadron. Soult himself (whose departure Joseph fervently hoped for) was to go back to Germany to take command of the Old Guard. He was replaced by General Gazan.

The year 1812 had been a difficult one for Wellington, for, after his early successes, he had had to return to Portugal. Even so, it had not been completely fruitless: Andalusia was lost to the French for good, and the Cortes, which had had its seat in Cadiz since 24 September 1810, had proclaimed the famous Constitution of 1812. Greeted with great joy throughout the land, this Constitution reinforced still more the Spaniards' determination to have done with King Joseph and the French occupation. Finally, in order to give maximum effectiveness to the command of operations, on 22 September 1812, a decree of the Assembly appointed Wellington Generalissimo of the Spanish armies.

After showing some unwillingness at first, Wellington established his general headquarters in Portugal, very close to the Spanish frontier, and re-formed his army with the numerous reinforcements from England. Soon he had 80,000 men at his disposal, and 50,000 Spaniards were distributed throughout Galicia and New Castile.

For the French, the situation was slowly going downhill. They knew that they were rather forgotten amid the giant conflagration whose echoes were reaching them. They knew that the 'Master' had given precise orders, '. . . only leave [in Spain] what is necessary'. The active presence of the Anglo-Sicilian troops at Alicante made them fear for their lines of communication with France. Everywhere loomed guerrillas. Their bands, led by 'El Pastor' (the Shepherd), 'El Capuchino' (the Capuchin), 'El Ferroro' (the Blacksmith), 'El Medico' (the Doctor), and 'El Abuelo' (the Grandfather) gave them no peace. Captain Marcel of the 69th Line tells us: 'Time and again the division ran its races, sometimes on the heels of "El Pastor", at other times on those of Mina or Longa, but they were useless fatigues. Seeing that we were not able to capture the bands during the daytime, General Foy gave the order to march by night. The thing did not go smoothly, especially the first few days, for, although we had good guides, we often managed to get lost in this pathless, mountainous country, and the darkness forced the soldiers to light the candles with which they were always furnished. One would have said we were a procession of penitents. But the enemy was always better informed than we were, and had inevitably just left whenever we arrived.'

It was now that Wellington, knowing the state of the French army, decided to leave Portugal and strike a major

Above: Joseph Bonaparte. He had left his capital for the third and last time on 17 March 1813.

Right: The 15th Hussars (Grant's brigade) cross the Tres Puentes bridge. (Caton Woodville)

Above: Francisco Longa, called 'Papel'. From 1811, he was the most important and most active chief of the Alava. At the head of 1,200 guerrillas, he harassed and attacked French outposts throughout the whole province. His band, periodically reinforced by the guerrillas of Pinto, 'El Pastor' and Mina, was to become more and more enterprising.

blow. Crossing the frontier on 22 May, he raised his hat: 'Goodbye Portugal – I shall never see you again.' This time he was determined to make a success of the Spanish campaign, which he had missed doing by such a narrow margin in the previous year. His objective was to cut off the French army from its communications with France. Four of his divisions took the Zamora road; he himself advanced on Salamanca by the direct Ciudad Rodrigo route. By the 26th, Salamanca had been occupied and, in order to avoid being outflanked, Joseph again abandoned Madrid (never to return) and concentrated his troops on the main road to Burgos. The British general crossed the Carrion at Palencia on 7 June and the following day established his troops along the French right flank, threatening to cut off their line of communication with Vitoria. On the 12th, the French army fell back on Burgos, which they abandoned almost as soon as the castle had been destroyed, and continued its retreat to the Ebro. On the 14th, the army crossed the Pancorvo defile and concentrated at the river. Joseph was expecting a frontal attack, but Wellington was manoeuvring. He crossed the Ebro on his left, via the bridges at San Martin and Fuente de Arenas, marched towards Bilbao and fell back on the right of the French. In an endeavour to retard this move, Reille engaged the Anglo-Portuguese army at Osma with some 10,000 men, but was forced to fall back.

To avoid being outflanked, Joseph pulled back to Vitoria and established his camp on the left bank of the Zadorra. His dispositions covered each of the three roads that converged on Vitoria. On the road from Bilbao he placed the Army of Portugal under Reille. On the Burgos road, he placed the Army of the South under General Gazan at the front, and, behind them, the Army of the Centre under General d'Erlon. Last of all, he positioned the Army of the North under Clausel on the road from Logroño. Clausel, meanwhile, was too far off to intervene. On 20 June, Wellington arrived from the northwest with 80,000 men, intending to join battle – he knew that the French numbers were only half his own. The day was spent in a reconnaissance of Joseph's positions, and Wellington then divided his army into three columns. On the left, Graham was opposing Reille. On the right, Hill was facing the Army of the South. The centre he kept for himself, with three divisions under Beresford, and found that Drouet d'Erlon was opposing him. At 4 o'clock on the morning of the 21st, the Allies attacked along the entire front-line.

Above: Marshal Beresford, Commander-in-Chief of the entire Portuguese army. (From a painting by Heaphy)

Above right: View of Vitoria. (Philippoteaux)

Above: General Drouet, Count d'Erlon (1765–1844). Commander-in-Chief of the Army of the Centre.

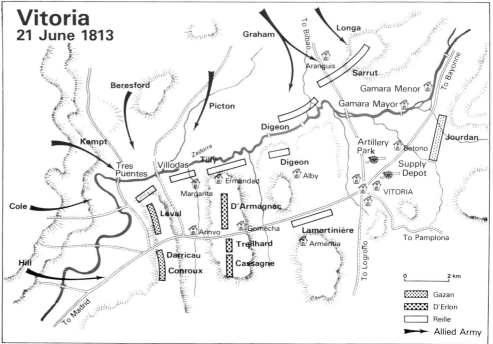

Above: The rout at Vitoria, 21 June 1813. 400 guns, a considerable amount of equipment and all the baggage of King Joseph and his partisans fell to the British and their allies. (Major Saint-Clair)

Above: Lieutenant-General Sir Edward Barnes (1776–1838). His brigade (7th Division) consisted of the 1st Battalion of the 6th Foot, 3rd Provisional Battalion and a company of Brunswick-Oels chasseurs.

Above: General Sir John Murray. His attempted landing on 2 June near Tarragona was repelled by Suchet's troops. (From a portrait by Sir T. Lawrence)

Above: General Count Reille (1775–1860) Commander-in-Chief of the Army of Portugal, which formed the French right.

Above: General of Division Baron Digeon (1771–1826) commanding the 2nd Division of dragoons of the Army of the South. He received four sabre cuts during the battle.

British and Spanish Armies, 1808–14

1. *2nd Regiment of Life Guards, marching order, 1813. The Household Brigade arrived in Spain in 1813. It probably wore the helmet, but certain documents show the hat of 1812.*

2. *2nd Regiment of Life Guards, 1813. In Spain this regiment certainly wore the plumed casque and not the bicorne.*

3. *2nd Regiment of Life Guards, dress uniform. Although in the regulations, the helmet had replaced the hat in about 1811, certain documents of the era show officers in old full dress uniform.*

4. *5th Dragoon Guards, 1813. The dragoons were formed from the dragoons of the Guard and dragoons of the Line. The 3rd, 4th and 5th Dragoon Guards and the 1st, 3rd and 4th Dragoons were present during the Spanish campaign.*

5. *Spanish Army, 'Ferdinand VII' Regiment, hussar officer in dress uniform.*

6. *Villaviciosa Dragoon Regiment, 1806.*

7. *Cavalry Regiment of Algarve, 1806.*

8. *2nd Regiment of Life Guards, officer in campaign dress, 1813. This is a transitionary uniform.*

9. *3rd 'King's Own' Dragoons. This unit was one of the three regiments of the Line which served in Spain.*

10. *4th Dragoons, campaign dress, 1809.*

11. *Lieutenant-General of the British Army in dress uniform. He wore six gold braids in groups of three on his cuffs, his lapels and his pockets. The major-general had these braids placed in pairs.*

12. *13th Light Dragoons, campaign dress, 1812. Certain regiments in Spain still wore the old 'tarleton' helmet with the new uniform.*

13. *16th Light Dragoons, major. Further example of a non-regulation uniform.*

14. *10th Light Dragoons (Hussars). Corporal in campaign dress, 1810.*

15. *42nd Royal Highland Regiment. Corporal of centre company, 1814.*

16. *57th Foot 'West Middlesex Regiment'. Light company, campaign dress, 1811.*

17. *87th 'Prince of Wales' Own Irish Regiment'. Light company, campaign dress, 1811.*

18. *'Voluntarios de la Patria' Regiment. This regiment was raised in New Castile by Colonel Don Fernando Mazarredo in September 1808.*

10. *'Cangas de Tineo' Regiment, fusilier. This regiment was raised in 1808. Like many new regiments, its uniform was brown.*

20. *Infantry Regiment of the Line 'El Rey', 1814. An example of a transitionary uniform. Before the Regulation of 1815 the Spanish Army wore many completely different uniforms.*

21. *Regiment of Infantry of the Line of Toledo, non-regulation uniform.*

22. *Walloon Guard, 1812.*

23 & 25. *Grenadier of the line and chasseur of the light. Regulation uniform of 1812.*

24. *'La Muerte' Regiment. This regiment was raised by Don Francisco Colombo in Galicia in 1809.*

Above: Landing the British troops. In June 1813 the Royal Navy, which had been constantly patrolling the coastline between Santander and San Sebastian, gave effective aid to the rebels by deliveries of arms and by landing operations. (By Dubourg, after J. A. Atkinson)

Below: The 85th Foot at the Battle of the Nivelle, 13 November 1813. (Watercolour by Simkin)

Above: Battle of Vitoria. Robinson's brigade capture the village of Gamara Mayor, defended by General Reille's infantry.

Below: The 119th Line at the Battle of Vitoria, 21 June 1813. (Musée de l'Armée)

Below: The Battle of Vitoria, second stage of the attack on the French centre. The 3rd (Picton) and 7th (Dalhousie) Divisions force a passage before the bridge of Zadorra, 21 June 1813.

Bottom: The flight of King Joseph. (After F. Motta)

At once, the two armies' skirmishers got to grips and the struggle continued until 9 o'clock without either side registering a real advantage. However, Wellington wanted to try and close the Bayonne road to the French, and so he sent General Graham on to the French right. With the divisions of Sarrut and Lamartinière, supported by Digeon's dragoon divisions, Reille resisted step by step, but was forced to fall back on the Zadorra, where General Sarrut was mortally wounded. On the left, the French army was losing ground despite the support of the artillery

set up by General Hugo, Chief of Staff (and father of the writer). By 4 o'clock, the French were forced to fall back on Vitoria and, because there was a lack of horses, the guns were spiked and abandoned. The order was given for a great convoy of the remnants of the Kingdom of Spain – treasure, archives and the refugees' luggage – to set off towards Pamplona, the only road still open. But it was too late. A vehicle that had overturned blocked the line of carts. The British hussars at the heels of the Army of the Centre fell upon the convoy and looted it. The road was littered with smashed-open boxes, ladies dresses and court effects. Joseph himself, lost in the throng with only a small escort, had only time to get out of his carriage and leap on horseback, leaving his papers and his sword to the British. Jourdan, ill and shaking with fever, had got up from his bed to take part in the end of the battle, and had to flee on horseback, leaving behind his marshal's baton.

A large number of the French troops continued their retreat without dispersing, and General Hugo distinguished himself by halting the enemy at the entry to the Pamplona road. This lamentable day, called 'the Leipzig of the South', put an end to French hopes in Spain. A total of 5,000 men, dead or wounded, remained on the battlefield. If this had not been the most murderous battle of the Spanish war, the number of prisoners taken was very high; although many of them managed to escape amid the disorder, 400 pieces of artillery and a considerable quantity of booty made Vitoria a glorious success for Wellington. Jomini has severely criticized Joseph's resolve to fight at this spot: 'It would have been difficult to have chosen a worse place to do battle, or to have joined it under more unfortunate auspices.' It was certain that his wish to keep the Bayonne road open had forced Joseph to detach Clausel to Logroño on the left, and Foy to the right to cover San Sebastian. These two worthy divisional commanders and their troops were sadly missed during the battle. He would have done better to have withdrawn along the Ebro to Saragossa to join Suchet. Wellington would not have dared to enter the Pyrenees leaving 100,000 Frenchmen behind him.

Meanwhile, the retreat was effected with fewer obstacles than had been expected. As usual, Wellington sought only feebly to exploit his victory. Foy, learning of the disaster, shut himself up in Tolosa, halted Graham, and withdrew via Irun and the Bidassoa, leaving a garrison in San Sebastian. Without any orders, Clausel had advanced on the 21st towards Vitoria via the Sierra de Audia. In the evening, he fell upon Hill's troops, but, having recognized them, decided to break contact because fugitives had told him of the day's disaster. He descended once more towards Logroño, took the Saragossa road and retreated into France via Jaca and the Canfran Pass. The main part of the army with Joseph and Jourdan arrived at Tolosa on the evening of the 23rd, and the corps reformed. Gazan continued towards Pamplona, Reille took the road leading to San Esteban, and the Army of the Centre under Joseph kept the rearguard. In spite of 'the wicked soldiers who, deaf to the voice of honour, had left their respective corps and made their way without orders towards the frontier', the reorganized French army was capable of holding Pamplona, which, situated at the foot of the Pyrenees, allowed Navarre to be watched over. Joseph left a garrison behind and continued his retreat. On the 27th, the Army of the South, led by General Gazan, arrived at St. Jean-Pied-de-Port via the Roncesvalles Pass. Drouet d'Erlon with the Army of the Centre descended via the Maya Pass

Above: General Lafon-Blagniac (1773–1833). Passed into the service of King Joseph to whom he was aide-de-camp in 1808, he became Governor of La Mancha, then of Madrid, and commanded the troops in the provinces of Madrid, Toledo and Guadalajara. He was wounded in the right arm during the Battle of Vitoria.

Below: The end of the Battle of Vitoria. General Reille's corps protects the retreat of the French army. (Philippoteaux)

Above: General Morillo. He commanded a division of Spanish infantry, about 4,500 men, at the Battle of Vitoria. (Contemporary engraving)

to Ainhoa. Reille, with the Army of Portugal, passed through San Esteban and Echalar and debouched at Sare. General Foy, who was to become the leading Bonapartist and Republican voice during the Restoration, held out against Graham, occupied Tolosa, and prevented the British from cutting off the retreat of the rest of the French army which was marching behind him. On 25 June, hard pressed by superior numbers, he was obliged to disengage and, after several quite violent actions, withdrew to Irun in good order after having reinforced the garrison at San Sebastian under the orders of the unyielding General Rey.

Now all that was left in Spain were the troops of Marshal Suchet. Since the beginning of the year, he had continued to hold the provinces committed to his authority. In Catalonia and Aragon, as well as in the province of Valencia, Generals Lamarque, Mathieu, Harispe and Habert proved their skill under his orders. In Catalonia, the resistance in March of the castle of Mora allowed the Duke of Albufera to thrust the Spanish rebels under Eroles back across the Ebro. In April, fearing a movement from the Allied forces stationed around Alicante, Suchet himself took up the offensive. He concentrated his divisions around Fuente de Higuera, and General Harispe made a stand at Yecla against two Spanish divisions, overcame them and occupied the fortress of Villena, after having beaten down its gate with cannon-fire. Followed by the reserves, Habert took the road to Castalla and captured the Biar defile, but Suchet failed to move General Murray's British, who were occupying an excellent position outside Castalla. After a violent but unsuccessful engagement, the French and British returned to their respective quarters.

On 31 May, Murray embarked his troops at Alicante and arrived at Tarragona on 2 June. The disembarkation was effected with great precision in broad daylight on 3 June. The British invested the town and took the fort on the Balaguer ridge by storm, so as to close the only possible route for Suchet's guns. While the siegeworks were being constructed, Elio took up position with his Spaniards in an endeavour to cut off Tarragona from any help that might come from Barcelona. As soon as Suchet learned of the landing, he set off without artillery at a forced pace along mountain paths, and emerged on the heights above Tarragona on the 12th. To bolster the morale of the garrison, great beacons were lit to signal his presence. Alerted, Mathieu set off from Barcelona and arrived at Villafranca on 11 June. On the 12th he sent his vanguard forward some thirty kilometres to reconnoitre. In all, some 16,000 Frenchmen were converging on Tarragona, and Murray, taking fright at the rapidity of the French reaction, decided to raise the siege and re-embark. Meanwhile, having withdrawn to the left bank of the Jucar with two infantry divisions and a brigade of cavalry, General Harispe was holding the Spaniards at bay, and, on 27 June, with the support of Suchet who had returned from Tarragona, forced them to retire on Castalla.

At this moment, news arrived of the disaster at Vitoria. The French had been thrust back beyond the Pyrenees and Suchet's position had become untenable. He decided to leave the garrisons, in particular the one at Sagunto (where General Rouelle was to hold out for eleven months, only surrendering when he had been ordered to do so), and the one at Tortosa (where General Robert was to do likewise). Retreating methodically, he collected up all the small detachments scattered throughout the region, crossed the Ebro on 14 and 15 July, and set up camp at Villafranca.

Above: At the beginning of 1813, the Spanish under General Copons were threatening the French Cerdagne. Following the orders of General Decaen (Commander-in-Chief in Lower Catalonia), General Lamarque marched to Ripoll where he drove off the enemy. The scene represents the crossing of the River Freser by the French infantry. (Lithograph by Langlois, Musée de l'Armée)
Below: Dragoon, élite company.

The Emperor was in Dresden when he learned of his brother's terrible defeat. The victories of Lutzen and Bautzen had led the Coalition to ask for an armistice, which was signed on 4 June at Pleiswitz and was to last until 10 August. Austria's secret manoeuvres annoyed him and he understood at once what disastrous consequences Vitoria could have in the forthcoming negotiations. His anger was appalling. He immediately relieved his brother of his command and sent him to the château of Mortefontaine, 'whence it would be fitting that neither he nor any officer of his household might come to trouble the administration of the Regency', as he said to Cambacérès, Archchancellor and President of the Regency Council. Jourdan, involved in this disgrace, was sent back to France in retirement . . . for several months. Things were moving swiftly. At the same time, Soult, Duke of Dalmatia, was appointed Lieutenant-General in Spain with full authority. Soult, who had just brought his family to Dresden, received the following letter: 'My cousin, you will leave here today before 10 o'clock. You will travel incognito, taking the name of one of your aides-de-camp. You will arrive in Paris on the 4th where you will go and see the Minister of War. He will give you the most up-to-date information about the situation. You will be in Paris for no longer than twelve hours. From there you are to continue your journey to go and take command of my armies of Spain. . . .' A master such as Napoleon brooks no delay and, by 12 July, the new Commander-in-Chief had arrived in Bayonne. His return was, for him, an indisputable matter of pride, for only a few months before it had been Joseph who had had him recalled. The taking up of his command was accomplished without incident, and Soult at once set himself to carry on the reorganization already begun by Jourdan.

With nearly 100,000 men, the French army had ten infantry divisions (one in reserve); two cavalry divisions under the Marshal's brother, Pierre Soult, and General Treilhard; and 86 guns. On the right, was Reille with Lamartinière (11th), Maucune (12th) and Foy (1st); in the centre, Drouet d'Erlon with Darricau (6th), Abbé (3rd) and Darmagnac (2nd); on the left, Clausel with Conroux (4th), Van der Maessen (5th) and Taupin (7th). Villatte commanded the reserve division. Opposing them, the Allies' forces were appreciably superior in numbers. They were commanded by Wellington in person, with Generals Hill and Graham, and with Beresford commanding the Portuguese army and the Spaniards Feyre and Mina, the latter being the famous partisan chief turned general. For the moment, the Allies were actively pursuing the sieges of San Sebastian and Pamplona and were occupying the ridges and defiles between Spain and France.

Having installed his general headquarters at St. Jean-Pied-de-Port, Soult displayed great activity. He had the old fortifications at Bayonne repaired, and raised fortified camps or suitable defences for the better protection of the approaches. He sent out proclamations to keep up the morale of the troops. Well provided for in food and munitions, he would have preferred to wait for some time before taking the offensive, but the Emperor's instructions were to act quickly, and the information he was receiving from the two garrisons at San Sebastian and Pamplona

Below: Action at La Salud on 9 July 1813. This took place during General Lamarque's move to strengthen the French frontier which was being threatened by Catalan troops. In the foreground General Beurmann is giving the order to attack. (Lithograph by Langlois, Musée de l'Armée)

Above: General Count Decaen (1769–1832). On 3 October 1811 he was appointed Commander-in-Chief of the Army of Catalonia.

Above: General Baron Lamarque (1770–1832). Commanding in Upper Catalonia, he took part, under Marshal Suchet, in the relief of Tarragona.

told him that the situation was becoming rather critical for them. He could choose to raise the blockade on one or other of those towns with more or less even chances of success. San Sebastian was nearer, but the road to it was better guarded and defended; Pamplona was farther off, and he would have to leave St. Jean-Pied-de-Port and cross the Roncesvalles Pass, but the surprise of such an attack might be greater and it would be possible to fall back on San Sebastian after the deliverance of the city. The latter plan was adopted.

On the morning of 24 July, Soult left St. Jean-Pied-de-Port with the corps of Reille and Clausel. On the right, Reille was occupying the Lindux Pass. On the left, Clausel was driving the enemy from the Ibaneta Pass, while Drouet d'Erlon captured the Maya Pass from the Anglo-Portuguese, and halted to await orders. This delay, coupled with the difficult conditions (Reille found himself in thick fog), held up the advance of the French army and gave Wellington time to rally his army and become strongly established on the heights of Zubiri. On the 27th, impatient that no British attack was forthcoming, Soult decided to act despite the fact that d'Erlon had not yet reached him. However, the Anglo-Portuguese army had received numerous reinforcements during the night, and the position they were occupying near Sorauren was difficult to reach, while the lie of the land prevented the French from deploying their columns of attack. One after another, the Duke of Dalmatia's divisions came up against murderous salvoes of gunfire. The tardy arrival of Drouet d'Erlon, who had forced his way to within six kilometres of Pamplona and then, hearing the gunfire to the rear of his left, had returned, could do nothing to change the day. Soult ordered the attacks to be suspended and, the next morning, began a general retreat. Drouet d'Erlon took the road along which he had come. Reille took the road to St. Jean-Pied-de-Port and Clausel set off on the left in the direction of Echalar and Sare. Mina's guerrilla corps tried unsuccessfully to cut off the French retreat, and on the 29th Reille and Clausel arrived at St. Jean-Pied-de-Port and Ascain, while Drouet d'Erlon took up his old positions before Ainhoa.

Within five days the operation had been completed. Having returned to their original positions, the French troops were discouraged and began to question the ability of their leaders. The losses were perhaps heavier for the Allies than for Soult's troops, but Wellington was able to receive the reinforcements he needed, which was not the case on the French side, where gaps could not be filled. Every defeat brought criticisms, and even Marshal Soult did not lack for them. However, Jomini wrote: 'This manoeuvre was a good one, but the harshness of the mountains, a little dilatoriness in marching and the stubborn defence of the British right under General Picton, all gave Wellington time to bring up his army. He was able to reinforce his army with Spanish troops, who were besieging Pamplona, and contained Soult at the same time as two British divisions under Hill and Dalhousie outflanked the right as far as the foot of the Arraiz pass and threatened our communications via Lanz. In his turn, Soult turned towards Ostiz in order to rally towards Drouet. He has quite ridiculously been reproached for this strategy. If his right had been forced and outflanked between Ostiz and Lanz, he would have suffered the fate of Joseph at Vitoria. He thought it prudent not to risk a general battle in such difficult terrain and, in fact, he had everything to lose and little to gain. . . . In the event, his

Above: General Baron Rey (1768–1846), glorious defender of San Sebastian. The siege lasted from 27 June to 9 September, during which the garrison effected two sorties and repulsed two attacks.

movement, conceived on excellent principles, would have had more success if the Roncesvalles road had been better and if more activity, precision and vigour had been put into the preliminary steps; but, as soon as the enemy had time to bring in superior forces, having all the advantages of the terrain and the high road behind them, the odds were no longer equal. . . .' It is quite true that, if Soult's offensive had been able to unfold, the Allied army might have been destroyed. But once again, though surprised to begin with, the crafty Wellington had chosen his battlefield well and exhausted the French attacks by his stubborn resistance.

Needing to get his breath back, Soult allowed the army to rest, but the news from San Sebastian was bad. In the face of Thomas Graham's British and Mendizabal's Spaniards, General Rey had managed to inspire his three thousand or so Frenchmen with an extraordinary spirit of resistance. Three times the British had opened up breaches and attacked, three times they had been repulsed with enormous losses. On 15 August, the garrison even celebrated the Emperor's birthday most heartily. The soldiers' singing mingled with the sound of bells, but it did not prevent their repelling an attack by the besiegers, who thought to take advantage of the defenders' inattention. All the same, this was quite worrying, because now the blockade was complete (the British Fleet had blocked the port) and Wellington, taking command himself, had decided to finish things off quickly.

On 30 August, Soult left Bayonne, crossed the Bidassoa between Vera and Biriatou, and marched on San Sebastian. So as not to be outflanked he left Conroux's division on his left, guarding the outflow of the Sare, and Abbé's division was posted at Urdax upstream on the Nivelle. Having had ample warning of the operation, Wellington had reinforced his support troops outside San Sebastian. While the British

Above: The mountain chasseurs. Destined originally for the protection of the Pyrenees, they were soon employed in the hunt for guerrillas and, to this end, participated in numerous actions. Their 3rd Battalion formed part of the garrison of San Sebastian, and its heroic defence of this fortress was to be its most handsome feat of arms. (J. Girbal)

Above: Colonel Sir Richard Fletcher, commanding the engineers. He built the lines of Torres Vedras. He was killed during the first assault on San Sebastian. (From a contemporary portrait)

were ceaselessly attacking the French left in order to worry Soult, Reille and Villatte were being defeated in their offensive against the Allied centre, held by the Anglo-Portuguese on the hills of San Marcial. Soult ordered a retreat, which was managed with difficulty. The heavy rains of the previous days had swelled the Bidassoa, and the army was forced to use the bridge at Berra because the bridge at Behobie had been destroyed. The crossing was made under fire from the British, and Generals Lamartinière and Van der Maessen lost their lives. The French army resumed its original positions.

The garrison at San Sebastian, finally left to itself, was soon obliged to cease all resistance. Since the last few days of June, the indomitable General Rey had been holding the town with some 3,200 soldiers. Opposing him were forces ten times their number, commanded by the Englishman Sir Thomas Graham. Annoyed by this resistance, Wellington brought up siege equipment, installed formidable batteries on the heights, and crushed the town under a deluge of fire. On 31 August, having blown up the walls with mines,

the British launched their attack. The battle was relentless and the losses of the assailants were considerable, but the town was taken and the defenders withdrew into the castle of La Mota, which served as the redoubt of Mount Orgullo overlooking the town. When the town fell, it became the theatre of dreadful scenes – rape, pillage and arson, which continued through the night. Despite his critical position, General Rey rejected all summonses to surrender, hoping to be extricated by Soult's attack. But soon its failure was known and, pinned down by overwhelming fire, without provisions or munitions, the French decided to surrender. At midday on the 9th, the 1,800 survivors marched out with the honours of war and laid down their arms amid the ruins of the town, where only seventeen houses remained standing. One month later, at the end of its provisions, the Pamplona garrison also surrendered, leaving Wellington a free hand to pursue his offensive and, this time, to invade France.

Having received a reinforcement of conscripts, Soult wasted no time. Redoubts and bastions were erected or

Left: The 119th Line at the siege of San Sebastian. (Musée de l'Armée)

Below: The capture of San Sebastian on 31 August 1813. After a magnificent defence the French garrison of 2,500 had to withdraw into the citadel, where it resisted until 8 September. The siege cost the assailants 8,000 men. The garrison was given the honours of war.

Above: General Thomas Graham, later Lord Lynedoch, commanded the British troops at the siege of San Sebastian (about 10,000 men, supported by 8,000 Spaniards guarding the lines of San Marcial which covered the besiegers). (Portrait by T. Lawrence)

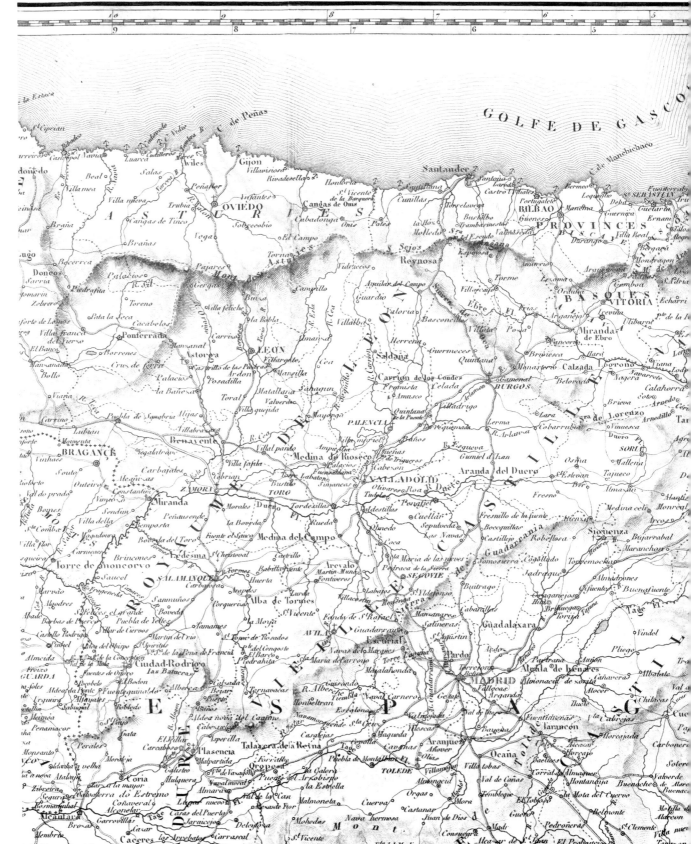

Right: North-east section of the theatre of war map in General Foy's 'Histoire de la Guerre de la Peninsule sous Napoleon' (1827).

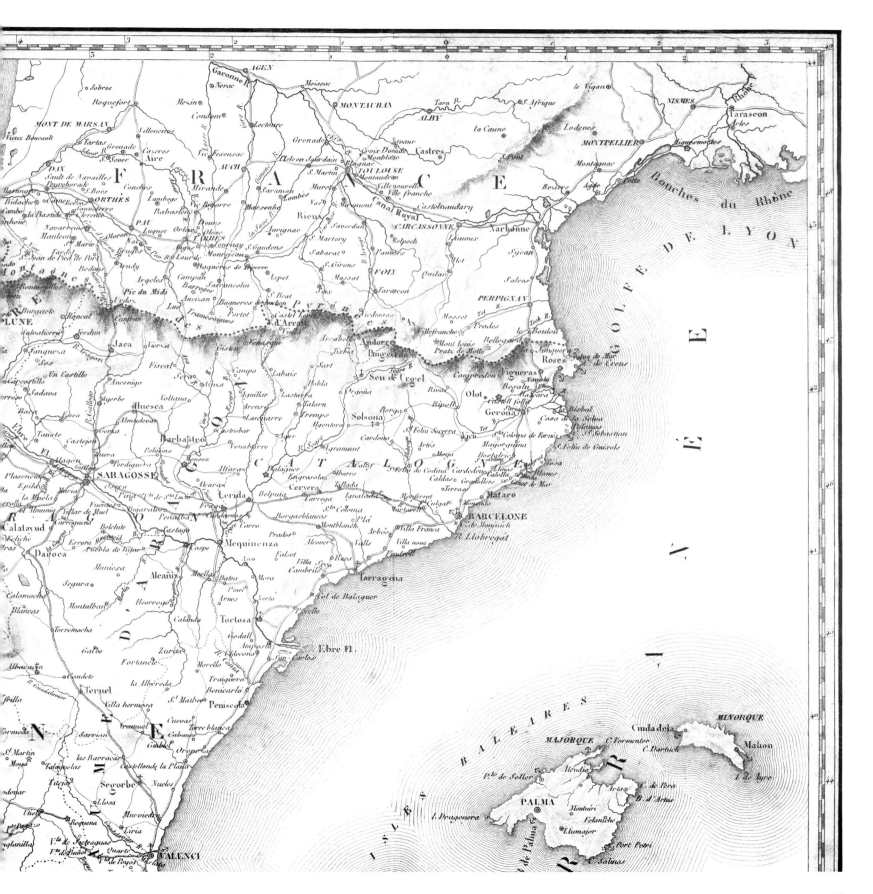

repaired to protect the four roads from Spain. If the Madrid – Bayonne and Pamplona – St. Jean-Pied-de-Port routes were relatively easy to defend, and if he could also hope to halt the enemy without too much difficulty by fortifying the twin routes from Maya towards Urdax and the Mondarran, this was not the case where the Sare was concerned. Here, in fact, the gap between the heights of the Rhune and the bridge of Amotz on the Nivelle presented an easy passage by which to enter France. Wellington was aware of this, and it was here, on 10 November, that he launched his attack. Conroux's division was dislodged from the Rhune and moved back to the plain, while its commander fell, hit in the chest by a bullet. Fearing that his defence might be outflanked, Soult decided to abandon the Nivelle line and withdrew to the Nive, which, swollen by the rains, presented a convenient line on which to halt. While Wellington was installing his general headquarters in St. Jean-de-Luz, Darricau's division took up a position opposite Ustaritz, Darmagnac's division occupied Ville-franque, General Abbé occupied St. Jean-le-Vieux-Mou-guerre, and Foy watched over the passage between Iatzu and Cambo. The divisions of Taupin, Maransin and Rey (successor to Conroux) formed the left wing of the army protecting Bayonne, while the divisions of Maucune, Boyer and Villatte on the right took up their positions on the St. Jean-de-Luz road, with their outposts level with Biarritz.

On 9 December, Wellington crossed the Nive, which was again fordable between Iatzu and Cambo. A savage action took place at the farm of Lormentua, where Abbé had come to support General Foy. However, Darmagnac was thrown out of Villefranque and Darricau from Ustaritz. By the evening of that day, the Anglo-Portuguese had crossed the

Nive at three places. The next day, Soult sent Reille with his right wing to attack Bidart, which was held by the British General Hope. Clausel carried the plateau of Bassussari with Taupin's division and marched on Ar-cangues, but was repulsed after a desperate struggle outside the village church.

During the night of the 10/11th, the Nassau Regiment and the Frankfurt Battalion, detailed to Villatte's division, deserted. This notably discouraged the French, and Wellington took advantage of it by launching an unsuccessful attack on Bassussari. Reille was held up outside Bidart and was not able to disengage. On the 13th, Soult decided to attack Hill's troops at St. Pierre-d'Irrube in force. The battle raged all day long and, here and there, the losses were very heavy. Arriving at the position with reinforcements, Wellington halted the French attack and pushed them once and for all beyond the Nive. From now on, the Allies had their left outside Bayonne, and occupied Hasparren and Labastide-Clairence, while the Duke of Dalmatia, who moved his general headquarters to Peyre-horade, was forced to occupy an arc extending from the mouth of the River Adour to St. Jean-Pied-de-Port, which was occupied by General Paris's brigade.

While the French army was moving back step by step through the Basque country, Suchet was still holding out with remarkable confidence in Catalonia. He had left his garrisons in Denia, Murviedro, Peniscola, Tarragona, Tortosa and Mequinenza and a few detachments such as the one at Monzon, which was to achieve uncommon fame. A hundred men, ninety of them gendarmes, shut up in the fort in this little town, held out for four and a half months against Mina's forces, who were fifty times their number. Saint-Jacques, an ordinary guard of the Engineers, was

Above: Action at San Privat del Mallol on 4 December 1813. This episode illustrates the retreat of the French troops after the disaster at Vitoria. The Army of Aragon successively evacuated the Kingdom of Valencia and Lower Catalonia. The scene depicts the action fought by Petit's Brigade against the Catalan division of Brigadier-General Villamil during which the Spaniards had to fall back to Joanetas. (Lithograph by Langlois, Musée de l'Armée)

Above right: View of St. Jean-de-Luz. (Drawing by Captain Batty)

Right: After the actions fought near Behobie, Vera and La Rhune, Marshal Soult established a new line of defence on the Nivelle. (Martinet)

Below: The Duke of Wellington at the Battle of the Nivelle on 10 November 1813. Debouching behind the Rhune, 30,000 Anglo-Portuguese outflanked the French defence lines between the Sare and the sea. The battle cost each side 4,000 men. On the evening of the 10th, Wellington moved his headquarters to St. Jean-de-Luz, while Marshal Soult withdrew to the River Nive outside Bayonne. This new line of defence was taken in the course of violent actions which took place on 10–13 December (Battle of St. Pierre-d'Irrube). The French army fell back on the River Adour after evacuating Bayonne. (From a painting by Heaphy)

Right: Return of the dragoons of the Army of Spain. (A. Lalauze)

Below right: Evacuation of Tarragona by Marshal Suchet's troops on 18 August 1813. The walls, dating from Roman times, which had had to be mined because of their solidity, collapsed in front of the retreating French army. (F. Blanch)

the moving spirit of this resistance. Omnipresent, making catapults, digging counter-mines, salvaging from the enemy whatever equipment he needed, he repelled all attacks and inflicted heavy losses on the besiegers. Before they would agree to leave, a captured French officer had to come and confirm that the neighbouring towns of Lerida and Mequinenza, had surrendered. These brave men then obtained permission to march out with their arms and baggage to rejoin the French army, dragging proudly with them a loaded cannon, with 'lighted match'. But the Spaniards did not respect the convention, and shortly afterwards they were taken prisoner. During the siege, 500 assailants had been laid low.

In August, the Duke of Albufera realized that Tarragona, besieged by Lord Bentinck, could not hold out for very long. By means of a skilful manoeuvre, he arrived outside the town without the British being able to stop him. With the aid of the garrison he blew up the Roman ramparts, whose solidity had given him some concern, and took everyone back with him to Catalonia. However, the events in the Pyrenees had left him unprotected, for his was the only army still stationed in Spain. At the end of December, having sent some 10,000 men back to France at the request of the Emperor, he established his general headquarters at Gerona, 80 kilometres north of Barcelona.

As the year 1813 drew to a close, French diplomacy was kept busy trying to separate the Allies. After his defeat at Leipzig, Napoleon knew that he was going to need all his resources, including his troops in Spain, which included some excellent units. Anyway, Soult, without any illusions, had warned the Emperor that Spain was lost for good. So, Napoleon decided to negotiate with Ferdinand VII, and cherished the hope that the restitution of their king would lead the Spanish people to dissociate their destiny from that of the British, who had been suffered by necessity, yet often detested. In November, Laforest, the former French Ambassador to Madrid, went to Valençay where Ferdinand had settled down very well in captivity. His 'gaoler', Talleyrand, had received instructions to entertain him and, in addition to theatres and other amusements, had not hesitated to present certain ladies of easy virtue who were always well received. At first, the ex-Crown Prince listened with a certain incredulity to the proposals that were being put to him. Only distorted news had reached his château, and the Emperor's about-face seemed to him incredible. To begin with, he suspected a trap. Then, advised by his faithful Canon Escoiquiz, he thought better of it and declared himself ready to examine the propositions that were being put to him: reciprocal evacuation of territories, exchange of prisoners, the breaking off of relations between Spain and the British, an allowance for the former king, Charles IV, and an amnesty for the Spaniards who had served King Joseph. In addition, it was suggested that Ferdinand marry a Bonaparte. Here was a problem, for the list of available ladies was practically nil. Nevertheless, Zénaïde, Joseph's daughter, was suggested, but she was thirteen and Ferdinand was twenty-nine. This inconvenience meant that this last 'arrangement' was left very vague. All at once, intoxicated by the thought of mounting the throne, Ferdinand signed and prepared to leave. There was one stumbling block, however. The Emperor had stipulated that the Cortes must approve the document, and they, having issued a decree on 1 January 1811 that refuted as invalid 'any act, treaty or convention which might be signed by Ferdinand during his captivity', equivocated. Finally, at the beginning of 1814, they decreed that the King 'would only be considered free if he swore allegiance to the Constitution', so Ferdinand, in no hurry, remained at Valençay.

1813 was drawing to a close. A tiny French army under Suchet still held a fragment of Spanish territory, but the Allies had crossed the Pyrenees and French territory had been invaded. The Rhine had also been outflanked. To the Senate, who were asking him to make peace, the Emperor replied: 'Béarn, Alsace, Franche-Comté and Brabant have been penetrated. The cries of this part of my family rend my soul! I call Frenchmen to the aid of Frenchmen. I call the Frenchmen of Paris, of Brittany, of Normandy, of Champagne, of Burgundy and the other departments to the aid of their brothers. At the sight of this whole nation in arms, the foreigner will flee or sign the peace. . . .' Alas, this was not to be! And yet this last effort was indeed to take place. In France, Champaubert, Montmirail and Montereau were to be so many battles in which the Imperial genius was to shine at its brightest; in which the 'Marie-Louises' were to show the veterans that they too knew how to cultivate heroism. But the end was near. By 31 March, Paris would surrender; in Toulouse on 10 April Soult would finally lose the last great battle of this war of Spain; while three days earlier, vanquished by force of numbers and betrayed by his marshals, the Emperor would sign his abdication.

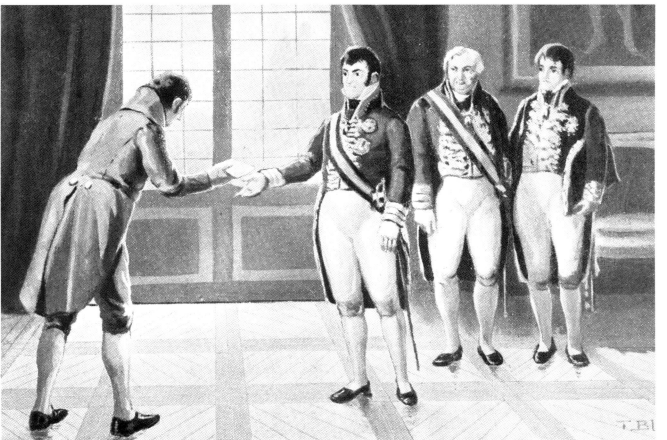

Left: Ferdinand VII, accompanied by his brother and his uncle, receives M. de Laforest, former French Ambassador in Madrid, sent by Napoleon to Valençay to negotiate a peace treaty and an offer to restore Ferdinand to his throne. By the terms of this treaty, signed on 11 December, Ferdinand VII was to recover his crown. The Continental and colonial integrity of Spain was to be guaranteed, and there was to be a general amnesty. The French garrisons were to evacuate those Spanish fortresses still occupied. The Spanish and British armies were to return across the Pyrenees. The treaty was submitted to the Regency in Madrid by the Duke of San Carlos and Palafox, the former defender of Saragossa who had been detained in France and who was set free for this occasion. The treaty having been rejected by the Regency on the pretext that the King had signed it in a state of captivity, Napoleon preferred to trust the word of Ferdinand VII, who pledged on his honour to respect it, and gave orders to set the Spanish prisoners free (6 March 1814).

1814

Position of the French army — British attack — Soult withdraws — Battle of Orthez — Bordeaux occupied by the British — Suchet welcomes Ferdinand in Catalonia — Soult arrives at Toulouse — Battle of Toulouse — Capture of the town by the British — French fall back towards Castelnaudary — Union with Suchet's troops — Soult agrees to recognize Louis XVIII — End of the campaign.

It was in the greyness of early January that Soult attempted to organize the line of defence to which he had been forced after his defeat at St. Pierre-d'Irrube. He had, moreover, to send to the Emperor three divisions, one of them a division of dragoons commanded by Treilhard. To the south, at St. Jean-Pied-de-Port, General Harispe, detached by Suchet, held the town with a small division. A fine figure of a Basque (he was born at St. Étienne-de-Baigorry), he recruited a free corps from among his countrymen to try to fill out the numerical weakness of the French.

With the exception of a few skirmishes, the two armies remained motionless until 14 February. On that date, in a temperature well below zero, Wellington decided to attack. General Hill, commanding the British right, marched on Helette, which Harispe was forced to evacuate. Mina, the partisan leader turned general, arrived at St. Étienne-de-Baigorry and Bidarray. This joint action forced the French to withdraw on Garris (near St. Palais) and to recross the Bidouze, whose bridges they destroyed. On the 15th, attacked once more on the right bank of the torrent of Mauléon, Harispe continued his withdrawal, installed his troops on the torrent of Oloron, then rejoined Soult who was manoeuvring around Orthez. The French marshal was being pressed by the troops of Picton and Beresford, and had taken the decision to fall back towards the east, leaving the Bordeaux road unprotected.

In this movement he hoped to entice Wellington to overextend his forces, and hoped that he might surprise and destroy some of the British corps at risk. He also considered that the British general could not march on Bordeaux, leaving his flank threatened. Meanwhile he had to cope with things as they were, so he pulled back to Orthez his troops which were drawn up on the torrent of Pau. At 7 o'clock on the morning of the 27th, the battle commenced. The troops of Reille on the right, Clausel on the left and Drouet d'Erlon in the centre were attacked by the British troops of Beresford, Walker, Picton and Clinton.

Commanding in person, Wellington grew impatient of the French resistance, and sent the squadrons of General Cotton and General Somerset against Darmagnac, a member of Drouet d'Erlon's staff. Darmagnac was forced back, taking with him the rest of the French forces, and soon Soult was ordering the retreat. This was accomplished in good order, but the action had been quite murderous. Foy had been gravely wounded and General Béchaud had been killed. Passing through Sault-de-Navailles, and followed cautiously by the British, Soult retired to St. Sever and Aire-sur-l'Adour, then to Tarbes. The effect on the populace was bad. It had not been a real defeat, but the enemy continued to advance and the royalist South began to move.

The Battle of Orthez. Above, the charge of the British 7th Hussars. (A contemporary engraving) Left, General Foy. (Painting by Cogniet, Musée de Bayonne) Below, General Baron Béchaud (1770–1814), commanding the 1st Brigade of the 8th Infantry Division, who was killed at Orthez.

Meanwhile, Wellington, who knew how to keep his head politically, thwarted Soult's calculations and decided to enter Bordeaux where the mayor, Lynch, declared himself ready to open the gates and recognize the King of France. The town's bourgeoisie, ruined by the Continental Blockade, had long been hostile to the Imperial régime and La Rochejaquelein, an emissary charged with convincing Wellington of their feelings, had been sent to him. Having received reinforcements, Wellington had sufficient troops to face Soult and so he detached Beresford with about 15,000 men. On 12 March they entered Bordeaux. The Duke of Angoulême, following with the baggage train, was received at the cathedral where a Te Deum was sung. The enthusiastic mayor declared to Wellington: 'It is in a city of our legitimate king, allied to yours, that we receive your Excellency. Long live the King, long live the English!' Wellington was a little less enthusiastic, and on 16 March he wrote to the Duke of Angoulême: 'I have no objection to your proclaiming the King, but I pray your Royal Highness to excuse me from taking any part in the actual proceedings.'

In northern Catalonia, Suchet was still holding out. At the Emperor's request, however, he was obliged to send some of his men to Lyons as reinforcements. After leaving a garrison at Gerona, he withdrew behind the Ter and thence to Figueras. It was there, on 24 March, that he welcomed Ferdinand, whom Napoleon, exasperated by the non-ratification of the treaty by the Cortes, had decided to set free. Suchet accompanied Ferdinand to the River Fluvia. The French Army was drawn up on the left bank; opposite, on the right bank, waited General Copons's Spanish army. The King reviewed the French troops, addressed compliments to the marshal, then crossed the river. As soon as he arrived, Copons presented him with a copy of the Constitution of 1812, which he immediately placed in his pocket. A few days later, having found General Elio's troops at Valencia, (whom he could count on) he threw off the mask once and for all and declared: '... in accord with the general demonstrations of the will of my people, which I find just and well-founded, I declare my royal intention to be not only never to accept or swear to this Constitution, nor any decree given by the Cortes, general, extraordinary or ordinary ... but to declare this constitution and its consequences null and void for the present and for the future....' France had lost Spain. But by giving them back their king, the Emperor, without realizing it, was wreaking the cruellest vengeance on the Spanish people....

During the month of March, Soult, who had pulled back to the Tarbes–Plaisance line, tried to impede Wellington's march, which was progressing slowly along difficult roads, harassed in his rear by the free corps. At Lembeye, Soult came up against 60,000 Anglo-Spanish and turned back towards Rabastens in order to cover the road to Toulouse. On 20 March the Allies crossed the Adour at Vic-en-Bigorre. While the bulk of the French made their way towards Toulouse along the St. Gaudens road, Clausel was detailed to lure their adversary along the shortest but worst route, which passed through Trie and Lombez. In the defiles at Sare, rendered impassable by the recent torrential rains, Wellington's artillery became bogged down. Clausel arrived at Boulogne-sur-Gesse thirty-six hours before the British and broke column to rejoin Soult. On the 24th, with the whole of his small army, Soult presented himself outside Toulouse and immediately placed the town in a state of defence.

On the right, Reille's corps settled into Blagnac and along the steep banks of the Touch. In the centre, Drouet d'Erlon held St. Martin-du-Touch and Tournefeuille. On the left, Clausel pushed Villatte's division on to Portet, situated at the confluence of the Garonne and the Ariège. General Soult's light cavalry reconnoitred towards Muret.

Above: Obelisk commemorating the Battle of Toulouse.

Below: Episode during the Battle of Toulouse, 10 April 1814. Picton's Scotsmen are repelled by Darricau's division at the Matabiau bridge. (Philippoteaux)

Behind this battle line, work was undertaken to fortify the suburb of St. Cyprien. The works were directed by General Travot, who was in command of a reserve of 6,000 men, mostly conscripts and battalions of the National Guard.

On the 28th, the French army was violently attacked by Wellington, and withdrew to the bridgehead at St. Cyprien. Here they made ready to defend the old walls, which could be closed by means of portcullises, as well as the bastions of the left bank and the fortified line of the right bank. The Allies' first crossing of the Garonne took place to the south of the town at Pinsaguel, where a pontoon bridge was used, but the appalling state of the roads prevented Wellington from continuing this manoeuvre, whereby he intended to outflank the French. He decided to cross the Garonne to the north, level with the village of Cagnac. On 5 April, Beresford crossed the river and occupied Grisolles, effectively cutting off the Montauban route to Paris.

On 10 April the last great battle of 1814 began. At first light, Hill attacked Reille at St. Cyprien, and Picton attacked Darricau at Ponts-Jumeaux. The Spaniard, Manuel Freyre, debouched from La Croix Daurade and made his way towards the hillock of La Pujade, dislodged Villatte and attacked the Matabiau bridge. With the divisions of Cole and Clinton, Beresford crossed the River Hers, arriving at the Caraman road at the redoubt of Sypierre, which he attacked. General Taupin, sent by Soult to the rescue, fought desperately and managed to repulse the assailants, but was hit and killed and the redoubt was retaken by the British. At 4 o'clock, the French, hard-pressed on all sides, withdrew beyond the Midi canal where they held out energetically until the evening. Losses were

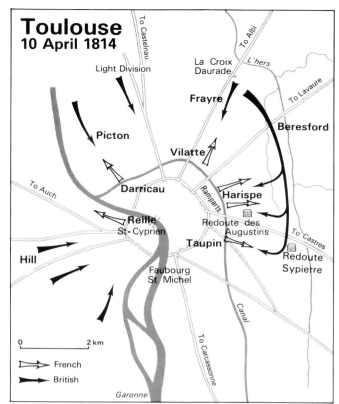

Toulouse
10 April 1814

To Castelnau
To Albi
La Croix Daurade
L'hers
To Lavaure
Light Division
Frayre
Beresford
Picton
Vilatte
To Auch
Darricau
Harispe
Ramparts
To Castres
Reille
St-Cyprien
Redoute des Augustins
Taupin
Redoute Sypierre
Hill
Faubourg St Michel
Canal
To Carcassonne

0   2 km

⇨ French
➤ British

Garonne

Right: The Battle of Toulouse, 10 April 1814. The French lost 3,200 men while the Allied losses amounted to 4,650 killed or wounded. (T. Sutherland)

Below right: View of Bayonne. (Drawing by Captain Batty)

Below: General Sir John Hope, Duke of Hopetown (1765–1823). He commanded the besieging forces at Bayonne, and was taken prisoner on 14 April when the French garrison left the town. (From a painting by Raeburn)

very heavy, especially on the Allied side. The British General Pack was killed, as were the Spanish Generals Espeletta and Mendizabal, and 12,000 men were put out of action at one place or another. Still master of the St. Michel suburb, Soult's retreat was assured, and it was not until the evening of the 11th that the French army began its withdrawal along the road to Carcassonne, beyond Villefranche de Lauragais.

On the 12th, Wellington entered the town and had not been there an hour when a messenger announced the Emperor's abdication. 'Hurrah, it was about time!' he replied, and decided to give a ball that very evening at the Prefecture, to which the pretty women of Toulouse would come, some for fear of reprisals, many to salute the man in whom they saw not the conqueror of France, but the hero of the peace. On the 13th, Wellington's senior aide-de-camp, Colonel Gordon, presented himself at the French outposts escorting Colonel Saint-Simon, who had been sent

by the provisional government to deliver despatches from the new Minister of War. Soult gathered together his generals and contested the authenticity of these documents. To Gordon, who was waiting, he made this proud reply: 'Tell Lord Wellington that I cannot put faith in any news of peace given to me by the leader of the army which I am fighting. Add that I have still to fight ten battles similar to that at Toulouse and that in the end, if our losses follow the same pattern as in the past, both he and I will become generals without armies. . . .' It seemed that this campaign would never end.

In Spain, the garrisons of Figueras, Peniscola, Barcelona, Tortosa and Sagunto still held out, and in France Bayonne was obstinately resisting. Better still, in mid-April, in the last action of this 'badly begun' war which had started some six years earlier, the garrison made a sortie and captured General Hope, leader of the besiegers. The final capitulation of the town did not take place until May.

174

French Allied Troops, 1808–14

In February 1808 the first Italian division entered Catalonia. It consisted of a battalion of the Vélites of the Guard, the 2nd Line, the 2nd Chasseurs à Cheval, a company of foot artillery and a section of the artillery train of the Guard. These troops were joined by a second contingent under General Pino consisting of the 4th, 6th and 7th Line and the 1st and 2nd Dragoons and Chasseurs à Cheval.

1. 2nd Light, skirmisher in campaign dress, 1808.
2. 7th Line, fusilier in dress uniform.
3. 5th Line, grenadier in dress uniform.
5. Vélites of the Guard (Veleti Reali), carabinier in dress uniform.
6. 'Napoleone' Dragoons (foot service), sapper in marching order, 1810.
7. 2nd Light, carabinier in dress uniform.
4 & 8. 'Regina' and 'Napoleone' Dragoon regiments. At the time of the Spanish campaign there were two dragoon regiments, but only the 2nd took part in the war. (4) Officer of the 'Regina' in dress uniform. (8) 'Napoleone' dragoon in campaign dress.
9. Chasseur à cheval, officer. In 1806 there were two regiments of chasseurs à cheval. The 3rd Regiment was raised in 1810 and the 4th in 1814.
10 & 11. Kingdom of Naples. A Neapolitan contingent of 2,100 men was added to General Lecchi's Italian division. Grenadier (10) and fusilier (11) of the 'Re' regiment.
12, 13 & 14. Grand Duchy of Cleves-Berg. The 1st and 2nd Infantry Regiments of Cleves-Berg arrived in

Spain in 1809 and participated in the siege of Gerona. The 3rd Regiment arrived in 1810. It was the only one to remain in the Peninsula. (12) Colour of the 1st Infantry Regiment, 1807–12. (13) Fusilier in campaign dress, 1810. (14) Skirmisher in marching order.
17. Berg Lancer, 1809–11.
15, 16, 18 & 19. Kingdom of Holland. This kingdom furnished Spain with a contingent composed of battalions of the 2nd and 4th of the Line, detachments of the 3rd Regiment of Hussars, a company of horse artillery, a detachment of the train and a detachment of sapper-miners. (15) Colour of the 1st Battalion of the 2nd Line, 1807. (16) Fusilier of the 2nd Line. (18) Grenadier of the 4th Line. (19) Hussar in dress uniform of the 3rd Regiment.
20, 21 & 22. Legion of the Vistula. This consisted of three regiments of infantry and a regiment of lancers. They set off for Spain in 1808 and took part in the Battle of Tudela and the siege of Saragossa. (20) Lancer. (21) Skirmisher of the 2nd Regiment. (22) Sapper of the 1st Regiment.

175

British Army and Auxiliary Troops, 1808–14

1. Duchy of Brunswick (Brunswick-Oels), infantry. Formed of prisoners and foreigners (Germans, Croats, Danes, Italians and Portuguese). Known as the 'Black Legion', they arrived in Portugal in 1810.
2. Duchy of Brunswick, hussar.
3. King's German Legion, 2nd Regiment of Heavy Dragoons, campaign dress, 1803–12.
4. King's German Legion, 3rd Regiment of Hussars, 1812. This legion consisted of three hussar regiments, often called light dragoons.
5. King's German Legion, 2nd Regiment of Heavy Dragoons, officer in marching order.
6. Sicilian Troops, grenadier of line infantry, 1812–15. In 1812 an Anglo-Sicilian army disembarked at Alicante, and remained there until 1814, principally opposed to the Army of Aragon (Suchet).
7. Sicilian skirmisher, 1809.
8. Sicilian Regiment of Grenadier-Guards, sergeant, 1812.
9. Sicilian volunteer, chasseur, 1810.

10. Sicilian Regiment, light infantry, officer, 1807.
11. Calabrian Free Corps, light infantry, officer, 1812. Certain documents affirm that this unit was raised in Sicily by Sir John Stuart; others say in Spain in 1809, under the command of Sir Octavius Carey.
12. Calabrian Free Corps, light infantry, private soldier.
13. King's German Legion, carabinier officer of the battalion of the line.
14. Carabinier in campaign dress, 1811.
15. King's German Legion, 2nd Battalion, officer of light company, 1814. The uniform shown here is that of Captain Georg Wacherhagen, who was wounded and taken prisoner at Bayonne in 1814.
16. King's German Legion, 2nd Battalion of light infantry, sergeant.
17. King's German Legion, 2nd Regiment of Dragoons, officer, 1803–12.
18. De Roll's Swiss Regiment, officer in dress uniform. This was the first Swiss regiment in the service of Britain. With five companies of Dillon's troops, it formed a provisional battalion in 1810.

19. British Chasseur Regiment, light company, officer, 1812. Formed in 1801 with émigrés from the army of Condé, this regiment served in Sicily, then in Spain. It took part in the Battle of Fuentes de Oñoro, but suffered a great number of desertions during the 1812–13 campaign.

Right: Napoleon signs his abdication on 4 April 1814. (Painting by Bouchot and Ferré)

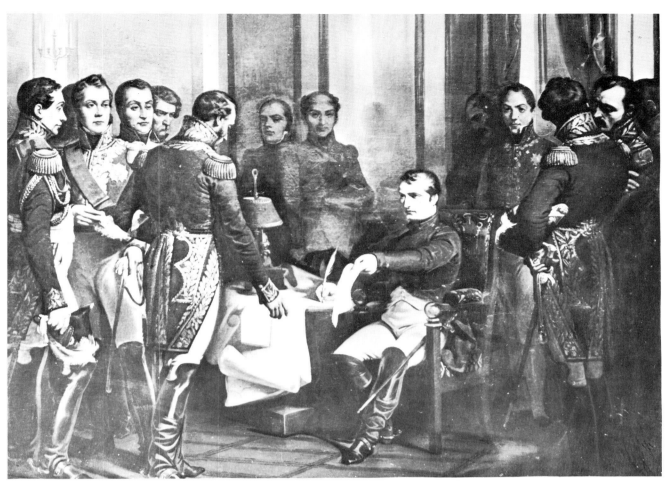

Right: Entry of Ferdinand VII into Madrid on 13 May 1814. (J. Calderé)

On 14 April, having through the fault of its leader, arrived too late for the Battle of Toulouse, Suchet's army rejoined that of Soult near Castelnaudary. On the 19th, finally convinced, the Duke of Dalmatia acknowledged Louis XVIII and was relieved of his command on the 22nd.

The war in Spain had been the 'dirty war' of the Empire. It had frequently whetted an appetite for power in the French commanders who had followed one another there. Soldiers of fortune, they saw themselves as kings or reigning princes, and their sense of rivalry made them forget their duty. The Emperor had underestimated the British, whom he had so easily defeated when he himself was in Spain, and had underestimated too the resistance of a ravaged nation with great national pride. He had wanted to direct operations himself from afar, and that had not been possible. However, this French army of the Peninsular War had written pages of glory that did honour to its eagles. When the Spanish prisoners returned home, they were to astonish their fellow-citizens with the stories of their captivity in a France that was organized, open to liberal ideas, and where they had not been mistreated. They were to help soften a little the tenacious hatred that these long years of war had anchored in the hearts of the Spanish people, while the ideas they brought back were to cause them difficulty in accepting the authoritarianism of Ferdinand VII, which only a Holy Alliance whose secular arm was royalist France, could sustain. For when, in 1823, suffocating under this king once so desired and now so abhorred, they rebelled, France returned once more to Spain, with the army of the Restoration. It travelled across the country and easily captured Cadiz, the symbol, along with the Cortes, of the relentless resistance to Napoleon.

Such is the way of history. . . .

Appendices

Scale:
0 — 100 — 200 miles
0 — 100 — 200 — 300 kilometres

Corunna
LUGO
VIGO
ASTORGA
Leon
Esla
SAHAGUN
BENAVENTE
PALENCIA
MEDINA DEL RIO SECO
Oporto
ZAMORA
Duero
TORDESILLAS
Valladolid
Douro
Salamanca
ALMEIDA
GUARDA
BUSSACO
Ciudad Rodrigo
FUENTES DE ONORO
COIMBRA
Mondego
ALBA DE TORMES
SOMOSIERRA
Segovia
AVILA
Zezere
PLASENCIA
Tagus
Madrid
TALAVERA
ARANJUEZ
ALCANTARA
ARSOBISPO
OCANA
VIMIERO
ABRANTES
Toledo
SANTAREM
TORRES VEDRAS
Lisbon
CAMPO MAYOR
MERIDA
Badajoz
MEDELLIN
ALBUERA
Guadiana
Jucar
SAGUNTO
Valencia
ALMANSA
CASTALLA
Alicante
BAYLEN
Cordova
Guadalquivir
Seville
Segura
CARTAGENA
Granada
Cadiz
CHICLANA
MALAGA
ALMERIA
Cape Trafalgar
Gibraltar

SAN SEBASTIAN
Bilbao
ESPINOSA
VITORIA
Bayonne
ORTHEZ
PAU
TARBES
Toulouse
Adour
Garonne
Bordeaux
TOLOSA
Pamplona
Burgos
LOGRONO
TUDELA
Saragossa
LERIDA
Ebro
Segre
MONTSERRAT
RIPOLI
GERONA
Perpignan
Barcelona
Tarragona
TORTOSA

Inset map:
FRANCE
ASTURIAS
GALICIA
CANTABRIAN MTS
LEON
NAVARRE
PYRENEES
OLD CASTILLE
ARAGON
CATALONIA
PORTUGAL
SIERRA DE GUADARRAMA
NEW CASTILLE
SPAIN
VALENCIA
ESTREMADURA
LA MANCHA
SIERRA MORENA
MURCIA
ANDALOUSIA
SIERRA NEVADA
DAG

The Peninsula

Chronology

Chronology of military events during the campaigns in Spain and Portugal from 1807 to 1814.
(Compiled from documents in the collection of Raoul and Jean Brunon, Musée de l'Empéri, Salon de Provence)

1807

18 October	Junot crosses the Bidassoa.
17 November	Dupont crosses the Bidassoa.
30 November	Junot enters Lisbon.

1808

9 February	Duhesme enters Catalonia.
2 May	Insurrection in Madrid.
6 June	Action at Logroño (Navarre); Verdier defeats the rebels.
6 June	Capture of Segovia (Old Castile) by General Frère.
7 June	Action at Tudela (Navarre); Lefebvre-Desnouëttes defeats the rebels.
8 June	Action at the bridge of Alcolea (Andalusia); Dupont defeats Etcheverria.
8 June	Capture of Cordoba by Dupont.
10 June	Action at Llobregat (Catalonia); Duhesme defeats the rebels.
12 June	Action at the bridge of Cabezon (Valladolid); Lasalle defeats de la Cuesta.
12 June	Action at Mallen (Aragon); Lefebvre-Desnouëttes defeats the Marquis of Lassan.
15 June	Capture of La Guarda (Portugal) by General Loison.
18 June	Action at Leiria (Portugal); Margaron defeats the rebels.
21 June	Action at Cabriel (Valencia); Moncey defeats the rebels.
24 June	Action at Las Cabreras (Valencia); Moncey defeats the rebels.
26 June	Action at Despeñaperros (New Castile); Vedel defeats the rebels.
28 June	Siege of Saragossa (Aragon); Verdier and Lefebvre-Desnouëttes besiege the city, defended by Palafox. They withdraw on 14 August, after the defeat at Baylen.
2 July	Action at Jaen (Andalusia); Cassagne defeats the rebels.
10 July	Action at Alcobaza (Portugal); Loison defeats the rebels.
14 July	Battle of Medina del Rio Seco (Leon); Bessières defeats de la Cuesta.
16 July	Action at Mengibar (Andalusia); Ligier-Belair repulses Castaños.
16 July	Action at Andujar (Andalusia); Lefranc repulses Castaños.
19 July	Battle of Baylen (Andalusia); Reding and Castaños defeat Dupont.
30 July	Action at Evora (Portugal); Loison defeats the rebels.
3 August	Disembarkation of the British army at Figueira (Portugal).
17 August	Battle of Roliça (Portugal); Delaborde repulses Wellesley.
21 August	Battle of Vimeiro (Portugal); Wellesley defeats Junot.
30 August	Convention of Cintra (Portugal) between Wellesley and Junot.
25 October	Action at Lerin (Navarre); Moncey defeats the rebels.
25 October	Capture of Logroño (Navarre) by Ney, who also defeats Pignatelli.
31 October	Action at Zornoza, or Durango (Biscay); Lefebvre defeats Blake.
31 October	Capture of Bilbaõ (Biscay) by Lefebvre.
5 November	Action at Balmaseda (Biscay); Villatte defeats Blake and de la Romana.
7 November	Action at Guenes (Biscay); Lefebvre defeats Blake.
9 November	Capture of Burgos (Old Castile) by Soult.
10 November	Action at Espinosa (Santander); Victor defeats Blake.
17 November	Capture of Santander by Soult.
23 November	Battle of Tudela (Navarre); Lannes defeats Palafox and Castaños.
30 November	Action at Somosierra (Old Castile); Victor defeats San Juan.
4 December	Capture of Madrid by Napoleon.
5 December	Capture of Rosas (Catalonia) by Gouvion Saint-Cyr.
16 December	Action at Cardedeu (Catalonia); Gouvion Saint-Cyr defeats Juan de Vives.
19 December	Second siege of Saragossa; Moncey, Junot, Mortier and Lannes besiege the city which is defended by Palafox and Saint-March. It falls on 20 February 1809.
21 December	Action at Puente del Rey (Catalonia); Gouvion Saint-Cyr defeats Juan de Vives.
22 December	Crossing of the Guadarrama by Napoleon.
26 December	Action at Benavente (Leon); Lefebvre-Desnouëttes is captured by Moore.
29 December	Action at Mancilla (Leon); Bessières defeats de la Romana.

1809

3 January	Action at Cacabelos (Galicia); during a skirmish with Moore, Colbert is killed.
9 January	Action at Lugo (Galicia); Soult engages Moore.
13 January	Action at Ucles (New Castile); Victor defeats Venegas.
16 January	Battle of Corunna (Galicia); Moore is killed and the British re-embark.
21 January	Capture of Ferrol (Galicia) by Soult.
25 February	Action at Valls (Catalonia); Gouvion Saint-Cyr defeats Reding.
5 March	Action at Monterey (Galicia); Soult defeats de la Romana.
12 March	Capture of Chaves (Portugal) by Soult.
16 March	Action at the bridge of Almaraz (Estremadura); Victor defeats de la Cuesta.
20 March	Action at Braga (Portugal); Soult defeats Freyre.

20 March	Action at Trujillo (Estremadura); Lasalle and Leval defeat de la Cuesta.
27 March	Battle of Ciudad Real (Mancha); Sebastiani defeats de la Cuesta.
28 March	Capture of Oporto (Portugal) by Soult.
28 March	Battle of Medellin (Estremadura); Victor defeats de la Cuesta.
16 April	Action at Amarante (Portugal); Loison defeats Sylveida.
12 May	Battle of Oporto; Wellesley defeats Soult, who evacuates Portugal.
18 May	Capture of Oviedo (Asturias); Kellermann defeats de la Romana.
22 May	Action at Lugo (Galicia); Soult defeats the Portuguese who are besieging Fournier.
4 June	Siege of Gerona (Catalonia) by Gouvion Saint-Cyr and Augereau. The city falls on 11 December.
15 June	Action at Maria (Aragon); Suchet defeats Blake.
18 June	Action at Belchite (Aragon); Suchet defeats Blake.
25 July	Action at Alcabon (Toledo); Sebastiani defeats de la Cuesta.
28 July	Battle of Talavera (New Castile). Joseph and Victor engage Wellesley and de la Cuesta; the battle is indecisive.
8 August	Action at the bridge of Arzobispo (New Castile); Mortier defeats Wellington.
11 August	Battle of Almonacid (Toledo); Sebastiani defeats Venegas.
12 August	Action at Col de Baños (Old Castile); Lorcet (Ney) defeats Wilson.
10 October	Action at Tamanes (Leon); the Duke del Parque defeats Marchand.
19 November	Battle of Ocaña (Toledo); Mortier defeats Juan Areizaga.
28 November	Action at Alba de Tormes (Leon); Kellermann defeats the Duke del Parque.
11 December	Fall of Gerona (Catalonia), which has been besieged since 4 June.
15 December	Capture of Ripoll (Catalonia) by Souham.

1810

1 January	Action at Sespina (Catalonia); Souham defeats O'Donnell.
3 January	Action at Mollet (Catalonia); the Marquis of Campo Verde defeats Colonel Guery.
21 January	Crossing of the Sierra Morena (La Mancha); Joseph defeats Areizaga.
28 January	Action at Alcala la Real (Andalusia); Sebastiani defeats Areizaga.
1 February	Capture of Seville by Soult.
5 February	Siege of Cadiz by Victor; it was to last for two years, until 9 February 1812.
5 February	Action at Malaga (Andalusia); Sebastiani defeats the Spanish.
9 February	Capture of Zafra (Estremadura) by Mortier.
22 February	Action at Vich (Catalonia); Souham defeats O'Donnell.
22 February	Action at Caceres (Estremadura); Foy repulses the Spanish cavalry.
21 March	Capture of Ronda (Andalusia) by Peyremond.
21 March	Action at Villafranca (Catalonia); Augereau defeats O'Donnell.
10 April	Seige of Lerida (Catalonia) by Suchet. The city falls on 14 May.
19 April	Siege of Astorga (Leon) by Junot. The city falls on 6 May.
22 April	Action at Margalef (Catalonia); Suchet defeats O'Donnell.

12 May	Capture of Fort Hostalrich (Catalonia) by Augereau.
20 May	Siege of Mequinenza (Catalonia) by Suchet. The town falls on 8 June.
6 June	Siege of Ciudad Rodrigo (Leon) by Masséna and Ney. The town falls on 10 July.
24 July	Action at the River Coa (Portugal); Ney defeats Craufurd.
11 August	Action at Villagarcia (Andalusia); Girard defeats de la Romana.
15 August	Siege of Almeida (Portugal) by Masséna. The town falls on 27 August.
24 August	Action at Rio Tinto and Moguer (Andalusia); Colonel Réymond against Copons.
29 August	Action at Siguenza (New Castile); Hugo defeats 'El Empecinado'.
4 September	Action fought by Macdonald at Cervera (Catalonia).
4 September	Action at La Bisbal (Catalonia); O'Donnell defeats Schwarz.
27 September	Battle of Bussaco (Portugal); Masséna fights Wellington in a drawn battle.
9 October	Action at Sobra (Portugal); Junot defeats the Anglo-Portuguese.
9 October	Investment of the lines of Torres Vedras (Portugal) by Masséna. He was to retire in March 1811.
30 October	Action at Alventosa (Aragon); Klopicki defeats Villacampa.
4 November	Action at Rio Almanzor (Granada); Sebastiani disperses Blake.
20 November	Action at Punhete (Portugal); Loison defeats the Anglo-Portuguese.
26 November	Action at Vilnaros (Catalonia); Musnier defeats the Spanish.
13 December	Action at Palamos (Catalonia); repulse of British landing.
19 December	Siege of Tortosa (Catalonia) by Suchet. The town falls on 18 January 1811.

1811

9 January	Capture of Fort St. Philip (Catalonia) by Suchet.
13 January	Action at Tarrega (Catalonia); Henriot defeats Campo Verde.
15 January	Action at Valls (Catalonia); Campo Verde defeats Palombini.
19 January	Action at Rio Mayor (Portugal); Junot against the Anglo-Portuguese.
21 January	Action at Villanuova de Castilleros (Estremadura); Gazan defeats Ballesteros.
22 January	Capture of Olivenza (Estremadura) by Soult.
27 January	Siege of Badajoz (Estremadura) by Soult and Mortier. The town, which is defended by Menacho, falls on 11 March.
19 February	Battle of the Gebora (Estremadura); Soult and Mortier defeat Mendizabal.
5 March	Battle of Chiclana-Barossa (Andalusia); Victor repulses Graham.
11 March	Action at Pombal (Portugal); Ney defeats Picton and Blake.
12 March	Action at Redinha (Portugal); Ney repulses Wellington.
15 March	Capture of Albuquerque (Estremadura) by Latour-Maubourg.
16 March	Action at Foz d'Arunce (Portugal); Wellington pursues Ney and Masséna.
27 March	Action at Campo Mayor (Estremadura); Beresford repulses Latour-Maubourg.

1 April	Siege of Figueras (Catalonia) by Macdonald. The town falls on 16 August.
3 April	Action at Sabugal (Portugal); Wellington repulses Reynier.
5 May	Battle of Fuentes de Oñoro (Leon); Wellington repulses Masséna.
16 May	Battle of Albuera (Estremadura); Beresford defeats Soult.
24 May	Siege of Tarragona (Catalonia) by Suchet. The city falls on 28 June.
14 June	Action at Sanguesa (Navarre); Caffarelli defeats Mina.
22 June	Action at Cifuentes (Old Castile); Hugo defeats 'El Empecinado.'
24 July	Capture of Montserrat (Catalonia) by General Abbé (under Suchet).
24 July	Action at Cuenca (Aragon); La Houssaye defeats Don Juan Martin.
25 August	Action at Astorga (Leon); Dorsenne defeats Abadia.
28 September	Siege of Sagunto (Valencia) by Suchet. The town falls on 26 October.
1 October	Action at Tarifa (Andalusia); the British repulse Godinot.
1 October	Action at Benaguasil (Valencia); Suchet defeats Blake.
21 October	Action at Arroyo de Molinos (Estremadura); Hill defeats Girard.
25 October	Battle of Sagunto (Valencia); Suchet defeats Blake.
10 November	Action at Bornos (Andalusia); Semelé defeats Ballesteros.
26 December	Siege of Valencia by Suchet. The city falls on 9 January 1812.
29 December	Action at Merida (Estremadura); Hill repulses Drouet d'Erlon.
29 December	Siege of Tarifa (Andalusia); failure of Leval against Skerret and Copons.

1812

19 January	Recapture by Wellington of Ciudad Rodrigo (Leon), which is defended by Berrié.
4 February	Capture of Peniscola (Valencia) by Severoli (under Suchet).
16 March	Siege of Badajoz (Estremadura) by Wellington. The town is defended by Philippon and surrenders on 6 July.
18 May	Destruction of the bridge at Almaraz (Estremadura) by Hill.
28 June	Wellington captures Salamanca (Leon) from Marmont.
18 July	Action at Tordesillas (Leon) between Marmont and Wellington.
21 July	Action at Castalla (Valencia); Delort disperses O'Donnell.
22 July	Battle of Arapiles, or Salamanca; Wellington defeats Marmont.
8 August	Action at Majahonda (Madrid); Treilhard attempts to repulse the Anglo-Portuguese.
13 August	Entry of Wellington into Madrid.
23 August	Action at Villadrigo (Burgos); Souham's cavalry pursue Wellington.

19 September	Siege of Burgos by Wellington. The city is defended by Dubreton and holds out until Wellington withdraws after 34 days.
2 November	Return of the French to Madrid.
9–15 December	Battle of Alba de Tormes (Leon); Jourdan against Wellington.

1813

12 June	The French evacuate Madrid.
12 June	Action at Alicante (Valencia); Suchet repels a landing by Murray.
21 June	Battle of Vitoria (Navarre), Wellington defeats Jourdan and Joseph.
21 June	Action at Rio Hormoza (Burgos); Reille tries to hold up the Anglo-Portuguese.
22 June	Siege of Pamplona (Navarre) by Wellington, The town, defended by Cassan, capitulates on 13 October.
23 June	Action at Palamos (Catalonia); Lamarque repulses the Anglo-Portuguese.
25 June	Action at Tolosa (Navarre); Graham defeats Foy.
27 June	Siege of San Sebastian (Biscay) by Graham. The town, defended by Rey, falls on 9 September.
25 July	Action at Col de Maya (Biscay); Drouet d'Erlon repulses the Anglo-Portuguese.
25 July	Evacuation of Valencia by Suchet.
25 August	Evacuation of Tarragona by Suchet.
31 August	Action at Irun (Biscay); Wellington repulses Soult.
1 September	Action at the bridge of Berra (Biscay); Wellington repulses Soult.
13 September	Action at Col d'Ordal (Catalonia); Suchet repulses Bentinck.
27 September	Defence of the fortress of Monzon (Catalonia). The fortress, which is defended by St. Jacques, capitulates on 14 February 1814.
7 October	Wellington crosses the Bidassoa.
7 October	Action at Hendaye; Wellington defeats Soult.
10 November	Battle around St. Jean-de-Luz (Nivelle); Wellington defeats Soult.
9 December	Action on the River Nive; Wellington repulses Soult.
13 December	Battle of St. Pierre-d'Irrube; Wellington repulses Soult.

1814

January	Actions around Bayonne.
27 January	Battle of Orthez; Wellington defeats Soult.
1 March	Action at Aire-sur-l'Adour.
13 March	Action at Viella.
10 April	Battle of Toulouse; Soult evacuates Toulouse during the night of the 11/12th.
14 April	Sortie by the garrison of Bayonne.

Select Bibliography

Abrantes, Laure Permon, Duchess of. *Mémoires ou Souvenirs Historiques sur Napoléon, la Révolution, le Directoire, le Consulat, l'Empire, et la Restoration.* Mame, Paris, 1835. Abridged English-language edition: *Memoirs of Napoleon, his Court and Family.* 2 vols. Bentley, London, 1836.

Boppe, Commandant P. *Les Espagnols à la Grande Armée.* Berger Levrault, Paris, 1899.

Bradford, W. 'Sketches of the Country, Character and Costume in Portugal and Spain, made during the Campaign, and on the route of the British Army, in 1808 and 1809'. London, 1812–13

Bucquoy, Commandant E. L. *Les Uniformes du Premier Empire.* Jacques Grancher, Paris, 1977 et seq.

Chardigny. *Les Maréchaux de Napoléon.* Flammarion, Paris, 1946.

Chastenet. *Wellington,* Fayard, Paris.

Clairval, H. de C. *Daumesnil.* Librairie Académique Perrin, Paris 1970.

Derozier, C. 'La guerre d'indépendance espagnole à travers l'estampé'. Atelier reproduction des thèses, University of Lille III, Honoré Champion, 1976.

Dubreton, J. L. *Napoléon Devant l'Espagne.* Fayard, Paris, 1946.

Fallou, L. *La Garde Impériale.* Paris, 1901.

Girod de L'Ain. *Mes souvenirs militaires.* Dumaine, Paris, 1873.

Grandmaison, G. de. *L'Espagne et Napoléon, 1804–1809.* Plon, Paris, 1908.

Grasset, A. L. *La Guerre d'Espagne 1807–1813.* Berger Levrault, Paris, 1926.

Guillon, E. *Les Guerres d'Espagne sous Napoléon.* Plon, Paris, 1902.

Hennet de Goutel, Baron. *Le Général Cassan et la Défense de Pampelune.* Librairie Académique Perrin, Paris, 1920.

Hugo, A. *France Militaire.* France Pittoresque, 1838.

Jomini, H. de. *Histoire Critique et Militaire des Guerres de la Révolution.* Anselin, Paris, 1820.

Knötel, R. and Sieg, H. *Handbuch der Uniformenkunde.* Helmut Gerhard Schulz, Hamburg, 1937. English-language editions: *Uniforms of the World,* Arms and Armour Press, London, 1980; Scribners, New York, 1979.

Lachouque, Commandant H. *Napoléon en 1814.* Hausmann, Paris, 1959.

– *Napoleon: Vingt Ans de Campagne.* Arthaud, Paris, 1964.

Lawford, Lieutenant-Colonel J. P. and Young, Brigadier P. *Wellington's Masterpiece: The Battle and Campaign of Salamanca.* Allen and Unwin, London, 1973.

Lawson, W. *A History of the Uniforms of the British Army.* Kaye and Ward, London, 1966–67.

Lefebvre, G. *Napoléon.* PUF, Paris, 1936. English-language edition: *Napoleon.* 2 vols. Routledge, Kegan, Paul, London, 1969.

Madelin, L. *Histoire du Consulat et de l'Empire.* 2 vols. Hachette, Paris, 1933.

Marbot, J. B. A. *Mémoires.* Plon, Paris, 1892. English-language edition: *Memoirs* (translation by A. J. Butler), Longmans, London, 1897.

Marshall Cornwall, Sir J. *Masséna, l'enfant chéri de la victoire.* Plon, Paris. English-language edition: *Marshal Massena.* Oxford University Press, 1965.

Martin, E. *La Gendarmerie Française en Espagne et au Portugal.* Leautey, Paris, 1898.

Napier, Sir W. F. P. *History of the War in the Peninsula, 1807–1814.* London, 1851; Armstrong, New York, 1882.

North, R. *Soldiers of the Peninsular War.* Almark, London, 1972.

Olague. *Histoire d'Espagne.* Paris, 1957.

Pivka, O. von. *The Portuguese Army of the Napoleonic War.* Men at Arms Series, Osprey, London.

Quennevat, J-C. *Atlas de la Grande Armée.* Sequoia, Paris, 1966.

Regnault, General J. *Les Aigles Impériales et le Drapeau Tricolore.* Peyronnet, Paris, 1967.

– 'Une leçon du feu et de la manoeuvre. Campagne d'Espagne 1809–1814', *Revue Historique de l'Armée* No 3, 1951.

Rousselot, L. 'L'Armée Française, ses Uniformes, son Armement, son Equipment'. Paris, 1943.

Ruby, General. 'Baylen'. *Sabretache* No 420, June 1960.

Saint-Pierre, L. and A. de. *Mémoires du Maréchal Soult,* Hachette, Paris.

Sarramon, J. *La Bataille des Arapiles.* University of Toulouse-Le-Mirail, 1978.

Sauzey, Colonel. *Les Allemands sous les Aigles Françaises.* Edition Art et Science, Bade.

Schuemans. *Itinéraire Général de Napoléon Ier.* Jouve, Paris, 1911.

Six, G. *Dictionnaire Biographique des Généraux et Amiraux Français de la Révolution et de l'Empire.* Georges Saffroy, Paris, 1934.

Solis, R. *La Guerra de la Independencia Española.* Noguer, Paris, 1973.

Suchet, Marshal L. G. *Mémoires.* Anselin, Paris. English-language edition: *Memoirs of the War in Spain from 1808 to 1814.* Colburn, London, 1829.

Thiers, L. A. *Histoire du Consulat et de l'Empire.* Paulin, Paris, 1845. English-language editions: *A History of the Consulate and Empire.* 20 vols. London, 1845 et seq; Lippincott, Philadelphia, 1893.

Var, Commandant. *Campagne du Capitaine Marcel.* Plon, Paris, 1913.

Windrow M., and Embleton, G. *Military Dress of the Peninsular War.* Ian Allen, Shepperton, 1974.

List of Sources

PICTORIAL SOURCES

Musée de l'Armée, Paris.
Authors' Collections.
Victor Balaguer Museum, Villanueva y Geltru, Barcelona.
Musée Basque, Bayonne.
Bibliothèque Nationale, Paris.
Collection of Raoul and Jean Brunon.
Cassel Museum.
Lazaro Galdiano Museum, Madrid.
Photos Giraudon, Paris.
Victor Hugo Collection, Paris.
Musée de la Legion d'Honneur, Paris.
Musée de la Marine, Paris.
Museum of Modern Art, Barcelona.
Musée Napoleonien, Antibes.
National Army Museum, London.
National Library, Madrid.
Prado Museum, Madrid.
Provincial Museum of Fine Arts, Saragossa.
Photos N. D. Roger-Viollet, Paris.
Royal Academy San Fernando, Madrid.
Royal Green Jackets, Winchester.
Musée de Versailles, Paris.
Collection Zuloaga-Zumaya.

PICTORIAL AND LITHOGRAPHIC SOURCES FOR THE PLATES OF UNIFORMS AND COLOUR

Achard-Bueno, *L'Armée Française et ses Allies en Espagne.*
Ales, S. *L'Esercito del Regno Italiano.*
Library of the Musée de l'Armée: Vanson Collection; Dubois de l'Etang, Historique des regiments, etc.
Barado y Font, Museo Militar.
Beaufort, L. de. Collection of drawings, notes and watercolours.
Bibliothèque Nationale, Paris: Ridder Collection, Valmont Collection, Marbot and Noirmont Collection.
Blanch, A. *Historia de la Guerra de Independencia en Cataluña.*
Boletin de la agrupacion de miniaturistas militares.
Bradford, W. 'Sketches of the Country, Character, and Costume in Portugal and Spain, made during the Campaign, and on the route of the British Army in 1808 and 1809'.
Bucquoy, E. L. *Les Uniforms du Premier Empire.*
British Museum Library.
Bueno, J. M. *Soldados de España.*
Clonard, Conde de. *Album de Caballeria Espanola.*
– *Album de la Infanteria Espanola.*
– *Historica Organica de las Armas de Infanteria y Caballeria.* 16 vols.
– *Memorias de las Academias e Escuelas Militares de España.*

– *Memorias para la Historia de Tropas de la Casa de España.*
Musée de l'Empéri: Library of Jean and Raoul Brunon.
Edinburgh Military Museum.
Engravings by D. and R. Dighton, Berenger, C. H. Smith and T. Saint-Clair.
Fallou, L. *La Garde Imperiale.*
Ferrer de Couto. *Album del Ejercito.* 3 vols.
Fieffe. *Troupes Étrangères.* 2 vols.
Forthoffer, R. *Soldats du Temps Jadis, fiches documentaires.*
Gimenez Gonzales. *Coleccion de Modeles de las Armas.*
Goddard and Booth. *The Military Costumes of Europe.*
Guerra de foresteros, estado militar.
Holtzmann, T. *Die Spanische Militar in Hamburg.*
Hourtoulle, F. G. *Soldats et Uniformes du Ier Empire.*
Job. *Tenues des Troupes de France.*
Knotel, R. and Sieg, H. *Handbuch der Uniformenkunde.*
Lawson, W. *A History of the Uniforms of the British Army.* vols IV and V.
Leinhardt and Humbert. *Les Uniforms et l'Armée Française.*
Lisbon: Military Museum, Military archives, Naval Museum.
London: National Army Museum, Library of the Victoria and Albert Museum.
Madrid: Military Museum, Naval Museum.
Martinet. *Troupes Étrangères.*
Museum of Monjuich, Barcelona.
Ministry of War Library, Paris.
North, R. *Soldiers of the Peninsular War.*
Olmes, J. Heere der Vergangenheit.
Ordavas, J. J. 'Coleccion de estad del ejercito y armado de J.M.C.'
Periodicals: *La Sabretache, Le Briquet, Tradition.*
Pivka, O. von. *The Portuguese Army of the Napoleonic War.*
Portugal: Plano para uniformes do exercito, maio 1806.
Portuguez: Ordenanzas militares.
Regimental museums in England and Scotland.
Reynolds manuscripts.
Ribeiro. 'Spanish Armies of the Napoleonic Wars'.
Rigo-Charrie. *Le Plumet.*
Rousselot, L. 'L'Armee Francaise ses Uniformes, son Armement, son Equipment'.
Rouen. *L'Armée Belge.*
Sauzey, Colonel. *Les Allemands sous les Aigles Françaises.*
Journal of the Society for Army International Research.
Suhr, C. *Abbildungen in Uniformen aller in Hamburg.*
– and P. *Uniformen der Division des Marques de la Romana.*
Terrel des Chenes. *Bourgeois de Hambourg.*
de Valliere. *Honneur et Fidélité.*
Weber, T. *Coleccion de las laminas del Marques de la Romana.*
Weiland, C. F. *Darstellung der Franzosischen Armée.*
Windrow, M. and Embleton, G. *Military Dress of the Peninsular War.*
Collection at Windsor Castle.

Index